Embracing the East

Embracing

the East

White Women
and American
Orientalism

Mari Yoshihara

OXFORD
UNIVERSITY PRESS

2003

Oxford   New York
Auckland   Bangkok   Buenos Aires   Cape Town   Chennai
Dar es Salaam   Delhi   Hong Kong   Istanbul   Karachi   Kolkata
Kuala Lumpur   Madrid   Melbourne   Mexico City   Mumbai
Nairobi   São Paulo   Shanghai   Taipei   Tokyo   Toronto

Published by Oxford University Press, Inc.
198 Madison Avenue, New York, New York 10016

www.oup.com

Oxford is a registered trademark of Oxford University Press

Library of Congress Cataloging-in-Publication Data
Yoshihara, Mari, 1968–
Embracing the East : white women and American orientalism / Mari Yoshihara
  p. cm.
Includes bibliographical references and index.
ISBN 0-19-514533-X; 0-19-514534-8 (pbk.)
1. White women—Race identity—United States. 2. White women—United States—Ethnic
identity. 3. Orientalism—Social aspects—United States. 4. Asia—Foreign public opinion,
American. 5. Public opinion—United States. 6. Asia—In literature. 7. East and West—History.
8. United States—Race relations. 9. United States—Ethnic relations. I. Title.
E184.A1 Y78 2002
305.4'0973—dc21   2002017060

9 8 7 6 5 4 3 2 1
Printed in the United States of America
on acid-free paper

ACKNOWLEDGMENTS

As I was making my entry into American academe and figuring out my relationship to various identity politics, I thought I had made a conscious choice *not* to be auto-biographical in my research project. It was not until recently that I realized how personal my project in fact turned out to be. Although I am not a white American woman attracted to Asia, I, a Japanese woman interested in American culture, am a mirror image of many of the women I depict in this book. My work in American Studies, U.S.-Asian relations, cultural history, and women's/gender studies has become something far beyond an academic pursuit and turned into an intensely personal exploration as well. Throughout the making of this book, my intellectual trajectory and personal journey has been guided and accompanied by a number of mentors, colleagues, and friends on both sides of the Pacific and on an island in the middle of it.

My interest in American Studies was first warmly nurtured by my professors at the University of Tokyo. Professor Kamei Shunsuke introduced me to the world of American literature and culture through his engaging lectures and the weekend "literature camps." He has always given me his tremendous support and affection, which I hope to return by continuing to be his drinking partner. Professor Shibata Motoyuki has always taken me seriously—often more seriously than I felt I deserved—and has shown great encouragement, understanding, and advice; I aspire to emulate his intellectual rigor, professionalism, and love of the subject. I would also like to thank Professors Takita Yoshiko, Kunishige Junji, Yui Daizaburo, and Endo Yasuo for giving me opportunities to present my work at various venues and making me feel that I have a welcoming home in Japanese academe.

The bulk of this project was done while I was a graduate student at the Department of American Civilization at Brown University, which provided a wonderfully collegial and supportive environment. Since my first year in graduate school, Professor Robert Lee has showered me with his enthusiasm, insight, and trust. His grounding in East Asian Studies as well as in American Studies and his creative and expansive mind have been extremely valuable for my project. Professor Susan Smulyan has taught me how to read, think, and write like a scholar; she trained me as a teacher and helped me grow as one. Professor Barton St. Armand has taught me the appreciation of literature, art, and culture and provided a thorough reading and comments on my chapters. The dissertation would not have been completed without the help and support of my dissertation group: Dan Cavicchi, Crista DeLuzio, Kristen Farmelant, Kathy Franz, Bill Hart, Joanne Melish, and Miriam Reumann. Just as important as their ideas and comments was the sense of intellectual community the group fostered. In particular, Joanne Melish's intelligence, generosity, and sense of humor have been a great inspiration, and her friendship has meant a great deal to me. I also thank the people who made me feel that I had a life, home, and family in Providence. Thanks to Natasha Zaretsky for friendship, laughs, and conversations. The company of Kashiwazaki Chikako and Suzuki Akira added to the cross-cultural dimension of the household. Max Wood-Lee, born two days after my prelims and therefore basically the same age as this project, grew a lot more quickly and became more articulate than my writing; when he is older I will remind him of the things he used to say and do when he was two. Thanks to the rest of the Wood-Lee family for making me part of their lives.

Living and working in Hawai'i has given me a much more immediate and nuanced understanding of how colonialism and Orientalism work. I have been fortunate to have friends, colleagues, and students at the University of Hawai'i with whom to explore these difficult issues in both scholarly and non-scholarly ways. My colleagues in the Department of American Studies have been supportive of my work; I am especially grateful to Paul Hooper for granting me teaching reductions so that I could move on with my writing and for supporting me in many other ways. Sandy Enoki and Gerry Uyeunten have made my life easier by always being competent, knowledgeable, and cordial. I have the greatest writing group of all, whose members generously read and gave me critical comments on many of the chapters: Marcus Daniel, Cindy Franklin, Linda Lierheimer, Kieko Matteson, Robert Perkinson, and Naoko Shibusawa. Not only have they been a wonderful intellectual community, but all the barbeques and dinners and trips to the beach—and, of course, jumping out of the plane—have been the main source of my well-being. Many thanks to Mark Helbling for the lunches, coffees, conversations, arguments, laughs, and all the weird things we share. High marks go to Paul Lyons for putting up with me during my grumpy moments, and I thank him for his affection and the good times. Andrea Feeser, Mark Helbing, and Paul Lyons read and carefully commented on many of the chapters. The East-West Center-University of Hawai'i International Cultural Studies Program has been a stimulating forum for interdisciplinary exchange, and I have learned a great deal from presenting my work and listening to others there. I am very proud of my students, especially Heather Diamond, Bich Do, Malin Glimang, Jinzhao Li, Hiromi Monobe, and Manako Ogawa, all of whom have made such an intellectual growth in the last few years, and I am grateful to them for making me feel that I make a difference.

My editor at Oxford University Press, Susan Ferber, has done an amazingly thorough and intelligent job on the manuscript, and my writing is so much clearer for all her help. I thank Jessica Ryan for patiently guiding me through the book's production. Heather Diamond's thorough proofreading saved me from many errors. I appreciate the extensive comments by Kristin Hoganson, Henry Yu, and an anonymous reader for Oxford University Press. Peggy Pascoe has also given me very helpful comments and suggestions on the manuscript. Adrienne Munich and Melissa Bradshaw provided precious feedback on one of the chapters. I am also grateful to Lisa Yoneyama for giving me the opportunity to present my work at the University of California—San Diego. At different stages of this project, Melani McAlister has shared with me her brilliant insights which always boggle my mind, and I thank her for the exchanges both scholarly and personal.

Two men deserve a separate paragraph of special thanks. Over the years, Yujin Yaguchi has become not only my professional and intellectual ally but a precious friend who truly understands and shares my bicultural world. It is impossible to express how important his friendship is to my life. Izumi Hirobe, without whom I may not have gone beyond a master's degree, has given me many forms of support. Most important, he has always made me laugh.

Needless to say, my family and friends in Japan and the United States who know me in non-academic contexts have been my lifeline. They are the ones who have been reading my other writings most eagerly, and they are probably the ones who have been most patiently waiting for this book to materialize. I won't name each of them, but I hope they know that this book is a testament to their love and support.

Very shortly before the publication of this book, Mr. Okayama Yoshinao, my piano teacher throughout my childhood and adolescent years, passed away. Mr. Okayama was one of the first teachers I had in my life who believed in my talent, pushed me to work hard, and encouraged my creativity. The fortune of having had a teacher like him made all the difference in the world for me, and it is my deepest regret that I could not present this book to him in person. I hope that as a scholar and teacher I will someday pass on to others the inspiration, guidance, and dedication he gave to me.

CONTENTS

A NOTE ON JAPANESE AND CHINESE NAMES

In this volume, Japanese and Chinese names are written with the family name first followed by the given name (e.g., Okakura Kakuzo, Chiang Kai-shek). Exceptions to this order are references to individuals who (1) follow the Western form (the given name first followed by the family name) and/or (2) have published their writings in English with their names in the Western form. In cases that may be unclear, I have indicated the family name in capital letters (e.g., Bunkio MATSUKI). As to Chinese proper nouns, I use the transliteration used by the author/text being discussed.

Embracing the East

*M*adame Butterfly has for over a century been one of the classic narratives of East-West relations. It tells the story of Lieutenant Benjamin Franklin Pinkerton, a U.S. naval officer stationed in Nagasaki who adds comfort and excitement to his foreign assignment by having a broker arrange his marriage with a "native" woman, Cho-Cho-San — or, Madame Butterfly. Innocently believing that the relationship is permanent, Cho-Cho-San severs ties with her Japanese family, converts to Christianity, and strives to acculturate to an American lifestyle in order to prepare for a life in America with her husband. After Pinkerton's departure to the United States, Cho-Cho-San gives birth to his child, and anxiously awaits his return to Japan. Pinkerton does return, but with his elegant American wife — Mrs. Pinkerton — and only to claim his child. Believing that death with honor is better than living a dishonorable life, Cho-Cho-San kills herself.[1]

Since the publication of John Luther Long's original story in 1898, David Belasco's stage production in 1900, and Giacomo Puccini's opera production in 1904, which coincided with the United States' full-fledged entry into the affairs of Asia and the Pacific, Madame Butterfly has provided a classic trope symbolizing the politics of race, nation, and gender in U.S.-Asian relations. It has traditionally been interpreted as a melodramatic construction of Orientalism — Western ways of perceiving, understanding, and representing the "Orient" that are founded upon the material reality of unequal power relations between the West and the East and upon the belief in the essential difference between the two. As many Euro-American cultural representations of the East attest, such notions of power and difference were typically expressed in gendered terms: the powerful West was associated with virile masculinity, and the subordinate East with passive femininity. Reading *Madame Butterfly* in this model, Lieutenant Pinkerton symbolizes the dominant, masculine America, while the fragile, exotic beauty Cho-Cho-San stands for the subordinated, feminized Asia.

However, the limits of such a simplistic binary become clear when one considers the critical role played by Mrs. Pinkerton. While the unequal power relationship between Lieutenant Pinkerton and Cho-Cho-San is clear from the beginning of the story, it is Mrs. Pinkerton—her absence from the Japanese scene, her presence "at home" as a white, upper-class, female guardian of American nationalism and expansionism, and her appearance in Japan at the end—who sheds light on the bigger picture of the gendered dynamics of U.S.-Japan relations. Adelaide Pinkerton, or "the Blonde Woman" as the author calls her, plays an active and aggressive role in showing that white women don't take Asian women seriously, that they are in alliance with American men rather than with Asian women, and that they are more concerned with their own womanhood at home than with the lot of women across the Pacific. Determined to claim Cho-Cho-San's and her husband's child, Mrs. Pinkerton goes to meet Cho-Cho-San at her house:

> As [Mrs. Pinkerton] advanced and saw Cho-Cho-San, she stopped in open admiration.
>
> "How very charming—how *lovely*—you are, dear! Will you kiss me, you pretty—*plaything*!"
>
> Cho-Cho-San stared at her with round eyes—as children do when afraid. Then her nostrils quivered and her lids slowly closed.
>
> "No," she said, very softly.
>
> "Ah, well," laughed the other. "I don't blame you. They say you don't do that sort of thing—to women, at any rate. I quite forgive our men for falling in love with you . . . Good day!"[2]

After the blond woman leaves, Cho-Cho-San says to her maid that Mrs. Pinkerton is "more beautiful than the Sun-Goddess," and "She—she thing me—jus' a—*play-thing*."[3]

The two women see each other in clearly sexualized terms. The sexual meanings each assigns to the other are expressed in Mrs. Pinkerton's and Cho-Cho-San's characterization of each other as "charming," "lovely," and "pretty" on the one hand, and "more beautiful than the Sun-Goddess" on the other, as well as in Mrs. Pinkerton's desire to have Cho-Cho-San kiss her (but not the other way around). Yet such eroticism is firmly grounded in racialized power dynamics. Mrs. Pinkerton infantalizes Cho-Cho-San while insinuating that Japanese women seduce American men with their innocent sexuality. She speaks on behalf of all white American women at home when she claims to forgive not only her husband but "our men" for falling in love with Japanese women. She addresses Cho-Cho-San not as "you" the individual but the objectified, collective body of Japanese women. Although Cho-Cho-San appears too innocent and ignorant to comprehend the situation, her comment that Mrs. Pinkerton thinks of her "jus'a—*play-thing*" shows that she instantly perceives the power differential between them.

It is also significant that Mrs. Pinkerton arrives at the scene to claim Cho-Cho-San's mixed-blood child and take him to America. Why does Mrs. Pinkerton want a half-Japanese, half-American child? At the turn of the century, many U.S. states had antimiscegenation laws; racial hybridity was viewed with suspicion at best; and the racial "inferiority" of certain peoples—as well as the "whiteness" of certain groups not yet firmly determined as "white"—was "proven" by scientific, legal, and "common sense" discourse.[4] This makes Mrs. Pinkerton's claim over Cho-Cho-San's child seem all the more remarkable. Does Mrs. Pinkerton's volunteering to bring the half-Japanese child to American civilization in the face of likely social opposition symbolize her nobility? Or does her taking the baby away from its mother symbolize her heartlessness and, in turn, the cruelty of America's racial and gender ideology which constructs Mrs. Pinkerton as the ideal mother while denying Cho-Cho-San her right to motherhood? Or does it represent the turn-of-the-century America's assimilationist racial ideology in that even a half-Japanese child can be made "American" by a white, middle-class woman?

Racial and gender dynamics symbolized not only by the relationship between Lieutenant Pinkerton and Cho-Cho-San but also by Mrs. Pinkerton are further complicated by the fact that *Madame Butterfly* is a text written and continually adapted by white men and widely enjoyed by white female audiences in America. Both Cho-Cho-San as the icon of exotic femininity *and* Mrs. Pinkerton as the symbol of white American womanhood are ideological constructions shared by white male creators and a considerable number of female audiences. To make matters even more complex, during the first half of the twentieth century, in stage productions—both the play and the opera—and on screen, not only Mrs. Pinkerton and other American characters but also the role of Cho-Cho-San was almost exclusively performed by white actresses/singers. Thus, in order to interpret *Madame Butterfly*, one needs to understand, among other things, the interplay among the white male producers' notions of Japanese femininity and American womanhood, the white female performers' enactment of the Japanese heroine, and the American audience's understanding of the racial and gendered meanings of U.S.-Japan relations. The questions that arise from the narrative of *Madame Butterfly* are just as much about white women and America's race and gender relations at home as they are about U.S. engagement with Asia.

Mrs. Pinkerton stands at a critical juncture in these questions, and her role in *Madame Butterfly* illustrates the larger issue of the role of white women in American Orientalism. While Mrs. Pinkerton enacts a crucial role in this fictional Orientalist narrative, real white women also played an integral and active part in American Orientalism. Women missionaries to China and Japan, who outnumbered their male counterparts at the turn of the century, played a significant role in spreading the gospel of Christianity, modernity, and gentility; and through their reports home in mission board publications and personal letters, they spread their views on Asia.[5] White, middle-class women consumed "Asian" objects—such as chinaware, silverware, bric-à-brac, furniture, and kimono—and assigned specific meanings to them. Artistic and intellectual women studied and appropriated Asian cultural texts—such as woodblock prints and poetry—and incorporated them into American arts and letters. White women performed Asian roles on stage, literally embodying Asian femininity. Women writers such as Pearl Buck produced enormously popular works about Asia, more influential than any text written by male scholars or writers. Early investigation about Asia in American academe included a significant number of female contributors; anthropologist Ruth Benedict's *The Chrysanthemum and the Sword* became one of the most authoritative texts about Japanese culture. These women "embraced" the East in multiple meanings of the word: they adored it, they eagerly adopted its ways, they believed in it, they brought it close to themselves, and they contained it—in gendered and sexualized ways. Although many of the women have been neglected, marginalized, or forgotten, white women were central to the shaping of American Orientalism.

This book examines how white American women helped construct American Orientalism in the period between the 1870s and 1940s. It analyzes the gender politics operating in American discourses about China and Japan in diverse sites of cultural production and consumption, including material culture, visual arts, performing arts, literature, and anthropology. White women played pivotal roles in inscribing gendered meanings to Asia, both complicating and replicating the dominant Orientalist discourse founded upon the notion of "West = male vs. East = female." Their participation in Orientalist discourse offered many American women an effective avenue through which to become part of a dominant American ideology and to gain authority and agency which were denied to them in other realms of sociopolitical life. By embracing Asia, women gained material and affective power both in relation to American society and vis-à-vis Asian subjects, which brought new meanings to their identities as white American women.

In addition to demonstrating white women's role in Orientalism, this book traces the cultural history of the relationship between white women and Orientalism. The nature of American Orientalism changed with the evolving relationship the United States had with the "Orient." Common expressions of Orientalism include objectifying, exoticizing, homogenizing, and feminizing the "Orient." These expressions are overlapping and interrelated but not always consistent with or supportive of each other. Historical and ideological contexts shape Orientalism—both its underlying ideology and its cultural manifestations—differently at different times. While most studies of Orientalism that have been produced since the publication of Edward Said's pivotal book in 1978 focus on European discourse about its colonial territories in the Middle East, in this book I use the term Orientalism specifically in reference to U.S. discourse about China and Japan during the period of U.S. empire-building in Asia-Pacific. This particular application of the concept of Orientalism requires specific historical and theoretical thinking. Unlike European relationships to the Middle East, U.S. involvement in China and Japan did not entail direct colonial rule in the form of territorial acquisition and political governance. Yet from the late nineteenth century, the United States built and consolidated its "informal empire" in China and Japan through the Open Door policy, unequal treaties, and the expansion of commerce and cultural exports. This "informal empire" in East Asia gave impetus to, and was supported by, the more direct and blatant forms of conquest and colonization in other parts of Asia-Pacific, such as the Philippines, Guam, and Hawai'i. In the same period, Japan emulated the Western powers and became Asia's own imperial power and eventually collided heads-on with the United States. These dramatic changes in the Pacific Rim were reflected in the different meanings Americans assigned to Japan and China, and the racialized and gendered tropes were deployed differently in each historical phase.

The roles of white women in American society also changed dramatically from the late nineteenth century to World War II. The Victorian "cult of true womanhood" was gradually replaced by new ideals for women's role, as white, middle-class women gained increasing access to higher education and professional opportunities in the twentieth century. Even as the ideals of domesticity and motherhood remained strong, in the twentieth century they were expressed in new ways, exemplified by Progressive social reformers both at home and abroad. The politics of suffragism and the culture of modernism gave birth to New Women and flappers. After the gender-segregated labor market produced the comradely ideal for families during the Depression era, the wartime economy created the image of Rosie the Riveter, "independent" women working in stereotypically male occupations.

The evolution of both U.S.-Asian relations and white women's social roles in America meant changes in white women's relationship to Orientalism. Among the roles that white women played in Orientalism were those of consumers, producers, practitioners, critics, and experts. These were not mutually exclusive categories, and often the same women played multiple, seemingly contradictory, roles simultaneously. But there were also changes in the way in which women's particular positions and perspectives were deployed or appreciated in the field of Orientalism by both male Orientalists and the women themselves. While women tended to be mostly consumers of Orientalism in the nineteenth century, the growing availability of "Asian" things and ideas from the turn of the century onward facilitated women's entry into the production of Orientalism. Furthermore, as gender became an increasingly effective tool with which to understand, negotiate, and represent the complex and intensifying U.S.-Asian relations, white women with material or discursive access to Asia came to play the role of expert authorities in American Orientalism. In this context, white women often used Orientalism not only to make their interventions in American ideas about Asia per se but also to assert, address, and/or challenge women's roles in American society.

My account of American Orientalism starts at a time when different strands of Orientalism converged and created a cultural discourse that extended over various segments of American society. One such strand was what historian John Kuo Wei Tchen calls "patrician Orientalism."[6] The China trade of the late eighteenth and early nineteenth centuries brought to the United States not only Chinese goods such as tea, silk, and porcelain, but also an imaginary vision of the Far East. In these early years of contact, American knowledge about Asia was extremely limited. In 1785, a year after the first American vessel to China, *The Empress of China*, reached Canton and brought tea, silk, and porcelain to the United States, George Washington was surprised to discover, by seeing the images drawn on Chinese porcelain, that the Chinese were not white.[7] Well into the mid-nineteenth century, the images and ideas Americans created and developed about China relied heavily on the Chinese goods brought to the American market through the trade. Wealthy American clients appreciated the exotic design, bright colors, and exquisite handicraft of Chinese goods, and some went beyond the mere purchasing of goods to build their own "Chinese-style" pavilions or pagodas in their gardens.[8] This mode of American Orientalism consisted largely of curiosity and exoticism.

Alongside the United States' commercial interests in China, American engagement with Asia also expanded because of evangelical efforts underway. American missionaries had begun to evangelize in China in the 1840s, and by the 1890s, the enterprise began to show significant results. By the end of the century, there were approximately one thousand American missionaries in China. American missionaries also went to Japan, where they had a significant influence through their educational work, particularly the establishment of girls' schools and women's colleges. Although the actual number of converts to Christianity remained relatively small in both countries, the missionary enterprise left broader legacies in the form of ideas about modernization and Westernization. Missionaries also contributed significantly to the shaping of American ideas about Asia in the early phase of U.S.-Asian contact. The letters and writings sent home by the missionaries—revealing their racist prejudices about the "heathen," uncivilized, barbaric peoples, colonialist condescension toward the native *amahs* and domestics, and compassionate affections for parishioners and students—informed and educated those in America about the distant land.[9] This sense of evangelical mission—and the reaction against it—constituted a significant component of American Orientalism in the decades after the peak of the missionary movement itself.

There was also a more intellectually-oriented strand of Orientalism. Following Commodore Matthew Perry's arrival in 1853, Japan opened its doors to foreign trade after two centuries of isolation. The encounter with the Western products, technology, and political system shook Japan's feudal government, leading to the fall of shogunate and the founding of the modern Meiji government in 1868. The newly established exchange between the United States and Japan took place on many levels, but one of the most influential was the hiring of American professionals by the Japanese government to teach and consult in many areas, including language, law, engineering, and science. A number of these Americans—most of whom were upper-class New England men—became pioneer "Japanologists" and played crucial roles in introducing Japanese culture and history to Americans.[10] One cannot understand American Orientalism without considering the intellectual and cultural work of men such as William Elliot Griffis, Edward Sylvester Morse, Ernest Fenollosa, and Lafcadio Hearn.

At the other end of the spectrum from this intellectual Orientalism was the highly charged political discourse regarding Asian immigrants that emerged on the West Coast of the United States and quickly became a national debate. With the arrival of Chinese laborers in the mid-nineteenth century, the heated debates around "free" and "coolie" labor swept across the country, producing images of the "Heathen Chinee" and "John Chinaman" and leading to the Chinese Exclusion Act of 1882. The wave of Japanese laborers arriving on the shores of Hawai'i and the West Coast further aggravated the racial construction of Asians as unassimilable aliens. Racialized discourse about labor was closely linked with gendered and sexualized notions of emasculated Asian men, Chinese prostitutes, and Japanese picture brides, generating a series of legislation and court rulings—including the Page Law of 1875, Chinese Exclusion Act of 1882, *Takao Ozawa v. United States*, and culminating in the Immigration Act of 1924—that located Asians outside of the American polity.

What spread American Orientalism into a broader cultural trend beyond either an intellectual discourse among the elites or politically charged debates around Asian immigration was the rise of "popular" Orientalism or, in John Tchen's words, "commercial Orientalism."[11] In the 1870s and 1880s, various sociocultural factors—such as the growth of consumer culture through venues such as mail order catalogues and department stores, cultural spectacles such as the world's fairs, and the fascination with the exotic as manifested in both highbrow and lowbrow theaters—turned the interest in Asian imports shared by some segments of the population into a more widespread form of popular culture. The penetration of Japanese goods into

Western markets brought about a kind of "Japan craze," following the European vogue of Japonisme in art and style. The entry of Japanese goods into the American market mingled with the images and ideas about Asia already created by the earlier China trade, and led to the conflation, confusion, and admixture of Chinese and Japanese traditions and styles along with other "Oriental" ones.[12] This popular Orientalism first emerged and grew in cosmopolitan cities such as New York and Boston and soon spread across the country. It is this popularization of Orientalism among the middle-class Americans that marks the beginning of my study.

This book will explore diverse modes and sites in which white women engaged in American Orientalism. Part I, "Materializing Asia," looks at white women's interactions with Asia as objects and tools by focusing on material culture and visual arts as a site of Orientalism. From the late nineteenth to the early twentieth century, the idea of Asia gradually changed from an esoteric body of knowledge held by a select group of male intellectuals to a popular commodity in the American market. Asia also became an important source for American cultural expression, and American artists deployed styles and methods as well as subject matters of "Asian" art to explore new themes and aesthetics in their work. Thus, Asia beckoned as "materials"—both in the form of commodified objects in the market and as styles and methods imported for use in "American" art. White, middle-class women played a central role in this process both as consumers and producers of such "materials." I will first examine the roles of white women in Orientalist consumption by looking at how "Asian" artifacts circulated in the American market in specifically gendered ways. I will then analyze the works of women artists who used the methods and themes of "Asian" art—namely, Mary Cassatt, Bertha Lum, and Helen Hyde—to see how "Asian" art methods and subject matters were useful for their feminist and/or aesthetic goals.

Part II, "Performing Asia," deals with the diverse ways in which white American women "performed" what they understood to be Asian-ness by engaging in different forms of racial and cultural cross-dressing. I examine how white women's performances of Asian-ness, and particularly their embodiment of "Asian" gender roles and sexualities, not only turned them into powerful agents in the production of Orientalism but also empowered them as American women. First I will look at literal "performances," that is, theatrical performances of Asian roles. Analyzing the works of actresses and singers who played the roles of Asian heroines on stage and debates surrounding their performances, I demonstrate how these productions were performances of modern American womanhood as well as enactments of Asian femininity. I will then look at more indirect forms of "performance" through artistic or political engagement with Asia. My discussion of Amy Lowell, who used Asian forms and themes in her poetry, shows that literary Orientalism made it possible for Lowell and her readers to "try on" Asian-ness and assume alternative gender roles and enjoy the pleasures of cultural cross-dressing. I will then examine the life and writings of Agnes Smedley, a radical activist who worked with the Communist army during the Chinese revolution. For Smedley, Asia was a site where she could shape her own gender and sexual identity in ways she could not in the West; putting on the uniform of the Chinese Communists, she was able to pursue not only the political goals of the Communist Revolution but also egalitarian gender relations not determined by sexuality.

In the last part, "Authorizing Asia," I will look at the discursive field in which American women became particularly influential "experts" and "authorities" on Asia. My discussion here shows that women's own gendered positions as well as their use of gender as a category of analysis provided them with a particular authority on Asian affairs at a time when sociopolitical conditions in the Pacific Rim were becoming increasingly tense. The two chapters in this final section will examine works of two well-known women—Pearl Buck and Ruth Benedict. Through a textual analysis of their classic texts—Buck's *The Good Earth* and Benedict's *The Chrysanthemum and the Sword*—I will demonstrate how the use of gender as a narrative tool and analytical category served to both revise and reinforce the dominant discourse of American Orientalism.

Materializing Asia

Asia as Spectacle and Commodity
Feminization of Orientalist Consumption

ight Cousins (1875), one of Louisa May Alcott's novels for girls, depicts the transformation of the heroine Rose from a sheltered, frail orphan to a healthy, strong young woman. Rose's new guardian Uncle Alec takes her from the stuffy world of great-aunts and transforms her into a new type of woman who practices a healthy diet, outdoor exercise, domestic industry, and intellectual curiosity.[1] Like the enormously popular *Little Women* and Alcott's numerous other stories, the novel portrays the material and moral lives of genteel girls and the emergence of a new type of womanhood in late nineteenth-century America. Alcott's proto-feminist ideals, which often conflicted with the dominant conventions of femininity and domesticity as well as the demands of the market, were expressed under the guise of conventional juvenile literature.[2]

Rose's transformation is symbolized by the material surroundings of her domestic environment. At the beginning of the novel, lonely, tearful Rose sits in a room that appears to be set up perfectly for her misery: "[the room] was dark and still, full of ancient furniture, sombre curtains, and hung all round with portraits of solemn old gentlemen in wigs, severe-nosed ladies in top-heavy caps, and staring children in little bob-tailed coats or short-waisted frocks."[3] A little later in the story, her discovery of wonderful, exotic treasures brought home by her family of sea captains raises

Rose's spirits. Refreshing herself with "Lumps of Delight" brought from Cairo, Rose indulges in this exotic pleasure, wearing a purple fez on her blonde head, brilliant scarves about her waist, a pair of Turkish slippers on her feet, holding a smelling-bottle in one hand and the "spicy box of oriental sweetmeats" in the other. "I feel like a girl in the 'Arabian Nights,'" she exclaims in joy. In the meantime, Uncle Alec transforms Rose's room, "once so shrouded, still and solitary, now so full of light and warmth and simple luxury":

> India matting covered the floor, with a gay rug here and there; the antique andirons shone on the wide hearth, where a cheery blaze dispelled the dampness of the long-closed room. Bamboo lounges and chairs stood about, and quaint little tables in cosey corners; one bearing a pretty basket, one a desk, and on a third lay several familiar-looking books. In a recess stood a narrow white bed, with a lovely madonna hanging over it. The Japanese screen half folded back showed a delicate toilet-service of blue and white set forth on a marble slab, and near by was the great bath-pan, with Turkish towels and a sponge as big as Rose's head.[4]

The encounter with these foreign objects—many of them from the Orient—takes place at a critical moment in the transformation of Rose's gendered identity, from the "proper" girlhood she abided by under the care of her elderly great-aunts to a new model of young womanhood. The influx of material objects from foreign lands into the domestic space exposes Rose to the world of adventure in her own home, and thus without endangering her genteel femininity. Rose makes an important leap to becoming a young woman of a new generation, curious and bold in the big world, without having to leave home or transgressing the bounds of gentility.

Rose's encounter with the Orient goes a little beyond the physical confines of her home, however. When one of her uncles' ships returns from Hong Kong, Uncle Alec takes her to the harbor for a "glimpse of China."

> "I'll show you two genuine Chinamen who have just arrived. You will like to welcome Whang Lo and Fun See, I'm sure."
>
> "Don't ask me to speak to them, uncle; I shall be sure to laugh at the odd names and the pig-tails and the slanting eyes. Please let me just trot round after you; I like that best."

At the harbor, Rose witnesses the importation of Chinese goods to America and is enraptured by the sensory feeling and spectacular scene: "Odd smells saluted her nose, and odd sights met her eyes, but Rose liked it all . . ."[5] Rose's gaze is directed not only to Chinese objects; however; her encounter with the two "Chinamen" is also an important element of her growth into a new woman. As the names Whang Lo and Fun See indicate, the Chinamen are curious spectacles that entertain Rose:

Mr. Whang Lo was an elderly gentleman in American costume, with his pig-tail neatly wound round his head. He spoke English, and was talking busily with Uncle Mac in the most commonplace way,—so Rose considered him a failure. But Fun See was delightfully Chinese from his junk-like shoes to the button of his pagodo [sic] hat; for he had got himself up in style, and was a mass of silk jackets and slouchy trousers. He was short and fat, and waddled comically; his eyes were very "slanting," as Rose said; his queue was long, so were his nails; his yellow face was plump and shiny, and he was altogether a highly satisfactory Chinaman.[6]

Fun See's foreignness thus makes him an ideal object of Rose's gaze, and the material elements that make up his Chinaman-ness serve as tools for Rose's education. Presented with a tea set and an "astonishing fan" by Fun See, a Chinese umbrella by Whang Lo, and lanterns to light her balcony by Uncle Alec, Rose goes home with souvenirs of her "trip to China." She later reports to her aunt that she collected "some useful information about China" and recites all the different kinds of tea produced in China; she further recounts that "[p]rincipal productions [of China] are porcelain, tea, cinnamon, shawls, tin, tamarinds, and opium."[7] Thus, the encounter with things and people Asian and the incorporation of Asian objects for her and her aunts' domestic consumption play an important role in the expansion of Rose's world and the making of a "new" young woman. In other words, the entry of Asian objects into her American home parallels the journey of this white, upper-middle-class girl into a new form of femininity—a journey that takes place right in, or just beyond, her own home.

Alcott's use of Asian objects and people to represent Rose's transformation is not simply an idiosyncratic literary device but an illustration of the material culture shaping the emerging ideals of femininity in postbellum America. The encounter with things Asian as spectacle and objects of consumption was an index of the expansion of women's/girls' imaginary, if not physical, sphere. It suggested a liberating potential for white, middle-class women whose rights and opportunities were limited by their gender yet whose racial, class, and national identities made the world come to them in the form of commodities.

This chapter traces the material culture of American Orientalism between the 1870s and the 1920s and the roles of various agents in bringing Asia to white women. Women encountered Asian objects first as public spectacles. These encounters led wealthy women to collect Asian artifacts, while middle-class women purchased more accessible "Asian" goods for personal and household consumption. Various cultural and social phenomena—including large-scale cultural apparatuses such as the world's fairs and museum collections, appropriations and adaptations of "Asian" art motifs by artists and manufacturers, the popularity of Oriental novelty stores and art dealers, and the proliferation of advice literature on interior decoration—helped transform ideas about Asia from what had been a highly specialized, esoteric knowledge of select male intellectuals to a popular commodity purchased and used not only in upper- but also middle-class American households, particularly by women. Thus, artistic Orientalism which manifested in the works of "high art" by painters such as William Paxton, William Merrit Chase, James Abbott McNeill Whistler, or Winslow Homer linked with the field of decorative arts and household goods, creating a culture of middlebrow Orientalism. The material culture of Orientalism packaged the mixed interests Americans had about Asia—Asia as seductive, aesthetic, refined culture, and Asia as foreign, premodern, Other—and made them into unthreatening objects for collection and consumption. This encounter with, and consumption of, Asian objects turned white, middle-class women into agents of the culture of Orientalism without their having to physically travel to the Orient. Consumption and material culture offered women a cultural, educational, and liberating experience akin to the grand tour of the world which their wealthy male counterparts undertook.

While Rose in *Eight Cousins* had a privileged access to the site of China imports because of her status as an heiress in a family of sea captains, it was not only women and girls of the wealthy class that encountered Asia as spectacle and objects in the nineteenth century. Especially after the mid-nineteenth century, Asian goods and peoples appeared frequently as public spectacles for American viewers. As historian John Kuo Wei Tchen shows, the marketplace economy and the commercial culture of New York in mid-nineteenth century produced new forms of representing Chinese things, ideas, and people. Not only Chinese objects but living Chinese people—such as "the Chinese Lady" Afong Moy, the "Siamese Twins" Chang and Eng, and "Miss Pwan-Ye-Koo" and her entourage—were displayed, mimicked, and mechanically simulated in theaters, dime museums, and public spectacles for the "edifying curiosities" of the American audience.[8]

This spectacular mode of representations of Asia was most vividly played out in the world's fairs of the late nineteenth and early twentieth centuries. The world's fairs in the United States—most notably the Philadelphia Centennial of 1876 and the Worlds' Columbian Exposition in Chicago in 1893—not only displayed the latest technologies, arts, and ideas, but visualized and presented to the public the global social system which produced them.[9] The spatial arrangement of the grounds, architectural and decorative themes, classification of various exhibits, and the use of technology all functioned to give "scientific" justification to the racial and civilizational hierarchy which placed Anglo-Saxons at the top. At the World's Columbian Exposition, the fair's concept of racial hierarchy was most symbolically epitomized by the layout of the fair ground: the White City with rows of white colossal monuments based on Greek and Roman classicism exhibited the technologies, products, and arts of European and North American nations, while the adjacent

Midway Plaisance, which was attached as an entertainment subordinate to the main part of the fair, displayed the "primitive" peoples and cultures forbidden to enter the White City.[10]

Asian goods and cultures were represented in the context of the racial logic of the fair. China refused to have an official exhibit at the Chicago fair in protest to the 1892 Geary Law, which renewed the restrictions placed on Chinese immigration by the 1882 Exclusion Act. However, since it seemed essential that China be represented in some capacity in an exposition supposedly international in character, the Chinese exhibit was leased to "patriotic and commercially interested Chinese" in America and was placed on the Midway Plaisance. The "Chinese Village" consisted of a theater, a joss house, a bazaar, a tea garden and a café. The actors and actresses in hand-embroidered silk costumes performed plays that were "identically the same as given in the larger cities in China," and Chinese musicians played native instruments. The joss house contained thousands of idols, representing "heaven from the Buddhist stand-point." The infernal regions, with the many different modes of punishment, were vividly illustrated. The joss house also included a store, a farmhouse and a house of royalty, and "in the latter [lived] a Chinese lady and two children, a little girl 2 ½ years old and a baby boy 11 months of age." In the tea garden and café, the visitor could sit down and have tea and fruit served while listening to the soft strains of the Chinese music.[11]

On the other hand, Japan made a quite different appearance at the fair. Having embarked on extensive political, economic, and social reforms under the new Meiji government, Japan eagerly pursued economic growth and military empowerment through the increased exports. Japan had participated in the Philadelphia Centennial Exhibition in 1876 and received high praise for the excellence and beauty of its products. With this experience, the Japanese had high hopes for the World's Columbian Exposition. Before an official invitation from the Columbian Exposition had even been received, Japan's Imperial Diet voluntarily proposed that provision be made for Japanese participation and agreed to appropriate the funds. The government further made a supplementary appropriation of 630,000 yen. The Emperor appointed a supervisory commission placed directly under the government's control, and the minister of agriculture and commerce became the ex officio president of the commission. To widen support and improve communication, an advisory council was appointed that included manufacturers and merchants.[12]

The most notable of the Japanese exhibits at the fair was Ho-ö-den, or the Phoenix Hall. On the Wooded Island in the Lagoon, a small piece of land located near the Fine Arts Building, the building provided visual relief from the overpowering classicism of the White City. Frederick Olmstead, who supervised the fair's landscaping, originally intended to keep the island a refuge from all formal fair activities. However, the Japanese, who promised to present their buildings as a gift to the people of Chicago, managed to change the commission's mind and obtain a

40,000 square foot site. Ho-ö-den was modeled after the mid-eleventh century palace built near Kyoto, consisting of three pavilions, each representing the decorative and architectural features of three prominent epochs in Japanese art. Kuru Masamichi, a government architect who was the director of Japanese work for the world's fair, designed the building; the Tokyo Art School furnished the interior decorations. Japanese carpenters, sent to Chicago expressly for the purpose, completed the construction of Ho-ö-den which was estimated to have cost $100,000.[13]

Independent of the intent of the Japanese government, however, Ho-ö-den reasserted the Orientalist vision of the Japanese as the peculiar Other. While the excellent proportions, superb craftsmanship, and exquisite design of the building and its interiors impressed American visitors, they were also fascinated by the spectacle of the construction process.[14] Even while the snow from Chicago's winter still covered the Wooded Island, Japanese carpenters began to construct the pavilion. The carpenters at work were soon surrounded by curious crowds intrigued by the raw examples of exotic peoples. "And what bright and nimble fellows these workmen were," reported *Harper's.* "It may be that they were picked men, selected for their skill and intelligence . . . It seems almost a pity that these carpenters could not be kept at work all during the fair."[15] The crowds that gathered to watch the workmen were so great that ropes had to be put up to keep them from the construction site, and they plied the workmen with questions about the novel techniques they employed. The carpenters, according to observers, retained their good humor and answered the inquiries. The Japanese carpenters assembling the Phoenix Hall became objects of the Western gaze, as much as the peoples displayed in the Midway Plaisance.

It was within the context of the fair's imperial worldview and its representation of nonwhite cultures as spectacles that a significant number of American women first encountered Asian arts and artifacts. The popular novel of the time, *Uncle Jeremiah and Family Go to the Fair,* depicts one such encounter. Uncle Jeremiah, perpetually awestruck at the sights and sounds he encountered in the Manufactures Building, saw two elderly ladies sit down in the Japanese section to admire a display of pottery and overheard their conversation. "I don't see the use of sending missionaries to Japan," said the first. Nodding her head in agreement, the other replied: "I don't believe they are so very bad after all. I can't believe that anyone who could make such things could be a very wicked heathen. I should think the Japanese would almost feel like sending missionaries over here."[16] While such renditions of women's responses to Asian displays reflected their racialized notions about Asian peoples as much as their openness to appreciating Asian goods, it is important to note the functions of public cultural apparatuses such as the world's fairs in introducing Asian culture to the American audience, particularly women, first and foremost as a spectacle and display.

Indeed, white women in this period typically encountered "Asia" as a spectacle and saw Asian artifacts as objects for display. This mode of encounter is evidenced by a small group of wealthy women who collected Asian arts and artifacts at the turn of the century. Like the world's fairs of the period, major collections of foreign arts and artifacts formed during this period publicly represented and celebrated America's expansionist and imperialist power.[17] Asian art collections by wealthy men such as Henry Havemeyer, Charles Lang Freer, and J. P. Morgan were part of such enterprise. Some wealthy women of the Gilded Age took active part in this project of collecting Asian arts. The women's wealth and class status, their physical location in the metropolitan cities on the East Coast, and their cultural and intellectual milieu offered them a special relationship with male Orientalists and Asian merchants.

The Isabella Stewart Gardner Museum which opened in Fenway Court in Boston in 1903 exemplified the ideals of the Gilded Age museums. Gardner's interest in, and acquisition of, Asian art took place in the context of America's imperial enterprise in Asia-Pacific. In her flamboyant social life as Boston's cultural matron in the 1880s, Gardner befriended male intellectuals and connoisseurs of Asian arts, such as Edward Sylvester Morse, William Sturgis Bigelow, and Percival Lowell. In 1882, Morse gave a series of lectures on Japan at Gardner's house, which stimulated her desire to see the Orient and led to her trip around the world in 1883. Gardner and her husband traveled in Japan, China, Cambodia, Singapore, Burma, and India. While Gardner was fascinated by the cultures and arts of each country she visited, to her Asia was clearly a spectacle. In a letter from Kyoto to a friend, she described her trip to a *sumo* wrestling match in Osaka, in a manner not unlike Rose's fascination with Chinese imports and "Chinamen" in *Eight Cousins*:

This man [sitting next to her] was intensely interested to know which wrestlers I thought would win and asked me each time. Once I couldn't form any idea, so he coached me and said it was a sure thing for the small lithe man against a huge great fellow, so I interested myself properly in the little one — and when he threw the big one most cleverly and wonderfully, I thought my friend would have convulsions of delight, as I clapped my hands and called out. Please don't be shocked, dear, at all these dreadful proceedings. "When in Turkey, etc." — I shall go to see the Missionaries when I go back to Osaka, to atone. And I am really interested in the work they do, for the poor Japanese *sorely* need help; but how beautiful are their Buddhist temples. When I get into one I never want to come away — I could lie on the mats and look forever through the dim light.[18]

As much as Gardner saw the Japanese as heathens in need of help, she was also drawn by the sight of *sumo* and the beauty of Buddhist temples, both of which were objects of her American gaze.

In the 1900s, Gardner's interest in Asian art was expressed in conspicuous ways. As soon as Okakura Kakuzo, a young Japanese artist, connoisseur, philosopher, and poet was appointed to the staff of the Boston Museum of Fine Arts in 1904, Gardner promptly added him to her entourage, and Okakura and Gardner spent time together whenever he was in Boston. Their friendship increased her interest in Asian art and culture, and in 1905 she turned her Music Room into a "Japanese village" and had herself carried around "in a genuine jinrikisha [rickshaw]." She had Joseph Lindon Smith write a Japanese play to be performed at repeated intervals on the stage of the Music Room. According to *Town Topics*, a New York magazine of social gossip, Gardner's "jinrikisha man was a real Japanese . . . All about were little pagoda-like booths with Japanese fittings and ornaments and . . . on the stage was a Japanese grove with a temple at one side and a Buddhist shrine nestled in the trees opposite. Japanese men and women wandered to and fro as villagers, some gazing at the booths as if seeking the most favorable chance to trade, while others were tradesmen themselves, saddled with trays of all kinds of attractive novelties of Japanese handicraft." In the opinion of this writer, the production was "a curious stage show."[19] Gardner's interest in, and accumulation of, Asian arts exemplified by this spectacular performance reflected the mode of Orientalist consumption of Asian cultures.

Abby Aldrich Rockefeller and her sister Lucy Truman Aldrich are further examples of patronesses of Asian arts and artifacts. Lucy (1869–1955) and Abby (1874–1948) Aldrich were born daughters of Abby Greene and Nelson Wilmarth Aldrich in Providence, Rhode Island. In the year of Lucy's birth, her father won a seat on the Providence Common Council; in 1879 he was elected to the U.S. House of Representatives and in 1881 to the U.S. Senate. Growing up in this privileged family in Providence, the Aldrich sisters were exposed to paintings, prints, rare books, and fine furniture, which their father collected from around the world. Each summer he traveled to Europe, sometimes with the children, purchasing china, silver, and other arts and artifacts. He also had a significant collection of Asian artifacts and books on Asia, which filled the boathouse he built in Warwick, Rhode Island, in 1896.[20]

In addition to the daily exposure to these objects and literatures, the Aldrich sisters were introduced to Asian art and culture through cultural events at the Providence Art Club, the Providence Athenaeum, and the Rhode Island School of Design. The activities related to Asian subjects offered in Providence during this period demonstrate the high level of interest in Asia among both the social elites and the city's residents in general. Starting in 1885 and continuing until his death in 1926, Edward Sylvester Morse gave a series of lectures in Providence on Japanese manners, customs, and household art. In the 1870s, the Providence Athenaeum began purchasing books on Asia for its extensive collection on travel and exploration.[21] By 1900, the collection included nearly every important book on Asia available in the United States. In 1878, the Providence Public Library opened with a collection of ten thousand volumes that also included many works on the Far East.

Private collectors in Providence were also assembling significant collections of Asian books and objects, such as the one by Brown University Professor Willard H. Munro, who acquired every work about Japan as it was published. During the 1890s, the Providence Art Club included in its annual exhibition paintings of Japan by John LaFarge. In 1901 it exhibited watercolors by the Pacific Painting Society, a group of Japanese artists working in the Western style. In 1898 the Museum of the Rhode Island School of Design exhibited Japanese prints, and in 1904 it also held a show of paintings by the members of the Pacific Painting Society.[22]

The exposure to these materials, as well as socializing with the leading collectors and connoisseurs of Asian art such as Henry Clay Frick, the Havemeyers, and J. P. Morgan cultivated the Aldrich sisters' interest in and taste for Asian arts and artifacts from an early age. Abby Aldrich's marriage to John D. Rockefeller, Jr. in 1901 added financial resources of the Rockefeller family to the sisters' interest in art. Lucy Aldrich was increasingly drawn into the Rockefeller orbit and became her sister's partner in art collecting. In April 1919, Lucy Aldrich sailed on *The Empress of Russia* to Japan, a trip which was arranged through the office of John D. Rockefeller, Jr. and escorted throughout by Standard Oil executives and wives. During this trip, Aldrich made her first visit to Yamanaka & Co. in Kyoto, from whom she would acquire much of her future collection. Aldrich admitted at this point that she knew "absolutely nothing about Oriental things," and that she was afraid of making mistakes, but that she was "learning fast."[23] She quickly developed her fascination with and admiration for Japan and things Japanese, and wrote to her sister, "I'd much rather be a Buddhist than a Baptist anyway—the whole thing appeals so much more to my temperamental, or is it emotional, love of color: the gold and lacquer, the beat of the drums and even the smell of the incense. I love it all."[24] Aldrich's claim of Japan's appeal to her senses and her reduction of Buddhism to color, smell, and sound echoes Gardner's attraction to Buddhist temples, illustrating the women's encounter with Asia as spectacle.

As she became more confident in her shopping, she purchased twenty-one prints for her sister, some Imari plates and bowls, four "pieces of curios," and a number of brocades including two Buddhist priests' robes. Once Aldrich arrived in China, Chinese merchants came to her with bundles of tapestry cushions, Taoist priests' robes, embroidered hangings, and hundreds of examples of court robes of the Ching Dynasty. Aldrich arrived in China as old imperial families, fallen from power, sought to sell off their elaborate robes, and Aldrich began to focus her interest on textiles. Aldrich had gained confidence in her expertise by the time she returned to Asia in 1920 and purchased $3,000 worth of textiles, furniture, and jade in Beijing. In 1923, she traveled to Asia again and wrote to her sister, "I have spent millions." The purchases from Yamanaka & Co. and Nomura Shojiro in Kyoto on that trip were enough to make Aldrich's group of priests' robes a real collection.[25] From 1924 to 1925, Aldrich traveled to Southeast Asia, and at each stop purchased bronzes, decorative wooden objects, and textiles. But her collection of Japanese textiles remained the most extensive, and the receipts of Yamanaka & Co. indicate that she spent $10,000 for costumes for Japanese *noh* theater. The thirty costumes she acquired in Japan in 1925 represent nearly every type of *noh* costume, and Yamanaka & Co. helped her to see that her collection was not only wide-ranging but adequately documented and stored, supplying wrappers with each robe and provenance when available and advising her on how to display and house them. From this time on, Lucy Aldrich clearly became one of Yamanaka & Co.'s best clients. In October 1925, Yamanaka Sadajiro visited her in Providence, and in November their Boston branch began sending her textiles on approval.[26]

While Aldrich thus amassed an impressive collection of Asian arts and artifacts, her interest was focused more on the objects than the culture that produced them. Despite her strong interest in textiles and Japanese *noh* costumes in particular, as curator Susan Hay points out, there is no evidence that Lucy Aldrich ever attended a performance of *noh* theater. It cannot be determined whether this was because of her deafness, because of the reputation of *noh* drama as a difficult art unapproachable for Westerners, or because it was simply impossible for a Western woman to attend a Japanese performance in this period. For many years she continued to call her collection "*noh* dance costumes," a designation given them by Yamanaka; however, attendance at a performance would have revealed that *noh*, which is an elusive combination of opera, drama, and stylized motion, can hardly be called dance in the Western sense.[27] Thus, Lucy Aldrich's collection of Japanese and other Asian textiles was clearly separated from the original cultural context of the objects themselves.

Lucy's younger sister, Abby Aldrich Rockefeller, was less free to travel, as she was married to the son of the Standard Oil magnate and was raising six children. Consequently, her interest in foreign arts and artifacts and her desire for acquisition was to a large extent fulfilled by requests to Aldrich to purchase various items for her. Through this indirect patronage, Rockefeller also formed a major collection of Asian art, most notable of which was her collection of Japanese *ukiyo-e* prints, particularly of birds and flowers. The over 700 prints which Abby Rockefeller collected through her own purchases from dealers and Lucy Aldrich's acquisitions during her travels constitute by far the largest collection of this genre in the world.[28] It is unclear what Rockefeller did with these prints before she donated her collection to the Museum of Art of the Rhode Island School of Design in 1934. Yet, the fact that Rockefeller, who had the opportunity to travel to Japan herself only once in 1921, amassed such an extensive collection of Japanese prints demonstrates that wealthy women such as Rockefeller could "encounter" Asia at home through collection of arts and artifacts.

Asian art collections by wealthy women such as Gardner, Aldrich, and Rockefeller set the standards of Orientalist consumption, serving as models of cultural refinement and taste for middle-class women who, in more modest ways, also eagerly consumed "Asian" goods. Asia gradually entered the more private space of the household, becoming part of the material culture of middle-class American homes. In this process, several key agents played crucial roles. One such agent was the manufacturers of goods of "Asian" design, such as furniture, silver, glass, porcelain, and textiles that catered specifically to female consumers.[29] The emergence and popularity of "Asian" style goods was part of the Aesthetic Movement in postbellum America. The development of the Aesthetic Movement in the United States, particularly its concern with the appearance of the home, was closely tied to the Victorian gender ideology of the separate spheres and the socioeconomic conditions of industrialization and modernization. As the urban, industrial, male-dominated "public" sphere became the world of "work," for white, middle-class families the home was constructed as the sacred, private domain presumably detached from the worldliness of the market economy. Through the aesthetic refinement of the domestic space, women promoted their family's love of beauty, educated their taste, and ultimately elevated the nation. In this cultural context, the Aesthetic Movement in the last one-third of the nineteenth century made a wide range of refined items of decorative arts available to upper and middle-class consumers, particularly women. The Aesthetic Movement provided white, middle-class women an idealized site for exercising their moral and cultural power within the dominant gender ideology. At the same time, aestheticism also transgressed Victorian conventions of domestic life and offered the power of liberation.[30] It was within this mix of convention and transgression that the Aesthetic Movement brought Asia to white, middle-class women.

The mode of appreciation and consumption of "Asian" art in America reflected the historical and political dynamics of U.S.-Asian relations and the nature of what historian Kristin Hoganson calls "cosmopolitan domesticity.[31] As art historian Roger Stein argues, "The vocabulary of art for art's sake partially masked the degree to which this stylistic appropriation was indeed a form of cultural appropriation, particularly over the non-Western regions of the Near East and the Orient."[32] This meant that a particular style was often dissociated from its historical or cultural context, and disparate cultural elements were artificially combined into an "aesthetic" unity. Whereas earlier interior styles that drew on exoticism (the Egyptian or Gothic Revivals, for instance) placed emphasis on historical accuracy and cultural integrity, the model aesthetic house during the 1870s and 1880s was a pastiche of unrelated, exotic formats (Greek, renaissance, medieval, "oriental," Moorish, or Japanese). Between this eclectic aestheticism and the expansionist drive of turn-of-the-century America, the American interior became a site for displaying such sensibilities. In historian Mary Blanchard's words, "[i]n short, domesticity was refashioned into an imagined exotic terrain."[33] It was common during this period, therefore, to see a Persian rug, a Chinese scroll, and a Japanese umbrella displayed in a single setting.

Yet at the same time, Orientalist discourse delineated a clear cultural hierarchy within the "Orient" that was directly related to current political events. Japan's rapidly increasing power as a modern nation and its importance in international politics—manifested in Japan's victory in the Sino-Japanese War of 1894–95 and the Russo-Japanese War of 1904–05—made Japanese culture more appealing and respectable for Americans. Reflecting this national status, Japan occupied by far the most prominent place in American Orientalism in this period. In contrast, other parts of Asia that were not yet recognized as directly relevant to the United States' national interests, like Korea and Indochina, or the areas that were colonized by the United States, such as the Philippines, were far less visible in the material culture of American Orientalism.

While Aesthetic Orientalism created both an admixture of different Asian cultures and a hierarchy among them, it discursively constructed a dichotomy between the West and the East. Constructing Asia as the West's "Other," American discussions of Asian art typically associated Asia with premodern simplicity, naturalness, tradition—in sum, Asia embodied what historian Jackson Lears calls "antimodernism."[34] In the age of industrialization, commercialization, and urbanization, many Americans were anxious to assert and maintain the ideas and values considered to be lost in modern society, such as purity and sincerity.[35] As Americans discovered such qualities in Asian arts and artifacts, they believed that the production, use, and display of Asian-style goods would represent and promote their moral and cultural refinement.[36] The commonalties between the qualities attributed to Asian arts and the roles assigned to white, middle-class women were particularly useful for defining and reinforcing the women's place in Victorian domesticity, while cloaking the gender and racial ideologies inherent in such practices under the language of cultural refinement.

These stylistic and discursive characteristics of Aesthetic Orientalism are exemplified by the products of Gorham Manufacturing Company, a silver manufacturer based in Providence, Rhode Island. Since the founding of the company in the early nineteenth century, Gorham had become one of the two leading silver manufacturers in America along with Tiffany & Co.[37] In the 1870s and 1880s, Gorham manufactured a line of products in "Japanesque" design, including kettles, pitchers, cups, tête-à-tête sets, flatware, cigarette cases, soap dishes, pendants, and card cases. The images, motifs, and designs used in Japanesque products included dragons, bamboo, spiders, birds, and Japanese men and women in traditional clothing. While some items depicted distinctly Japanese settings (such as a tray with the design of several Japanese children playing, a perfume pendant engraved with an old Japanese man fishing in a sea, or a kettle embellished with a Japanese woman carrying a bucket of water), others simply used parts or combinations of images (such as bamboo, birds, butterflies) and design features (such as the combinations of straight and curvilinear lines) to evoke exoticism. This line quickly became one of Gorham's best-selling designs. In Gorham's 1875 photograph book of silverware, work distinctly influenced by Japanese (and some Chinese) designs constituted approximately one out of twenty to twenty-five products, suggesting that the company still considered the Japanesque design as experimental,[38] but four years later, they comprised approximately one out of twelve to fifteen products.[39] By 1883, Japanese-style goods made up approximately one out of four to five products, having clearly become one of Gorham's most important lines.[40] The increase in the company's Japanesque goods reflected the expansion of public interest in Japanese art, objects, and design, in part precipitated by the Philadelphia Centennial of 1876[41] (fig. 1.1).

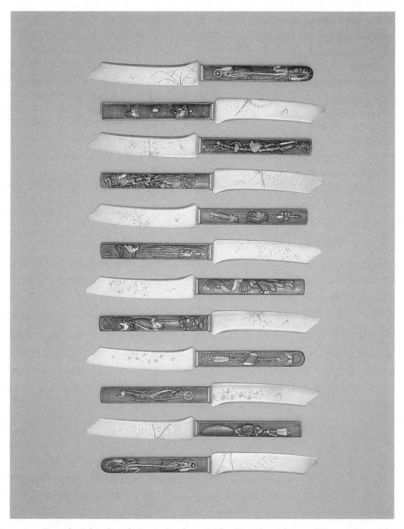

Figure 1.1 Set of twelve fruit knives. Gorham Mfg. Co., Providence, RI, ca. 1880. Silver, bronze, and gilding. Dallas Museum of Art.

Gorham's enthusiasm for the Japanesque style fits the common pattern of Orientalist discourse of the period. Promotional publication from 1876 expressed the company's ideas about Japanese art and design:

> The Japanesque style of decoration is justly popular, for it is the outcome of a careful study of Nature. The ordinary Japanese forms for design are not great in number, yet they constantly recur in great and endless variety, and always with fresh and pleasing novelty of combination. Coming straight from Nature, the fountain head of all good design, it is perhaps one of the chief reasons why it impresses us with a freshness which gives great effect with few lines. Truth and simplicity, grace and harmony are characteristics of the work sent out by the untutored native of Japan, who with an intuitive sense of the beautiful, furnishes models for artistic decoration surpassing in many respects the more elaborate and theoretic efforts of our schools of art.[42]

Like many other proponents of Japanese design in the late nineteenth century, the writer of this passage saw "truth and simplicity, grace and harmony" in Japanese art, created by the "untutored native" using "intuitive sense," the antithesis of the art of the modern, industrial, civilized West. By returning to this primitive stage of appreciating Nature—or, by assimilating Japanese art into a "theoretic" and civilized framework of American environment—the company suggested, Americans could attain a higher level of artistic sophistication.

The circulation of Japanesque Gorham—and more generally of Orientalism in material culture—was gendered: men produced the goods, while women consumed them. Gorham hired a number of European-trained designers who had studied Japonisme in French and English arts. American manufacturers worked hard to attract and retain these trained designers and craftsmen who often moved from one company to another for better working conditions. Frederick A. Jordan, for example, worked as a chaser in Tiffany & Co. in the 1870s where he was trained in Japanese design. Gorham hired him away in 1878, and he contributed a wealth of information about the new Japanesque design forms to the company.[43] At Gorham, as well as in most other manufacturers in this period, men gained training and expertise in classic Orientalist knowledge and reproduced Orientalist sensibilities through the production of styles and motifs, while women played only a marginal role in the production of Japanesque design and goods. Although a significant number of women workers were employed by Gorham by the 1880s, their jobs were limited to those secondary to the main line of production, such as lining the cases, blocking, and organizing photographs.[44] Designers and craftspeople were exclusively men, and, with a few exceptions of those who worked as assistants in the enamelling department, women were not part of the production process itself. While women were not engaged in its production, the targeted clients of Japanesque Gorham were clearly women. The Japanesque products, such as tea sets, trays, and perfume pendants suggest that Gorham designed a number of products specifically for women users. Women customers played a significant role in choosing and purchasing the many wares, such as tête-à-tête sets and cutlery sets, sold as wedding gifts.[45]

The female consumers of Japanesque Gorham were of the upper- and upper-middle classes. Although the technological innovations in silver manufacturing considerably lowered the cost of production in the course of the nineteenth century, silver was still beyond the reach of most Americans. Japanesque Gorham was Orientalism for the Victorian upper-class. However, manufacturers of Orientalist material culture did not limit their clients to the wealthy. The advertisements for other, more inexpensive goods using Asian images and motifs indicate the presence of a widespread material culture of Orientalism among middle-class women during this period.

For example, in the early 1900s, the *Ladies' Home Journal*—widely read by middle-class women at the time—ran a series of advertisements for "Jap Rose Soap" distributed by Chicago's James S. Kirk & Co.[46] These advertisements show images of kimono-clad Japanese women in various settings, with a picture of a soap with "JAP ROSE" carved in it. Words such as "transparent," "healing," "natural," and "pure" used in the text suggest the qualities attributed to Japanese femininity. The visual image and the text together construct Japanese women as aesthetic models for the readers of the *Journal*. The juxtaposition of the racialized term "Jap"—which evokes the fear of the "yellow peril"—with the implication of pure, white skin presents an intriguing example of racialized and gendered Orientalism which constructed Asia as both threatening and desirable. These mixed interests of Orientalism were contained and packaged in the form of a non-durable commodity, soap, and entered American homes and women's lives.

Around the same period as the Jap Rose Soap, a varnish company in Cleveland marketed a product named "Jap-a-lac." Jap-a-lac was also advertised in middle-class women's magazines such as *Ladies' Home Journal*, often on the same page as the advertisement for Jap Rose Soap. The company's trade catalogue has a cover with a presumably Japanese woman dancing in kimono, but the attire of musicians in the back as well as other material objects in the scene have other Asian, perhaps Chinese, attributes.[47] The 18-page catalogue describes the product—the "home beautifier"—and gives directions for use. Its targeted clients were white, middle-class women: all of the six illustrations that appear in the catalogue are of well-dressed women in Victorian interiors applying the product to their furniture. With one exception, all the letters from clients printed in the catalogue are written by women. The company thus appeals to middle-class women's desire to beautify the home. A letter from one such client reads: "JAP-A-LAC is not a luxury, but is a necessity, if one must have the home beautiful."[48] Interestingly, throughout the catalogue there is no mention of Japan or Japanese lacquer. The targeted client is presumed to be familiar with the high quality of Japanese lacquer and to find the name and the image of the product appealing. This suggests the knowledge of the material culture of Orientalism that was already popular among middle-class women at the turn of the century.

While Jap Rose Soap promised the whiteness of skin, the racial implications of Jap-a-lac as expressed in the catalogue's text are more complex and can be read as sinister. The opening section, "What Jap-a-lac Is," reads:

> JAP-A-LAC is a varnish and stain combined. But it is more than that—it is a mixture, not merely of a varnish and stain, but of the very best varnish we know how to make and of the purest of pigment colors, ground in oil. This insures two things: Wonderful wearing qualities and permanence of color.
>
> JAP-A-LAC stains and varnishes at the same time.
>
> We also make Natural of Clear JAP-A-LAC which contains no coloring matter whatever, but it is a beautiful, clear, transparent varnish and which dries with all the brilliancy and luster characteristic of the colored JAP-A-LAC.[49]

In the period when a series of federal acts and state statutes defined Asian immigrants as unassimilable aliens ineligible for citizenship, the connection drawn between the product "Jap-a-lac" and "permanence of color" clearly participates in the racialized discourse about the Japanese. The combination of "varnish and stain" creating the "beautiful, clear, transparent" effect out of the "colored" product reflects the mixture of aesthetic appeal and the fear of the racial Other that was at the foundation of Orientalist discourse. Like Jap Rose Soap, Jap-a-lac literally smoothed and glossed over these conflicted interests and entered the middle-class American homes to be consumed by women.

The manufacturers of Aesthetic Orientalism thus played a crucial role in creating the material culture of Orientalism and bringing Asia to female consumers in America. Whether they were luxury wares such as Japanesque Gorham or items for everyday use by middle-class women such as Jap Rose Soap and Jap-a-lac, Orientalist objects entered the American home and functioned as signifiers of aesthetics and therefore class status for women who possessed and consumed them, marking them as sophisticated, refined women.

By the turn of the century, Japanesque goods and Orientalism in general were popularized and commodified, and permeated into a realm beyond that of the wealthy class. The commodification of "Asian" goods in the consumer market made Orientalism available to a larger middle-class audience across the country. In particular, stores specializing in "Asian" goods—variously referred to as "novelty stores," "curio shops," "antique stores," or "Oriental stores"—became key players in Orientalist material culture. While they had existed and were popular during the 1870s and 1880s, they came to exert their full power as dealers of "Asia" as commodity around the turn of the century.[50] The popularity of these specialized stores was accompanied by the contemporary innovation in store displays which featured merchandise as spectacles.[51] The development of a consumer market where Asian goods were circulated as commodities provided a site for a large number of middle-class women to be participants in the culture of Orientalism.[52] While women consumers did not have the same type of agency as male producers of Orientalism who created, selected, and/or sold Asian objects for the American market, the act of consumption opened a way for women to partake in the ideology and practice of Orientalism.

One "Oriental store" that flourished around the turn of the century was A. A. Vantine's of New York. Ashley A. Vantine, who ran a general provision and supply business in San Francisco, moved to Manhattan in 1869 to establish an Oriental goods business on Broadway and within a decade had gained a reputation as the foremost dealer of Oriental goods.[53] Vantine's trade catalogues and advertisements vividly illustrate the store's typically Orientalist representations of the "Orient." Vantine's definition of the "Orient" was quite broad and flexible. The illustrated catalogue from the 1890s shows "A. A. Vantine & Co" floating across the cover diagonally in artistic script, followed by the self-identification, "Importers From the Empires of Japan, China, India, Turkey, Persia, and the East."[54] The last of their list, "the East," seems to designate all the other countries and cultures besides the five "empires" they identified. The content of the 112-page catalogue makes a clearer demarcation and creates a hierarchy among these different cultures. In Vantine's hierarchy, Japan is at the top in artistic and material accomplishment. In the preface, the author comments that "[w]ith an increasing knowledge of the country [Japan] came a deeper enthusiasm and appreciation for her productions. What appeared strange and fantastic to the superficial observer, acquired a different meaning when the underlying spirit of the representations were understood."[55]

Vantine's assigned clearly gendered meanings to their merchandise. Vantine's Orientalism, in its gendered form, is most vividly revealed in their catalogue, *The Wonder Book*.[56] This catalogue has colorfully designed cloth covers with images of Buddha and is bound with colored ribbons. The costly form and the emphasis on image instead of detailed descriptions or price of products suggest that the catalogue was intended as a souvenir rather than as a general promotional catalogue. The presentation and the content of the catalogue blur the boundaries between consumption of goods and travel to foreign places, creating an armchair traveler out of a consumer. The inside of this 16-page booklet is filled with photographs and illustrations not only of items being sold—such as ivory carvings, embroideries, porcelains, "Oriental perfumes," incense, Oriental rugs, lamps, etc.—but also of landscapes, people, and various images of the "Orient." Yet these images do not necessarily correspond to the items on the page. For example, a photograph entitled "The Villagers," which shows about a dozen young Japanese children in the field, appears on the page that lists "Objects of Art" (including "vases, koros, jardinières, urns, candlesticks, umbrella stands, figures, in a wide and comprehensive variety of shapes and wares") and "Bronze, Brass, Cloisonné." On the same page as the illustration of "Vantine's Steamer Basket" is photograph, "Idle Hours at Home," in which two Japanese women are shown in a traditional Japanese home, one playing the *koto* (Japanese harp) while the other, holding a Japanese fan, watches. All of these images capture and emphasize the dainty, feminine, picturesque, and archaic nature of the "Orient." All of the images show children or women, or "exotic" scenes such as the Ganges or a teahouse in Kyoto.

In addition to these images, the catalogue contains several poems illustrative of its intentions. On the first and the last page of the catalogue is the poem, "Two Views of Japan" (whose verse attunes the melody to the song, "America the Beautiful," which came out in 1893). The first, "Oh, Fair Japan" depicts the idealized view of Japan:

Oh, fair Japan; Oh, rare Japan
Though land of ancient trees,
Where lotus blossoms fringe thy paths
And perfume every breeze . . .
Oh, sweet it is to dwell with thee!
'Land of the Rising Sun,'
Where beauty, art and mystery
Combine themselves in one.

The second, "Oh, Fair (?) [*sic*] Japan" conveys another view:

Oh hang Japan; oh dang Japan,
A land of gnats and fleas,
Where noisome odors fill the air
And float on every breeze.
Where men run naked on the streets,
Wear spectacles for clothes,
And old and young, and rich and poor
Eschews the use of hose . . .
Boy, bring my clothes up from the wash
As quickly as you can,
Sir Edwin Arnold writes a lot
Of bosh about Japan.
I'm shivering cold, I'm wringing wet,
I've been an idle dreamer
To Yokohama let me get,
And there, thank God, a steamer.[57]

The contrasting poems vividly portray the two contradictory images Americans had of Japan: the dainty, artistic, ancient culture and the primitive, uncivilized society.

They also represent the different American interests in Asian things and people: clearly, it was much easier for American consumers to deal with the picturesque images and static objects symbolizing the former world than with the live Japanese people represented in the latter. Furthermore, the two renditions of Japan are specifically gendered: the former poem evokes femininity with the image of lotus blossoms and the verb "perfume," whereas the latter explicitly depicts naked men with body odor. As Vantine's was clearly selling the former image while explicitly acknowledging the presence of the latter "reality," the store was actively engaged in feminizing the Oriental world it constructed. Furthermore, this depiction of "reality" juxtaposed with the "fair Japan" served to reassure the consumers that they had access to Japanese and other Asian goods without having to deal with the real "Orient" and its people. Such packaging of the "wonders" of the Orient aroused the curiosity and desire for the goods presented in the catalogue while affirming the notion of essential difference between the Orient and the West and making Asia unthreatening to American consumers.

As Vantine's thus extracted the "Orient" from its people and feminized it, it also saw its American customers as female. The types of products shown in the catalogues—such as lamps, kimonos, perfumes, bric-à-brac—clearly targeted women. The gender and class of Vantine's targeted clientele is also detected in the wide-ranging prices of Vantine's goods. While some of their goods were very pricey—a Chinese embroidered shawl was sold for $285 and a Persian rug for $550—the store also carried a wide range of gift items, bric-à-brac, and accessories that were less than $5[58] (fig. 1.2–1.3). The store's advertisements repeatedly stressed the affordability of items, as this one from 1895 does:

> "Have you seen any of the new pieces of Oriental furniture that fashionable folk are using?" is a question often heard these days. . . . The cost of furnishing an apartment in Oriental fashion is not great, and a very few dollars judicially expended will accomplish wonderful results. Mantel covers, Oriental rugs, or the cheap Japanese copies of them, made of jute or cotton, fine bric-à-brac and table porcelains, and handsome screens are all within the reach of persons of moderate means. A wonderful collection of such goods as those alluded to may be seen in the establishment of A. A. Vantine & Co., 877 & 879 Broadway. A trip through their store is an education.[59]

Clearly, the store tried to attract not only wealthy collectors of Asian objects but the wider market of middle-class consumers in search of furnishings or gift items. Furthermore, the phrase "a trip through their store is an education" suggests that a visit to Vantine's—like Rose's trip to the trade vessel at the harbor in *Eight Cousins*—was like the grand tour usually reserved for upper-class men, since women could shop the store as an education and cultural refinement without the expense or trouble of physically traveling abroad.

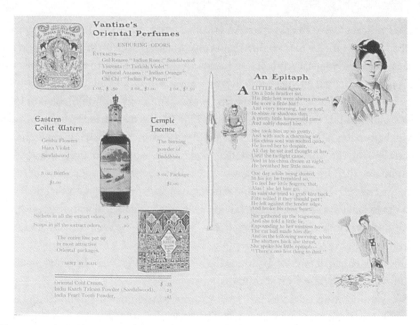

Figure 1.2 A. A. Vantine's, *The Wonder Book*, n.d. pp. 8–9. Courtesy, The Winterthur Library, Printed Book and Periodical Collection.

Figure 1.3 A. A. Vantine's, *Entrance to Vantine's: The House of the Orient*, n.d., pp. 44–45. Courtesy, The Winterthur Library, Printed Book and Periodical Collection.

Yet simply purchasing "Oriental" goods alone did not constitute proper Orientalist consumption. Women needed to be educated as to how to incorporate Oriental items into their homes in a tasteful fashion. Thus, Vantine's mimicked a living room tea service when they opened a tearoom on the ground floor of their Broadway shop in 1898. Vantine's furnished the room with chairs and tables containing tea sets, and white women dressed in kimonos, "experts in the art of making tea and who [took] great pleasure in giving instruction to anyone who desires information on the subject," served customers.[60] Persian rugs covered the floor, and Chinese porcelains, tapestry, vases, and other pieces of bric-à-brac decorated the walls. The drapes shed a subdued light through the room, and the Japanese bells jingled softly in the breezes. The photograph of the tearoom confirms that the patrons of the tearoom, and most likely of the store in general, were women (fig. 1.4).

At the same time Vantine's wanted to spread the popularity of its Orientalist products, it wanted to maintain an image of high quality and exclusivity, thus warning its customers not to be taken in by cheaper and inferior products sold elsewhere. For example, the store's catalogue expressed the fear that Japan's purity might be corrupted by exposure to industry:

Figure 1.4 Vantine's Tea Room, 1906. Museum of the City of New York, The Byron Collection.

At the present time when the dilettante justly mourns the decline of handicrafts, and the consequent loss of individuality and beauty, especially in its relation to industries caused by the constantly increasing use of machinery as a creative force, in Japan, the hand of the humblest workman is still guided by his mind, or rather by an inherited freedom of touch that prevents the tiresome uniformity or sameness so common to ordinary productions of pottery, metal, &c.; and it is at least to be hoped that the art instinct of the Japanese will be strong enough to live down or resist the inroads of cheap and vulgar manufactures that the rapid progressiveness of these times gives out in such abundance.[61]

By commenting on the "cheap and vulgar manufactures," Vantine's claimed that the products they sold were pure, authentic artifacts of Japan. The juxtaposition between the industrialized and mechanized West and Japan echoed the Orientalist tone deployed by Gorham Manufacturing Company, but Vantine's audience was much larger than Gorham's. By fashioning itself as the cultivator of "educated taste," Vantine's claimed to serve not simply as a commercial store but as a cultural arbiter for the middle-class. Another of Vantine's turn-of-the-century catalogues, entitled *Entrance to Vantine's: The House of the Orient*, presents its claims as an authority:

> Vantine's reputation depends upon the genuineness of the Oriental articles offered and the fact that they are not the ordinary, cheaply commercialized articles from the Far East which any shop may buy from an importer. This confidence has been carefully nurtured for more than half a century and whether your purchase be large or small, you may make it with the absolute assurance that "If you buy at Vantine's, you will be proud to say so."[62]

Differentiating itself from "any shop" and its goods from "the ordinary, commercialized articles," Vantine's claimed authority and authenticity in the Oriental goods trade. Vantine's claim to be a cultural, rather than a solely commercial, establishment was also carried out in a series of exhibits put on by the store. In February 1894, Vantine's exhibited two Inca mummies.[63] In October of the same year, the store put together an exhibit of "thirteen pictures, which portray vividly the horrible modes of punishment dealt out by the Chinese authorities to criminals, political and otherwise."[64] Two years later, the store opened an exhibit of antique Oriental rugs. According to the *New York Times*, "They are spoils from the temples, mosques, and palaces of those mysterious and wonderful countries, and were obtained at great expense by agents of the company, some of them only after years of secret negotiation."[65] Many of these exhibitions were obviously not intended to sell the objects they displayed but to promote the store's reputation as an expert in Orientalism.

While increasing commodification made it possible for the middle-class to consume Orientalist products, Asian goods continued to circulate among the more wealthy classes as well. An example of Oriental goods stores catering to a more wealthy clientele—such as Lucy Aldrich—was Yamanaka & Co. The store was established by Yamanaka Sadajiro, from a family of antique art dealers in Japan. Sailing to the United States on the *Empress of China* in 1893, Yamanaka opened a small shop on 27th Street in New York through the assistance of William Bigelow, Edward Morse, and Ernest Fenollosa, three prominent experts of Japanese art and culture who by this time had already established their reputation among America's intellectual and cultural elites. Having achieved an unexpected success in this small experimental shop, Yamanaka opened a new store in the following year which became the first branch of Yamanaka & Co. outside of Japan. In 1898, Yamanaka opened a Boston branch, where they sold Chinese art objects, Japanese crafts, and bric-à-brac. In 1904, the company established a new factory in Osaka, hiring over one hundred craftsmen to manufacture high-class room decorations and furniture for export to the Boston branch. After a factory fire in 1912, business declined and the company considered temporarily closing the Boston store. A number of Yamanaka's loyal Boston clients lobbied for action by the Consul General of Japan in New York, leading to a hearing by Japan's Foreign Ministry, which eventually saved the store from closing. The company also opened branches in Chicago and Bar Harbor. Yamanaka was active until his death in 1936 and gained the trust of a number of prominent clients in the United States and Europe.[66]

Yamanaka clearly targeted more upscale clients than Vantine's middle-class customers. Yamanaka's catalogues show that they sold exclusively expensive, high-quality goods. The quality of the catalogues themselves suggests that they had a limited distribution, probably only to patrons likely to make purchases. For example, *Catalogue of Room Decorations and Artistic Furniture* has silk-embroidered covers, is bound with silk strings, and contains 36 plates of elaborately carved, gilded, lacquered, or upholstered objects.[67] Yamanaka & Co. held auctions at art galleries but took no mail orders.

A notable feature of Yamanaka's marketing strategy is that he energetically manufactured goods that were made expressly for the American market and was proud of the modifications and adjustments they made to please the Western taste. Whereas Vantine's claimed authenticity by stressing that their goods were "pure," un-Westernized imports from Asia, Yamanaka decided that it was essential to research and accommodate the tastes of their Western customers. He thus hired foreign designers to produce novel "Japanese" crafts specifically for the Western market. Yamanaka himself made numerous research trips in the United States and Europe, and he also hired foreign craftsmen for his factory. Yamanaka's efforts to accommodate Western tastes show that American Orientalism in art and material culture was not simply a Western creation but that Asians themselves exercised agency and complicity.[68]

Like Gorham Manufacturing Company and Vantine's, most of Yamanaka's products were manufactured expressly for women and catered to what the company considered distinctly feminine taste. According to Kume Keiichiro, a prominent scholar at the Tokyo Art Institute during Yamanaka's time,

> What dominates the fashion and trend in general is women's taste. Across the national borders, women are adherents of classical art, and they desire orderliness of lines and purity of materials. The excessive concern with elegance often leads to delicacy and fragility, thus causing feminine taste to be regarded as inferior; however, the ways in which the bold and novel methods of masculine hands are skillfully controlled are decidedly attributed to the power of women.[69]

Japanese shapers of Western Orientalism such as Yamanaka thus deployed these seemingly transnational assumptions about "feminine taste" and capitalized on the association made between the qualities of female customers and the nature of Asian crafts through words such as "orderliness," "purity," "delicacy," and "fragility." Yamanaka's success with his female clients is evidenced by the list of women sending letters of eulogy to the editors of Yamanaka's biography.

Like Vantine's, Yamanaka & Co. claimed to serve not simply as merchants but as connoisseurs of Asian art and as liaisons between Western clients and Asian objects. Believing that the dealer should sell objects to clients who fully understood and appreciated their value rather than simply pursuing a profit, Yamanaka produced catalogues and pamphlets which provided detailed descriptions of the objects and explained their historical and artistic significance.[70] In addition to providing accurate and detailed information about their products, the company held a number of exhibitions in their New York store. Particularly during the 1920s and 1930s, Yamanaka arranged various art exhibits in their Fifth Avenue galleries. While they held large-scale auctions for their collections where art dealers purchased a Japanese *noh* costume for $350, a pair of carved jade vases for $700, and a pair of Ming wine jars for $6,800, they also put together exhibits of art that was not intended for sale.[71] In May 1934, they arranged an exhibit of more than a hundred pieces of Japanese ceramics;[72] in September of the same year, they held an exhibition of ceramics of Chinese horses and camels from the Han Dynasty to the twentieth century;[73] in January 1936, they displayed a collection of Chinese portrait paintings from the late fourteenth to middle seventeenth centuries.[74] These exhibitions suggest that Yamanaka & Co., like Vantine's, tried to serve as connoisseurs and taste-makers by bringing Oriental art objects to the public.

The intersections of gender, class, and Orientalist authority in the Oriental goods trade can be further traced in the career of Bunkio MATSUKI. Matsuki was born in 1867 in Kami-Suwa, Japan, to a family of merchants and manufacturers of household goods. He moved to Tokyo in 1882 to train as a Buddhist monk. From 1886 to 1888, he studied in China, where he encountered a number of Japanese and American businessmen, gained familiarity with commercial enterprises, and set his sights on the United States. In May 1888, Matsuki arrived in San Francisco, and was soon introduced to Edward Sylvester Morse in Salem, Massachusetts. Morse, who had acquired an immense collection of Japanese pottery from all regions of Japan while living in Tokyo as a professor of zoology, became an official guardian of Matsuki. Matsuki soon became an important figure in the Salem community. In 1890, he opened a Japanese section in a leading department store, Almy, Bigelow, & Washburn, where he sold Japanese works of art and household items he imported from Japan. Initially planned as a temporary arrangement, the Japanese section became a permanent feature of Almy's. Matsuki stocked more than twenty thousand items, allowing him to conduct a wholesale business, supplying a teachers' fair in Boston, as well as providing for the needs of collectors and even museums. In the midst of this success, Matsuki opened a store in Boston and decided to make Boston his permanent base while continuing to live and work in Salem. Matsuki's growing prestige as a purveyor of Japanese merchandise prompted the Japanese government to invite him to inspect the items that were to be displayed at the Columbian Exposition. After his trip to Kyoto in 1895, Matsuki shifted his focus to business, and concentrated on developing his Boston store and supplying Japanese works of art to collectors and museums such as the Museum of Fine Arts in Boston. He also opened a branch in Newport, Rhode Island, which catered to upscale clients. After 1897, Matsuki accelerated his shift from Salem to Boston, as well as changed his focus from general merchandise to fine arts, and consolidated his position as a market leader in the field of Japanese artists' supplies.[75]

Matsuki's business offers an interesting comparison to both Vantine's and Yamanaka & Co. The range of goods Matsuki dealt with and the clientele he served encompassed all the niches targeted by both Vantine's and Yamanaka & Co., and represented a wider spectrum than either of the two stores in terms of "authenticity," price, and types of merchandise. While Matsuki expressed disdain for "inauthentic" Japanese goods produced expressly for export to the West, his merchandise included a full spectrum of objects, ranging widely in their market orientation from obviously export goods to strictly domestic ones.[76] In historian Hina HIRAYAMA's words, "Despite his persistent claim that his merchandise was of uniformly high quality and genuinely Japanese, Matsuki's imports were, in reality, a cross section of Japan's decorative arts production. His wares varied widely, if not evenly, in character from ancient to modern, artistic to utilitarian, genuinely Japanese to Western influenced, well crafted to crude, fancy to plain, and expensive to cheap."[77] Matsuki's early business strategy represented his ability to cater to a diverse range of customers with separate classes of merchandise.

While the diversity of Matsuki's products makes it difficult to discern the gender and class of his clientele, the gradual shift in his business toward artists' materials suggests that a significant number of his customers were middle-class women who, as I will show in the next chapter, created their own artistic niche in Orientalism. Whereas the 1904 artists' materials catalogue includes photographs and descriptions of items as well as instructions on how to use them, these are absent from the 1908 catalogue, suggesting that the store already had a body of customers who were familiar with their merchandise by this time.[78] The 1908 catalogue also represents a wider range of goods than the earlier catalogue, ranging from water color brushes (costing from 8 to 75 cents), Japanese paper lanterns for school use (15 cents), a collection of Hiroshige's masterpieces ($2), and still life drawing models ($1.75–$5), to Japanese towels (15 cents), and "Matsuki novelties" (hanging well buckets, bamboo artists' bags, table lamp screen, etc. from 25 cents to $2). The advertisement for corsets that appears in the catalogue suggests that a significant portion of customers buying the artists' materials were middle-class women.

Matsuki ventured into other cultural enterprises, including the inauguration of a journal in 1903. *Lotus* was intended to be a quarterly journal which introduced various facets of Japanese art and culture to American readers.[79] The first issue, a special holiday number, focused on James McNeill Whistler, a "canonical" painter influenced by Japanese art. The articles included "The Place in History of Mr. Whistler's Art," "Whistler and the Ukiyo-ye," and "Japanese Influence in American Schools." Matsuki's engagement with these topics in his journal demonstrates the intersection of "high art" Orientalism exemplified by Whistler and consumer Orientalism for Matsuki's middle-class clients.

There were a number of other stores, large and small, across the country which served to distribute and popularize "Asia" as commodity in the consumer market. In New York City, there were the First Japanese Manufacturing and Trading Co., H. C. Parke, Morimura Bros. & Co.; in San Francisco was Ichi Bangi's Japanese Bazaar; in Hartford, Connecticut was A. D. Vorce & Co.; in Cincinnati was Marsh & Co.[80] Each store had its own targeted group of clients and types of merchandise, but all the Oriental goods stores capitalized on the existing Orientalist discourse and feminized both their merchandise and their clientele while establishing their own authority.

While retail stores such as Vantine's, Yamanaka, and Matsuki provided Oriental goods for middle-class women, the print media also played an important role in popularizing Orientalism and defining the value and the place of Asian objects in the American home. The uses of Asian goods in the home were discussed frequently in magazines of art and architecture (such as *Architectural Record, Art Amateur, Art Interchange, Decorator and Furnisher,* and *Good Furniture*) and general and/or literary magazines (such as *Atlantic Monthly, Cosmopolitan, Frank Leslie's Popular Monthly, Harper's Weekly, Scribner's Magazine,* and *Overland Monthly*), as well as in women's magazines (such as *Godey's Lady's Book, Harper's Bazar, House and Garden, House Beautiful,* and *Ladies' Home Journal*). As textiles scholar Jane Converse Brown's extensive study shows, the discussions of Japanese art in these magazines illustrate how middle-class consumers saw the functions of Japanese objects in their homes: "Economical and readily available to the middle class, the Japanese art object was useful in creating the right atmosphere in the home. Thus, by including Japanese objects and design in her home, a woman could use the Japanese Taste to present herself and her family as educated, artistically aware, religious, and concerned for the development of the children."[81]

The descriptions of Asian objects in these magazines echo advertisements of Oriental goods stores, demonstrating both the popularity of Orientalist material culture and the prescriptive role played by both retailers and the press in educating the female consumers about the use of Asian goods. *Godey's Lady's Book*, for example, guides its readers to Vantine's:

> If you want to revel in a perfect dream of Oriental color and beauty, wander in your own sweet will—for no attendant follows to mar your enjoyment—through the newly arranged interiors at Vantine's, which are the special attraction this season. Take, for example, the fascinating little Japanese boudoir, arranged in light color effects, and delightfully suggestive of the land of chrysanthemums, of brightness, and of sunshine. A careful examination of the manner in which this dainty room is fitted up proves how perfectly simple and inexpensive the furnishings are, and how readily they can be adapted to our ordinary and conventionally shaped rooms.[82]

The emphasis on "color," "beauty," "brightness," and "sunshine" reflects women's interest in Asia as spectacle appealing to the senses. The article also assures the readers—middle-class readers who have "ordinary and conventionally shaped rooms"—that Oriental furnishings are simple and inexpensive.

The magazines provided female readers with concrete models to follow in furnishing their homes in Oriental fashion. Magazines such as *The House Beautiful*, *Ladies' Home Journal*, and *Harper's New Monthly Magazine* published numerous illustrations of objects of Asian design—such as furniture, textile, porcelain, screens, scrolls, plates, fans, and lanterns—and how they are used in American homes. For example, in 1878, *The House Beautiful* printed an illustration of a Victorian parlor filled with such Asian objects as a scroll, porcelain, and plates with a woman sitting in a chair.[83] An 1886 issue of *Harper's* carried an illustration of a woman and her young daughter decorating their porch with Japanese lanterns.[84] *Ladies' Home Journal* showed an example of a "Japanese room" with Japanese-style ceiling, window, screen panels, fans, and porcelain in 1895.[85] In 1908, the *Journal* carried a number of illustrations of Asian-style screens that women could design themselves.[86] The captions for these illustrations, such as "Much in Little Space," or "Screens for the Clever Woman to Make," demonstrate the magazines' understanding of the limited resources—financial and spatial—their readers had in furnishing their homes as well as the educational and cultural qualities Asian-style decoration had for women.

As the commodification of Asian goods accelerated and as they became more readily available to middle- and upper-class women in the early twentieth century, the place of Asian goods in the domestic sphere came to be more clearly defined. The advice literature on the proper uses of Asian arts and artifacts in the home echoed America's larger political and ideological relations with Asia in this period. On the whole, Asian-style goods were appreciated as fine additions to already established furnishings, rather than as a dominant feature of household decoration. As the author of a magazine article explained, "Decoration on an oriental vase allowed it to blend into the room as an element in a picture; while that on a Sèvres vase was agreeable in itself but was too assertive as a room decoration and created a confused mass."[87] The entry of Asia into household art was thus carefully monitored and regulated so that it remained within the bounds of artistic whimsy. In other words, Asian objects were "domesticated" as an additional yet subordinate element of home aesthetics. William Hosley suggests that "the Japan idea" was "an image and not a complete life-style," and that "[f]urniture was usually too important a component of a room's furnishings to sustain the frivolity associated with Japanesque design. The Japanese style was a nice embellishment, but most people didn't want it to dominate their lives."[88] Although a number of wealthy, fervent art collectors like William Vanderbilt and Henry Havemeyer went beyond the confines of "slight impressions" and decorated entire rooms in Japanese style,[89] such enterprises were more artistic whimsies of the leisure class than a possible decorating scheme for an average American home, and most people who adopted Japanesque style, particularly women, used it in a more confined space and scale.

The literature on interior decoration in this period represents the recurrent notions about Asian goods: Asia represented exotic Otherness which was to be carefully contained, manipulated, and domesticated in the American scene; Asian arts and artifacts could serve as a fine artistic whimsy as long as they did not transgress the boundaries of cultural difference. A commentary which appeared in *Good Furniture* in 1916 exemplifies the dominant idea about Asian goods:

> It comes down to the fact that it is merely a question of keeping the Chinese taste in its proper place. Its proper place, as a seasoning where it gives variety and interest, and possibly wards off an approaching sense of monotony, should not be overstepped, for, extended out of bounds and used as a universal scheme, like an overdose of strychnine pills, it ruins everything.[90]

In other words, Asian goods were to be used as "slight impressions," which do not threaten the cohesiveness of the whole. The expressions used in this passage, such as "keeping . . . its proper place," "should not be overstepped," "extended out of bounds," correspond to the kinds of arguments made concerning the Asian immigrants in the United States in this same period.

Between the 1870s and the 1920s, China went through a series of revolutions and vastly transformed its political and social structure; Japan accelerated its modernization and Westernization and became one of the world's industrial and military powers; and Chinese and Japanese immigration heightened social tensions in Hawai'i and on America's West Coast. Against this background, Americans sought to deal with "Asia" in ways that allowed the United States to contain the threat of Asia and Asians while fulfilling its exoticist desire for the beauty of Asian cultures. In order to do so, Americans carefully and skillfully detached Asian arts and artifacts from their historical and cultural contexts, commodified them as objects, and confined them in the feminized space of the American household. White upper- and middle-class women became central players in this material culture of American Orientalism that collected and consumed "Asian" objects.

While white women became important participants in the material culture of American Orientalism, they did not do so on their own. Just as Uncle Alec in *Eight Cousins* was the one who took Rose to the China trade vessel and decorated her room with exotic objects, male practitioners of Orientalism—from European-trained designers at Gorham to Bunkio Matsuki—played a critical role in bringing white women and "Asia" together in a "proper" form that was compatible with the dominant racial and gender ideology. Owing to these key agents of Orientalism, white women who first encountered Asia as spectacles and objects increasingly became active consumers of "Asia" as commodified objects that embellished their homes. While few white women physically traveled to Asia during this period, women could experience "foreign" travel and education through purchasing Asian goods and incorporating them into their homes. This domestic Orientalism offered white, middle- and upper-class women a way to express the expansion of their gendered sphere without having to deal with the real people of Asia or endangering their Victorian womanhood. Orientalist material culture signified the formation of a new type of womanhood, one that offered adventure as well as cultural refinement.

Visualizing Orientalism
Women Artists' "Asian" Prints

*W*hite women's relationships to Asian objects were vividly portrayed in a series of paintings by William McGregor Paxton, a turn-of-the-century American Impressionist. Just as Edith Wharton's novels recall the morals, protocols, and women's place in Old New York, Paxton's paintings depict the physical, social, and mental space in which women lived in turn-of-the-century America. Whether they be kitchen maids or socialites in shimmering gowns, Paxton's female figures are part of the domestic landscape, the nature of their existence defined by the visual objects and physical space surrounding them. These women are, as cultural historian Jean-Christophe Agnew comments, "the primary compositional links between household objects from which they are, in visual and tactile terms, indistinguishable."[1] Important elements of Paxton's paintings are various Asian objects such as vases, figurines, and silk gowns. While they are rarely the central focus of the paintings, the frequency and the consistency of the ways in which they are used in Paxton's works demonstrates the unique significance of Asian objects in this cultural landscape.

For instance, in *The Housemaid* of 1910, a young maid with a duster under her arm is absorbed in her reading as she stands behind a table, on which stand a few porcelain vases and a figurine (fig. 2.1). While the porcelains are recognizably

Figure 2.1 William McGregor Paxton, *The House Maid*, 1910. Oil on canvas. In the Collection of the Corcoran Gallery of Art, Museum Purchase, Gallery Fund.

Japanese, they are made distinct more through the light shining on their surface than through the specific features or details of their design. The whiteness and the smooth surface of the porcelains blend with the maid's pale, soft neck, her white apron, and the pages of the book she holds. Furthermore, like the maid's physical contours and facial expression as well as the pages of her book, the faces and the design on the porcelain are deliberately blurred or made blank. The young woman's absorption in her reading in the midst of her chores suggests her agency and mental autonomy; however, the composition and the tone of the painting place her in a position more synonymous with that of the porcelain objects than that of an individual taking care of those objects. In this secluded domestic space with bare gray walls, both the Asian objects and the maid are reflected upon by the light, the painter's eyes, and the viewer's gaze.

The 1914 painting entitled *1875* shows a woman of a very different class than *The Housemaid*. In this painting, a woman in an elaborate green dress leans onto a table and earnestly studies an Asian (probably Chinese) figurine in a glass case. Against the dark background, the rich texture of her green dress occupies the bulk of the painting's visual space. Whereas the housemaid was lost in her reading and not paying attention to the Asian porcelains, this woman has all her thoughts focused on the figurine. Yet, as in *The Housemaid*, the careful depiction of the gown's texture and the light shed upon the woman is in clear contrast with her blurred face. In fact, despite the difference in size and the presence of the vitrine which stands between them, the symmetry of the posture, color, and lighting of the woman and the figurine suggest their similarity rather than difference. Both women—one live, adorned in ruffles and ribbons, and the other static, encased in a vitrine—are "imprisoned" in their respective spaces. One can read the woman's preoccupation with the figurine in two ways: she could be enchanted by the figurine without being aware of her own encasement; or, she could be conscious of her own imprisonment and seeking guidance from the figurine as to how to live in a world where women are defined by their adornment and display. In either case, the painting draws a clear connection between the upper-class American woman and the Asian figurine.

The Figurine (1921) depicts a woman's even closer engagement with an Asian object—the same figurine as the one used in *1875* (fig. 2.2). In this painting, a housemaid—perhaps Irish—is cleaning the vitrine holding the Asian figurine. Alongside the vitrine is another Asian-looking jar placed on the table. As she gently holds the vitrine with one hand while polishing the glass with the other, her eyes are cast low toward the object in her care, and the figurine's eyes too are pointed in the same direction. Unlike the adorned woman in *1875* and her figurine, both of which were resplendent objects of display, the housemaid and the figurine here are drawn with soft contours, color, and tone, highlighting the modesty of their role in the domestic space they occupy. As in *The Housemaid*, the color of the woman's attire, the tone of her skin, and her features mesh with the rest of the room, making her part of the visual space. The centrality of the vitrine and the housemaid's careful handling of it suggest that the two figures share the contained space they occupy—physically and socially—in the household.

Paxton was not unique in placing Asian objects with white women in their work. The use of Asian arts, motifs, and styles to portray women of leisure in Victorian interiors was a widely shared practice among contemporaneous New York- and New England-based artists such as William Merrit Chase, Joseph DeCamp, Thomas Dewing, Robert Reid, Frank Benson, Edmund Tarbell, Childe Hassam, and Albert

Figure 2.2 William McGregor Paxton, *The Figurine*, 1921. Oil on canvas. National Collection of Fine Arts, Smithsonian Institution.

Herter. The message about Asian objects and white women in many of these works are quite different from the liberating and transformative effect the encounter with Asian objects had for women's gendered identities as discussed in the last chapter. In these paintings, the figures of white women with Asian objects and clothing reflect the artists' and patrons' wish to link the stereotypical images of Asian docility, gentleness, and aesthetics with American middle- and upper-class opposition to suffrage. The association between Asian objects and white women in domestic settings thus served to project the male artists' and patrons' conservative gender politics.[2]

However, the visual uses of Asian objects and arts were certainly not an exclusively male domain. Women artists made active use of Asian objects, motifs, and styles in their work, often in ways quite different from their male counterparts. Whereas male artists such as Paxton used Asian objects to highlight the aesthetics as well as the conventions and constraints of Victorian femininity, for female artists Asian art offered a powerful tool for not only their aesthetic but also social and political explorations. The adoption of Asian themes and methods provided women with an entry into the male-dominated profession of art as well as new aesthetic expressions and artistic themes. In short, through the deployment of Asian materials, women artists gained a new way of seeing the world and new forms of power. By looking at women artists who used Asian art in their work, this chapter examines the different modes, conditions, and effects of their engagement with Asia and Asian art. All the women artists discussed below worked primarily with the themes of women and children, which were considered "feminine" subjects by the artistic tradition of the time. Yet, Asian art—specifically Japanese prints—provided the artists with new ways to address this theme. Sometimes, the adoption of a new way of seeing presented an alternative to the Western male gaze that traditionally objectified women's sexuality in art. In other cases, working with Asian methods and subject matters led women artists to adopt the masculinist vision that feminized Asia. White women artists' engagement with Asian subjects and methods was also based on the material power relations between them and Asian artists and craftsmen they worked with, and the women's practice of studying and producing Asian art in Asia often reinforced such dynamics while granting women professional recognition. These different functions of Asian art for women artists demonstrate the power of artistic Orientalism in which aesthetics and power worked together.

Mary Cassatt, a leading Impressionist in both the American and French art scenes at the turn of the century, used a Chinese export tea set in her 1883–85 painting, *Lady at a Tea Table*. In some ways, the tea set functions in a similar fashion to Asian objects in Paxton's works. A white woman in a Victorian interior sits at a table and looks into the distance as she holds the handle of a teapot. Along with the teapot are several items from a tea set with blue-and-white drip patterns. As feminist art historian Linda Nochlin points out, the texture and color of the tea set are strategically used against the delicate, transparent lace *coiffe*—also blue and white—of the sitter. The glitter of the porcelain is picked up by the subdued glow and color on the sitter's face.[3] One can read the Chinese tea set as illuminating the place of the upper-class woman in Victorian America—whose vocation is to drink tea with proper company, arrange her clothing and household décor, and exercise her aesthetic sensibility—by drawing a parallel between the decorative objects and the women who use them.

However, the image of the woman in Cassatt's painting is also strikingly unlike Paxton's ladies and housemaids because the work does not project any sentimentality or romanticism onto the female figure. Unlike many portraits of upper-class women by male Impressionists such as John Singer Sargent, the sitter in Cassatt's portrait is more rigid, her costume and décor are more severe, and the details of her face do not hide the signs of her age. By depicting the sitter's character and maturity instead of the glossy elegance of a woman on display, Cassatt conveys the sitter's psychological interiority.[4] Reading the painting this way, one can see the Chinese tea set as highlighting the woman's mental autonomy by drawing attention to the contrast between the surface beauty of the tea set and the woman's face. Throughout her career, Cassatt explored new ways of depicting women — "modern" women who possessed and exercised intellectual and mental autonomy by, for example, reading the newspaper (Reading "Le Figaro") or being an active subject of seeing the opera rather than being an object of the male gaze (At the Opera). Placed in this context, as Nochlin suggests, even the conventionally feminine space of the parlor could serve as a site for intellectual and creative production.[5] In this sense, the Chinese tea set, which signifies the feminine space, could suggest the strength and autonomy of the woman in the domestic milieu. Cassatt does assign gendered meanings to the tea set, but its function is different from Paxton's Asian objects: rather than illustrating the woman's confined and peripheral role in the domestic space, Asian objects suggest her autonomy and empowerment.

The depiction of actual Asian objects in her paintings, however, was not the only way in which Cassatt used Asian arts in her work. The influence of Asian art is, in fact, much more direct and pronounced in the series of color prints she made in 1890–91. As French artists and collectors had developed a vogue for Japonisme since the 1860s (Cassatt had lived permanently in France since 1875), Cassatt had for some time collected Japanese porcelains, decorative fans, and woodcut prints, especially the work of Kitagawa Utamaro. Yet the decisive inspiration of Japanese prints came to Cassatt at an exhibition at the Ecole des Beaux-Arts in Paris on April 15, 1890, where 725 Japanese ukiyo-e prints, albums, and illustrated books by prominent printmakers such as Kitagawa Utamaro and Ando Hiroshige were exhibited. The impact of these prints led her to produce the set of ten color prints that depict diverse moments of women's daily lives.[6]

Cassatt was certainly not alone in being influenced by Japanese prints. Ukiyo-e, or "pictures of the floating world," occupied a singular position in Western art; a number of prominent artists such as Whistler, Manet, Degas, and van Gogh had collected them and used their styles and motifs in their works in different ways. The Japanese prints were created by artists and craftsmen of plebian or low samurai background, and depicted scenes from the everyday life and entertainment of the urban classes. Originally associated with a Buddhist world view and alluding to the ephemerality of human experience, the phrase "floating world" subsequently came to suggest a hedonistic preoccupation with the present, with the latest fashions, pursuits, and lifestyles of urban culture, and implied a certain chicness. Their popularity lay among the townspeople portrayed in the prints, many of which focused on the manners and customs of the pleasure quarters and theater districts and portraits of beautiful women.[7] The styles and methods used in *ukiyo-e* were dramatically different from the traditions of Western art and introduced new aesthetic sensibility to Western artists. First, the images drew figures without shadows and made no attempt to represent the play of light and shade, and the diffusion of light was almost perfectly uniform, creating flatness and denying linear perspective. Second, the populist nature of *ukiyo-e* as an art of the people gained wide support among contemporary Western artists moving to break the elitist orientation of painting through both medium and subject matter.[8]

While *ukiyo-e* thus appealed to many of Cassatt's male contemporaries, Cassatt's *ukiyo-e*-inspired color prints illustrate a unique engagement with the Japanese art form. All of Cassatt's ten color prints portray scenes from upper-class white American women's lives. Cassatt, unlike other women artists I will discuss in this chapter, did not use actual Asian figures or scenes in her work. For Cassatt, Japanese prints became models for her *form* rather than her subject matter. It was the *form* of Japanese prints that enabled Cassatt to not only experiment with new aesthetics but also explore new ways of engaging her long-standing pursuit: the depiction of the female experience. The simplified composition and emphasis on line, which highlight the presentness and anti-narrative surface, allowed Cassatt to transform undramatic scenes of domestic life—such as morning rituals, daily errands, afternoon socializing, evening entertaining, and bedtime rituals—into works of formal rigor and emotional distance. This rendered Cassatt's women much more complex and ambivalent subjects than objects of sentimentality or erotic gaze as was often the case in works of male Impressionists, notably Renoir. Furthermore, Japanese prints offered Cassatt a way to engage themes and subjects that few other artistic traditions available to female artists allowed, such as women's labor and the female nude.

As she incorporated formalistic elements of *ukiyo-e* into her prints, Cassatt also adapted the methods and styles of Japanese prints to suit her project. For example, while in Japan there was no such person as a *peintre-graveur* since each stage of the printmaking process required its own atelier and training in special skills, as a painter Cassatt was only interested in the etching where she could actively participate in all stages of the process. She never considered the woodcut medium, and all of her Japanese-inspired color prints were done in drypoint, softground etching, and aquatint.[9] Cassatt's use of color was also radically different from the Japanese prototypes. Whereas Japanese prints typically use such vivid colors as red, orange, dark blue, yellow, and silver, Cassatt's colors are much more ambiguous and soft—taupes and terracottas, muted roses and pale creams. Furthermore, the often blatantly sexualized female subjects of Japanese prints—many of which were explicitly pornographic, while others portrayed women of the pleasure quarters—were replaced by the women of Cassatt's own social class in the West.

In this sense, one could argue that Cassatt extracted certain features of the Asian art form from their original context and appropriated them for her own purposes. However, neither the goals nor the effects of Cassatt's appropriations were to construct Asia in a particular way or to intervene in the racialized discourse about Asia. Rather, Cassatt's use of the *ukiyo-e* form was a feminist project. Her appropriations and adaptations of Japanese prints enabled her to pursue her project of depicting bourgeois women and female sexuality in ways that were clearly distinct from both the conventions of Western art and the tradition of Japanese prototypes.

For example, the print *The Lamp* captures a woman sitting in a parlor from her back (fig. 2.3). Showing a woman's neck from behind was a common device in Japanese prints, particularly those that depicted sexualized images of dancers and courtesans. The fine lines depicting the woman's hair also show the influence of *ukiyo-e*. Yet in Cassatt's print, the composition, color, and lines function to offset the angle on the woman. The woman's flesh shares the same tone (albeit with different shades) of pink as the wall, the floral patterns on the chair, and the lamp's shade. The woman's dress and her fan are colored with the same shade of light gold and green. The flatness created by these color configurations alters the erotic charge that could arise from foregrounding the woman's exposed neck into something more psychological, urging the viewer to see beyond the surface. Furthermore, the lines trace the contours of the woman's body in the same manner as any other objects in the setting. This color scheme and the line, combined with the mirror on the wall and the expression in the left half of the woman's face that is seen, convey the materiality of this domestic setting rather than valorizing or critiquing the woman's place in it.

The materiality of domestic femininity is also depicted in *The Fitting*, which portrays a woman standing in front of the mirror to have her dress adjusted by a seamstress (fig. 2.4). While the setting illustrates the everyday life of a woman of leisure, the design, composition, and color of the print highlight the material creation of such leisure rather than romanticizing Victorian femininity. The different shades of gray, yellow, and pink on the customer's flesh and dress, the wall, the mirror, and the carpet place the woman as a naturalized part of the setting by embedding her into the environment. On the other hand, the darker brown of the seamstress' dress and her black hair in the foreground make her, rather than her upper-class customer, a more sharpened focus of the image. The striped patterns on the customer's and the seamstress' dresses visually bring the two women even closer to one another, highlighting the class juxtaposition as well as the act of material creation of the customer's Victorian femininity. One could read this as an expression of the tension in Cassatt's own identity as a woman artist. On the one hand, she was a woman of leisure who had privileges of upper-class life and upon whom Victorian notions of

Figure 2.3 Mary Cassatt, American, 1844–1926, *The Lamp*, 1890–1891. Drypoint, soft-ground and aquatint, from three plates, in color on off-white laid paper, 43.2 × 29.7 cm, Bequest of Janis H. (Mrs. Gordon) Palmer, 1985.485. © The Art Institute of Chicago. All Rights Reserved.

femininity were imposed both socially and professionally. On the other hand, she was a rare female professional artist who entered the largely male world of "fine art" at a time when most bourgeois women engaged in amateur art or "minor" art, which operated on fundamentally different assumptions and practices from fine art. When there were few male artists who portrayed bourgeois women engaged in productive labor, and when there were few artistic traditions available to female artists for depicting alternative images of women, Cassatt asks the viewer to think about the materiality and labor involved in creating femininity rather than valorizing the leisure and décor. While Cassatt engaged in similar projects in her oil paintings as well, the simple composition and the flatness of the image of the print medium allowed her to express her sensibilities more explicitly.

Figure 2.4 Mary Cassatt, American, 1844–1926, *The Fitting*, 1890–91. Drypoint and aquatint, from three plates, in color and off-white laid paper, 37.7 × 25.6 cm, Mr. and Mrs. Martin A. Ryerson Collection, 1932.1283 © The Art Institute of Chicago. All Rights Reserved.

Woman Bathing and *The Coiffure* are two prints that show partially nude women in their intimate settings (fig. 2.5). It is highly significant that when Cassatt—who was becoming the most important American artist associated with Impressionism and who gained more acclaim in the world of "fine arts" than any other female artist at the time—engaged the nude, she turned to something outside the Western artistic tradition. As art historian Anne Higonnet points out, *ukiyo-e* for Cassatt—and her French contemporary Berthe Morisot—was a liberating tool: Japanese

Figure 2.5 Mary Cassatt, American, 1844–1926, *Woman Bathing*, 1890/91. Drypoint and aquatint, from three plates, in color on off-white laid paper, 36.8 × 26.3 cm, Mr. and Mrs. Martin A. Ryerson Collection, 1932.1281 © The Art Institute of Chicago. All Rights Reserved.

prints enabled these women painters to represent women's bodies in their own terms.[10] Cassatt's depictions of the toilette were influenced by both Degas's series of "bathers" and Japanese prints, but Cassatt adapted both influences so that the woman's body in Cassatt's prints is not sexualized in the same way it is in many contemporaneous Western paintings and in Japanese *ukiyo-e*. In *Woman Bathing*, the model's exposed upper body is captured from the back, and the mirror reflects only part of her head and hand in the water bowl. The soft, pale tone of the skin and the curvilinear contours of the body signify feminine sensuality, but the relative modesty of the setting and the woman's simple, striped dress, as well as the simplicity of lines, reduce the eroticism. In *The Coiffure*, the woman's bare chest that is reflected in the mirror, the floral patterns on the wall and the carpet, and the overall soft pink tone of the print convey the intimacy of the feminine space and the woman's sexuality. However, in contrast to a Japanese print which Cassatt owned, Kitagawa Utamaro's *Takashima Ohisa Using Two Mirrors to Observe Her Coiffure*, in which the woman's face is clearly reflected in her mirror, the face of the woman in Cassatt's print is blurred. And unlike Katsushika Hokusai's *Woman Adjusting Her Hair*, which shows remarkable similarity with Cassatt's print in the position of the hands, the tilt of the head, the folds of the drapery around the waist, Cassatt's print does not invite the viewer's attention to the woman's nipples or the drapery covering her lower body. Ensconced in the protective chair, the woman in *The Coiffure* appears to be attending to her toilette for her own comfort and in the privacy of the feminine space, rather than in preparation for a social outing (as in the case of *Takashima Ohisa*, subtitled *Night of the Asakusa Marketing Festival*) or posing for the male gaze (as in Degas's paintings of prostitutes). While the artistic conventions of the time made the female nude available only to a masculine vision, Cassatt could present an alternative to the male gaze on the female body by strategically using a foreign art form.[11] Deploying the formal devices of Japanese *ukiyo-e*, Cassatt turned the tools around to depict women's sexuality and Victorian femininity in a way that was different from either her Western male contemporaries or her Japanese prototypes.

As Cassatt did not depict Asian figures or subject matters but rather used an Asian art *form* for her alternative vision of bourgeois white womanhood, her role in Orientalism was quite different from that of those who intervened in the racialized and gendered constructions of Asia much more directly. Yet Cassatt's example shows how a formalistic engagement with Orientalism could have not only aesthetic but also powerful political and cultural potential for white women living within the dominant gender ideology that constrained their creative and professional activities.

It was not only upper-class women such as Cassatt that pursued artistic occupations at the turn of the century. After the Civil War, the middle-class women's need to earn a viable living through respectable means, combined with the socioeconomic conditions of modernization and the gender ideology of the separate spheres, led to the growing acceptance of women's enlarged cultural responsibilities. One visible sign of this process was the entry of many middle-class women into the field of artistic production.[12] Furthermore, the Aesthetic Movement of the post-Civil War period offered liberation and opportunities beyond the confined space of the household, and women came to play key roles in the movement. For a number of women, aestheticism became a tool of covert resistance to the Victorian conventions of family life as it provided not only a forum for women's artistic talents but also an expression of subversive gender norms and sexuality.[13]

As Reina Lewis's study of representation and femininity demonstrates, Orientalism played a significant role in the construction of professional creative opportunities for European women.[14] At the time of American expansion in Asia-Pacific, this was true in the United States as well. By using Asian media, styles, and subject matter, women artists could work in relatively unexplored methods and themes that were curious and fascinating to the American audience with a growing interest in things Asian. Bertha Lum and Helen Hyde are two examples of such women artists relying heavily on Asian art. Both women worked contemporaneously in the same medium of prints. Neither of their careers would have been possible without their interest in Japanese and Chinese arts and culture. Both artists spent a long time in Asia, studied printmaking there, and incorporated Asian methods and images extensively into their work. Both women's works created gendered images of Asia, many of which reinforced, consciously or not, the existing Orientalist discourse.

Bertha Lum (a Caucasian) was born Bertha Boynton Bull in Iowa in 1869. Her father, a lawyer, and her mother were both amateur artists, and she was exposed to Asian art from an early age. Like many American and European artists of the time, she was particularly inspired by the work of Katsushika Hokusai and Ando Hiroshige, as well as by the writings of Arthur Wesley Dow who was the first to incorporate Japanese artistic elements into American art education. In 1895, Lum enrolled for a year in the design department of the Art Institute of Chicago. As Chicagoans had been exposed to Japanese art at the World's Columbian Exposition in 1893, in her art education there must have been a significant Japanese influence as well as the impact of the arts and crafts movement which was particularly strong in the city. In the late 1890s she studied with stained glass artist Anna Weston and illustrator and printmaker Frank Holme. In 1903 she married Burt F. Lum, a corporate lawyer in Minneapolis, and they went on a six-week honeymoon to Japan. In Yokohama, she found an old artisan and spent an hour with him learning about the process and buying the tools for printmaking. After returning to Minneapolis, Lum began using those tools to produce Japanese-style color woodcuts. These early prints portrayed subjects and scenes that were then considered in the West as typically Japanese: images of geishas, street scenes, and Hiroshige-like images of landscapes.[15]

After this initial encounter with Japanese prints, she made many journeys to Japan, and with each trip Lum became more devoted to her study of Japanese printmaking. In 1907, Lum returned to Japan for a fourteen-week stay. Her ability to make such an extended trip and the connections she managed to make with Japanese artists and artisans indicate Lum's privileged status as a white American woman with means. Lum made contact with Igami Bonkotsu, a block cutter who lived and worked in a poor quarter far from the urban center of Tokyo. In contrast to Cassatt, who only took the stylistic elements of *ukiyo-e* but did not adopt its printmaking process, Lum was eager to learn the Japanese method of print production. Lum worked there every day for two months and learned printmaking from the block cutter and his helpers. She was then introduced to a printer who agreed to teach her his part of the craft, which proved even more difficult than block cutting. Her intensive work on this trip was manifested in a series of prints which showed distinctively Japanese pictorial devices, such as subtly graduated tones, soft hues, slanting lines of rain, and figures leaning into the wind.

On her third trip to Japan in 1911, she stayed in Tokyo for six months with her two small children. During this stay, her role was quite different from the one during her previous trips. Rather than studying under a Japanese teacher, Lum hired local craftsmen to do the printing, the most labor-intensive part of the printmaking process, under her supervision in her house. Her work received unusual attention in Japan, and in 1912 Lum became the only foreign woodcut artist to show at the Annual Art Exhibition in Tokyo. Lum's acclaim spread rapidly after this exhibition, and between 1915 and 1919 she made two more extensive trips to Japan, while continuing to produce numerous prints in her home in Minneapolis and later in San Francisco. Some of Lum's prints depicted scenes and ceremonies of Japanese life; some created new iconography for Japanese tales and legends retold by the classic Japanologist Lafcadio Hearn; others combined Western tales with Japanese myths. While Lum was never part of the network of American artists, as her acclaim rose in both Japan and the United States she came to see herself as a professional artist and began to seek shows in galleries and museum exhibitions in cities such as San Francisco, New York, Chicago, and Washington.

In 1922, Lum and her two daughters traveled to Beijing for the first time, where she learned Chinese methods of woodcut production. As the Chinese method of printing (the paper is placed on a block, and charcoal, an ink stick, or a stiff brush is rubbed over the block) was quite different from the Japanese one (the block is inked and the paper is pressed against it), studying Chinese printmaking led to a new area of Lum's work. Although Lum's "raised-line" Chinese prints never became as popular as the woodcut prints she created with the Japanese method, she often made prints of the same image using both methods, juxtaposing the different effects. The 1920s were the golden years for Lum's career, and she attained artistic and financial success. During the difficult years of the Depression, Lum managed to make a living by selling her prints and doing some illustration work for books, newspapers, and magazines such as the *New York Herald Tribune*, *Good Housekeeping*, and *World Traveller*. She spent much of the 1930s in China where her two daughters, now married to an Italian businessman in Beijing and a British diplomat in Shanghai, lived. As World War II approached, she left China to spend the war years in the United States, and had her last exhibition in 1941.

In many ways, Lum's use of Japanese and Chinese subjects and printmaking methods served to reproduce the gendered images of Asia. As art critics Meike Bal and Norman Bryson demonstrate, the use of visual images "involves an insertion into pre-established systems of visual discourse that lay down in advance the paths or net-works that the speaker's words are obliged to follow."[16] In this sense, Lum's images draw upon, and participate in, a genealogy of visual, material, and literary discourse of Orientalism. Furthermore, the use of Japanese printmaking methods functions to highlight the foreignness of both the subject matter and form while masking the ways of seeing that are firmly grounded in the Western conventions of visual practices as well as in the Western discourse of Orientalism. Most of the Japanese or Chinese fig-ures in Lum's prints are women and children, whereas depictions of male figures are rare. Her early works, such as O Yuki (1904) and Geisha Girls (1908) (fig. 2.6), clearly draw upon existing images of Japanese women that heighten the exotic femininity. Yet these images do not convey the potential danger of their sexuality that might se-duce Western men, as in the narrative of Madame Butterfly. They are images of Japanese women wearing kimono, captured from the side as they turn their heads with a slightly coquettish tilt to look straight at the viewer. This sweet and gentle eroti-cism, echoing the fashion plates and popular illustrations of the period as seen in the images of the Gibson Girl, foregrounds the women's surface rather than psychologi-cal interiority depicted in Cassatt's work. Most of Lum's female figures have the same facial features and expressions—small and slightly slanted eyes, small, closed lips, and tilted head—and the distinctions between each figure are minimal. While the women's kimonos and hairdoes indicate the exotic setting, the images say little about the specific scene or the moment, and the static quality of the prints freezes these feminine images in a timeless frame. Lum's work fits into Linda Nochlin's argument about the work of the nineteenth century neoclassical painter Gérôme, in which the "Oriental world is a world without change, a world of timeless, atemporal customs and rituals, untouched by the historical processes that were 'afflicting' or 'improving' but, at any rate, drastically altering Western societies at the time."[17]

Other images, such as Aoyagi (1907) (fig. 2.7) and Fox Women (1907), draw upon Japanese tales and legends introduced to an American audience by Lafcadio Hearn. In these prints, too, all the women look practically the same—in terms of their facial features, expressions, and their robes—making them more of folkloric archetypes than individual figures. While these tales have Japanese origins and therefore are not entirely a construction of Western Orientalism, by selecting these particular tales in which beautiful women are symbols of supernatural power and creating vi-sual iconography for them, Lum joined other contemporary Orientalists in femi-nizing Japan and relegating its images to myths and legends.

In her later prints, Lum's subjects become somewhat more diverse as she de-picted various scenes, locations, and ceremonies, yet the feminine quality of the images remains. The feminine quality is created in part through the frequent use of female figures even when the image is not a portrait but captures scenery, as in Pro-cession (1916). It is also achieved through the soft contours and graduated colors,

Figure 2.6
Bertha Lum,
Geisha Girls,
1908. Color
woodcut.

which distinguish Lum's prints from the Japanese prototypes on which she draws. For example, *A Rainy Twilight* (1905), *Bamboo Road* (1912), and *Winter* (1909) all draw upon Japanese landscape prints in terms of the composition, slanting lines of rain, and figures leaning into the wind. Yet while the Japanese original usually presents a more stoic, crisp, and severe image, Lum's prints are much softer in tone.

Figure 2.7
Bertha Lum,
Aoyagi, 1907.
Color woodcut.

The printmaking method she adapted for herself—she often used no defining outlines and almost entirely dispensed with the key-block—helped to create a sense of
depth that is more characteristic of Western paintings than Japanese *ukiyo-e*.[18]
These adaptations, combined with her replacement of male figures in Hiroshige's
original with female figures, reinforce feminized impressions of Japan.

On the other hand, Lum was also aware of the gendered nature of American Orientalism and in some ways consciously resisted falling into the stereotypes and
myths about Japanese women. In Lum's second book, *Gangplanks to the East*, she
explained why geishas, so frequent a subject in the *ukiyo-e* tradition, appeared seldom in her work.

Perhaps it is best to carry away the remembrance of an hour of unusual beauty and not stop to think and study the lives of these pretty playthings, but if one does inquire into them, one finds that it is not so often happiness as sadness and often tragedy that runs through their days. First, a geisha is always a slave—if she has beauty she is sold when very small by parents too poor to keep her and, almost before she can walk, she is taught to exist only for the pleasure of others. She gives her body, soul and every thought to those owning her, for which she is clothed, fed, and trained. . . She has only one desire and that is that someone will care enough to buy her freedom and take her away.[19]

By pointing out the material conditions in which the beauty of the geisha and pleasure of her client are created, Lum deconstructs and diverges from the Orientalist fantasy about the geisha as the icon of Japanese femininity. That Lum was conscious and articulate about the problems of idolizing geisha while she, perhaps unconsciously, feminized Japanese subjects in her own work demonstrates the seductive and naturalized appeal of visual iconographies of Orientalism that often overpowered alternative, non-visual, narratives about Japan and women.

In further understanding the gender as well as racial and class politics involved in Lum's Orientalism, it is important to note that the production of her prints was made possible by Japanese and Chinese craftsmen. Although little is known about the individual craftsmen Lum employed, a memoir by Lum's daughter gives a glimpse of the dynamics involved in her printmaking. The writer's—and likely her mother Lum's own—high admiration and respect for Japanese artistry is expressed in passages such as: "Only the Japanese seem to have just the right touch, the deft stroke that blends light and dark shading on a single block, the patience to print the same block over and over again to get a deep color, the constant turning of the paper to keep an even dampness, the quick fitting of each sheet to get a perfect register." At the same time, such admiration is mixed with a stereotypical, feminizing depiction of the male craftsmen ("the right touch," "the deft stroke," "the patience") and a patronizing attitude toward the craftsmen with artistic sensibilities foreign to Lum's, which justified the supervision and control Lum exercised over them: "Our paintings were inevitably somewhat alien to them, and if you took your eyes off what they were doing they might suddenly print a bright red where it should have been a soft, rosy shade, or a solid blue sky instead of a pale and misty one."[20] Thus, Lum's deep interest and involvement in Asian arts was accompanied by, and was made possible by, her status as a white American woman of means, which situated her in a position of power vis-à-vis Asian craftsmen.

One sees another example of American women artists' engagement with Asian art and the conditions of their artistic production in Lum's contemporary, Helen Hyde. The parallels in Hyde's and Lum's interests and careers make it curious that the two artists were not even acquainted with one another. Helen Hyde was born in 1868 to a wealthy family in San Francisco. The family money and her outgoing personality gained her easy access to a life of privilege and fine art instruction which began in California and continued in Europe before she traveled to Japan. Hyde lived in Paris from 1891–1894, and studied with influential artists such as Félix Régamy, who published *Japan in Art and Industry* in 1893 and had a decisive impact on Hyde's interest in Japanese art. Hyde was in Paris at the time of the *ukiyo-e* exhibit at the Ecole des Beaux-Arts which influenced Cassatt. Although Hyde missed the first exhibition of Cassatt's Japanese-inspired color prints in 1891, she saw them at the Durand-Ruel Galleries in 1893, and Cassatt's Japanese style and the mother-and-child theme became an inspiration for Hyde's work throughout her career.

Upon returning from Europe to San Francisco in 1894, Hyde began producing color etchings depicting scenes of the city's Chinatown. These Chinatown prints brought her to the attention of one of New York's most important art dealers, William Macbeth, who was to become critical to Hyde's career as an artist. In 1899, at age thirty-one, Hyde sailed to Japan for the first time. She would spend about half of her adult life in Tokyo and Nikko, studying and producing prints. Like Lum, Hyde's economic means as well as her status as a white American woman provided her with access and connection to the Japanese art world that would not have been normally available to women in Japan. Upon her first arrival, she and her friend Josephine Hyde (no relation to Hyde) began taking lessons in brush drawing from the revered Kano Tomonobu, and for eighteen months they studied the classic Japanese methods of brush painting. Hyde's attention was soon drawn to woodcut prints, and by April 1900 she was making arrangements for her first color woodcut, *A Japanese Madonna*, to be transferred to blocks by craftsmen. As in the case of Bertha Lum, Hyde engaged cutters and printers in the employ of a Tokyo print publisher and art dealer Kobayashi Bunshichi. She became increasingly familiar with the Japanese workshop system and tried to control the work by understanding each step of the production. Between April 1900 and her return to San Francisco in October 1901, Hyde produced twelve woodcuts and four etchings, editions ranging from 100 to 250 impressions.

After a brief visit home in 1901–02, Hyde returned to Japan, this time for eight years. She had a house in Tokyo and engaged the celebrated printer Murata Shohiro and a cutter named Matsumoto. By choosing to work within the Japanese system of production, Hyde made remarkable progress in her work and produced some of her most well-known prints, such as *The Mirror* (1904) (fig. 2.8) and *Baby Talk* (1908). As in her earlier works, Hyde's figures, mostly women and children, are often depicted in a domestic interior or garden landscape. The influence of *ukiyo-e* masters is apparent in both her style (e.g., sharp foreshortening, images cut off or overlapped by the frame, figures seen from behind, and decorative patterning) and

Figure 2.8
Helen Hyde,
The Mirror, 1904.
Color woodcut.

subject matter (e.g., figures in the rain or snow, folding screens, kimonos, and clogs). During this extensive stay in Japan, Hyde espoused Japanese life: she wore kimonos at home, had her crest embroidered on her garments and emblazoned in gold leaf on her rickshaw, had her Japanese name "Hatono" imprinted in her works, and collected a large number of kimonos and other Japanese artifacts. In the meantime, her reputation was growing in both the United States and Europe as some of her prints won awards in reputable exhibitions. When she returned to San Francisco in 1910, local newspapers ran articles featuring her life in Japan.

After her trip to Mexico in 1910–1912 to seek a warmer climate after her operation, she returned to Tokyo in early 1912, which was to be her last residence in Japan. In

October 1914, she closed her home in Tokyo and returned to the United States, settling in Chicago with her sister Mabel. Her prints were exhibited at the Panama-Pacific International Exhibition where she won a Bronze Medal. Despite her poor health and the absence of skilled cutters and printers to assist her, Hyde continued to work and in 1918 produced posters and intaglios for the war effort. Hyde died of cancer in California in 1919.

Although Hyde's choice to spend so many years in Japan and to devote her artistic career to Japanese subjects and style suggests her deep sympathy for Japanese culture, as in the case of Bertha Lum, Hyde's prints inherited and reproduced many of the racialized and gendered images of Asia that already existed in American discourse. Her close exposure to dominant American views of San Francisco's Chinatown and her own portrayals of the Chinese in the early phase of her career no doubt informed both the subject matter and style of her Japanese works. Her brother-in-law, Will Irwin, wrote the text accompanying the photographs by Arnold Genthe in *Pictures of Old Chinatown*. Irwin's text mixed his sympathetic rendition of the history of Chinese in America ("Why this thing [the persecution of the Chinese] began, what quality in the Chinese nature irritated our pioneers beyond all justice and sense of decency, remains a little dim and uncomprehended to this generation. They were an honest people — honest beyond our strictest ideas.") with the description of the world of opium dens, gambling parlors, slave girls, Tong wars, and underground tunnels, along with more racist accounts of the people:

> And as they drank and played, and played and drank, something deep below the surface came out in them. Their shouts became squalls; lips drew back from teeth, beady little eyes blazed; their very cheek bones seemed to rise higher on their faces. I thought as I watched of wars of the past; these were not refined Cantonese, with a surface gentility and grace in life greater than anything that our masses know; they were those old yellow people with whom our fathers fought before the Caucusus was set as a boundary between the dark race and the light; the hordes of Ghengis Khan; the looters of Atilla.[21]

Hyde's visual depictions of San Francisco's Chinatown were softer and more benign than Irwin's, yet Hyde's images were no less exoticized than Genthe's photographs.[22] Nor were her visual images less shaped by the racial dynamics surrounding the Chinese in California than Irwin's text. Bertha Jaques, who befriended Hyde and later wrote a book introducing her work, claims that Hyde referred to her two Chinatown etchings, *The Mandarin* and *Little Plum Blossom*, as her "little heathen[s]."[23] In another letter, Hyde talked of going to Chinatown and studying the people in New Year's costumes as "like hunting for tropical birds," which suggests that Hyde saw Chinatown and the Chinese as a curious and colorful spectacle.[24] From these early Chinatown etchings, Hyde carved a niche for her work by singling out women and children as her subjects. The combination of Japanese-influenced composition and lines, the exotic attire of the Chinese figures, and the warm and round images of women and children created distinctive portrayals of a life that was gendered feminine and was both fascinating and unthreatening to an American audience in the midst of the Chinese exclusion years.

Jingles from Japan (1901) (fig. 2.9), a book of verses by her sister Mabel Hyde and illustrated by Helen, shows a remarkable example of Hyde's Orientalism.[25] The book consists of twenty-five verses depicting diverse scenes of life in Japan, which highlight Japan's exoticness and mock its eccentricities. While many of Mabel's verses, evidently written for children, are non-sensical plays on words with minstrel-like portrayals of the Japanese, what is notable about the book is the visual way in which Helen's illustrations position the subjects in relation to the reader. Throughout the book, the illustrations in black and red show a little girl with long red hair pulled above her head and tied with a ribbon. Her hair and her dress, socks, and shoes identify her as an American, and the reader follows her journey through curious scenes and customs of Japanese life. On the front cover and accompanying a few of the poems is an older, taller girl with long, black hair. Two pages in the frontspiece show the red-haired girl writing on the scroll and the black-haired girl painting with a brush. Therefore, these two figures may be depictions of the Hyde sisters themselves, whereby Helen, the older of the sisters, takes the younger Mabel through the wonders—and dangers—of Japan. In many of the pages, the red-haired girl stands above Japanese children, either physically or symbolically. For example, the poem, "The Land of Approximate Time," portrays Japan as lacking in order or industry:

Here's to the Land of Approximate Time!

Where it is very ill bred to go straight to the point.
Where one bargains at leisure all day,
Where with method unique 'at once' means a week,
In the cool, easy Japanese way. . . .

. . . Where the overcharged West may learn how to rest,
The Land of Inconsequent Now!

While the verse thus constructs Japan as a relaxed, disorganized, and lazy antithesis to the West, the accompanying illustration shows the red-haired girl standing and toasting (to the Land of Approximate Time) as three little Japanese children sit on their feet and drink from their cups. In "The Sonnet," a verse about the *tatami* mattress and the Japanese practice of taking one's shoes off in the house, the girl is laboriously taking her shoes off on the verandah while a kimono-clad Japanese girl, presumably a servant, awaits bowing in respect. These images, by implication, place the American reader in a position of superiority over the Japanese subjects that is established by the content of the verses.

Figure 2.9 Helen Hyde, *Jingles from Japan*, cover.

In other parts of the book, the red-haired girl glimpses the undesirable, potentially fearful elements of "Japanese life." A poem entitled, "Would You Like to Be a Coolie?" combines the racialized language about the Chinese "coolie" labor with the portrayal of the Japanese as backwards, impoverished, and lacking in industrial work ethic:

> Would you like to be a coolie,
> Where hurry there is none,
> Where there's ever time to smoke and drink your tea,
> Where your pay is by the load,
> Where your conscience does not goad,
> A quiet-minded coolie would you be? . . .

In the illustration, a group of Japanese men in worker's gown beckons the girl who has a look of consternation. The Hyde sisters' depiction thus expresses confusion about the types of labor Chinese workers engaged in, conflation of Chinese in America and Japanese in Japan, and racist notion of Asian men threatening young white women and girls.[26] Another poem, "The Lay of the Doguya," represents Japanese merchants as constantly attempting to cheat foreign customers. While her sister looks admiringly at the merchandise, the red-haired girl peeks at the conniving men. In the images where the little girl is pictured with Japanese children, she is depicted as being in control and superior to the children, while the facial and bodily features do not differ dramatically between her and the Japanese children. On the other hand, when she is portrayed with Japanese men, she looks threatened. These images thus capitalize on and reinforce the racialized and sexualized images of Japanese men as a threat to the moral fabric of American society and in particular to white female sexuality.

The Hyde sisters' racialized and sexualized construction of Japan in *Jingles* was also well manifested in their portrayal of Japanese women in the poem, "The Little Geisha." Since there is no other poem in the book that is specifically about Japanese women or girls, this poem, like many other Western texts about Japan, implicitly equates the geisha with Japanese women. Moreover, unlike Lum, who had a more nuanced understanding of the profession, this poem replicates the popular Western notion of the geisha while taking out the explicitly sexual reference as appropriate for children:

> Wandering out o' mornings,
>   One hears the dulcet tones
> Of samisens and quavers,
>   Of trilling and of groans.
> And through the latticed doorways,
>   With eyes applied below,
> One sees the busy geishas
>   Who live in Geisha Row.
>
> The floor is strewn with obis,
>   And rouge in tiny pots,
> They kneel before steel mirrors
>   And dab the beauty-spots.
> Now some are loudly singing,
>   Some dance with rhythmic beat.
> Those naughty little geishas
>   Who live in Geisha street.
>
> Again, when day is older
>   While still the sun is high,
> Bedecked in silks and tassels,
>   They come a-riding by,

Their eyes with mischief gleaming,
    Lips carmine, brows of snow,
Those coquettish little geisha
    Who live in Geisha Row!

And should one go a dining,
    With chopsticks on the floor,
One hears a teasing laughter
    As they push the sliding door.
They come, those fairy beings,
    And sway on gliding feet;
Those bewitching little geisha
    Who live in Geisha Street!

By combining the adjectives "naughty," "coquettish," "bewitching" with "little,"
and by emphasizing their adornment, noise, laughter, and mischief, the poem creates an image of the geisha as playful and pleasurable beings outside of social conventions. Helen's illustrations portray women in identical kimonos from their back,
one sitting in front of her mirror to put on her makeup and the other four dancing
with fans in hand, presumably in front of their customers. This image constructed
by both Mabel's verse and Helen's illustration became an archetype used consistently in Helen's printmaking career.

In the context of racial, gender, and class politics of these verses and illustrations,
what is even more striking is that the book is subtitled, *As Set Forth by the Chinks*,
even though there is not a single reference to a Chinese figure in the content of the
book. Does this mean that these verses are to be read as composed by the Chinese?
Are the two girls—particularly the older girl with long, black hair, who is wearing a
kimono-like long robe—supposed to be "the Chinks"? Perhaps this is a remnant of
the childhood of the Hyde sisters who, growing up in San Francisco and being familiar with the city's Chinatown, called themselves "Chinks" and played a game
among themselves. Or perhaps this reference is a ploy on the part of the author/
illustrator to absolve themselves of racist depictions of the Japanese by attributing
them to "the Chinks." Although there are no clear answers to these questions, one
thing that *Jingles* does demonstrate is that Hyde's portrayals of the Japanese were
shaped as much by the racialized discourse around Chinese labor in California as
by Hyde's own sympathy for and interest in Japanese culture.

Hyde's "Japanese" prints during the height of her career are in direct conversation with the dominant Orientalist discourse of the time and provide visual materiality to the popular images of the Japanese. Even more clearly and consciously than
Lum, Hyde focused on women and children as the subjects of her Japanese prints.
Together with the absence of Japanese men in the prints, the images she chose to

portray reinforce the gendered construction of the Japanese woman in contemporary American discourse, particularly the image of the geisha (as expressed in the poem in *Jingles*) and the icon of Madame Butterfly. Both *The Mirror* and *Baby Talk*, two of Hyde's most well-known works, depict a Japanese woman in a kimono holding and talking affectionately to a baby. With the distinct and round lines of the woman's body which heighten her sensuousness, detailed depictions of the kimono and the domestic interiors (mirror, sliding doors) which accentuate the exoticness of the cultural context, and the woman's domesticity underscored by the baby, these images could very well be illustrations for *Madame Butterfly*. Practically all of Hyde's Japanese prints were versions of this image of Japanese women and children, thus reproducing and giving visual reference to the dominant Orientalist discourse.

What is notable about Hyde's work is that the more experience she gained in depicting Asian subjects later in her career, the less individuated and more cartoonish her figures became. In her early work, such as *A Monarch of Japan* (1901) and *Day Dreams* (1901), Hyde captured the domestic image that conveyed the emotional depth and the relations between the mother and her child. The color soft-ground etching, *The Daimio's Daughter* (1901), and the watercolor, *The Kettle Lullaby* (1903), both portray Japanese women sitting on the floor in their domestic spaces and express their social position and emotional state, somewhat similar to Cassatt's work. In contrast, the figures in Hyde's later prints become increasingly uniform in their facial features and expression and are depicted more as types than individuals. For example, *My Neighbors* (1913) depicts the same mother-and-child image as her earlier works but the faces of the mother and the child are not very distinct from each other, and there is little psychological depth to the image beyond its cute, sweet quality. In *Blossom Time in Tokyo* (1914), figures—all women and children— are portrayed with the same distinct lines, round contours, and tone (fig. 2.10). One could interpret this evolution of Hyde's work either as her growing mastery of the flat and surface-oriented quality of Japanese prints or as her decreasing engagement with Japanese subjects as individuals. In either case, her increasingly uniform archetype of Japanese women and children provided tangible icons for the feminized vision of Japan already popular in America's Orientalist discourse.

As with Lum, Hyde's hiring of Japanese craftsmen—celebrated ones at that— demonstrates the material conditions which enabled her artistic production. While Hyde either conflated Japanese male workers with "coolie" laborers (as she did in *Jingles*) or made them invisible in her prints, her own artistic production was highly dependent on the labor of Japanese craftsmen. Bertha Jaques describes Hyde's printmaking:

When the little pile of boards were done, Muratta san [*sic*], her printer, presented himself at her studio with a deep bow and prepared for the fray. With his legs neatly tucked away beneath him, Muratta san seated himself on the floor and was

Figure 2.10 Helen Hyde, *Blossom Time in Tokyo*, 1914.

nearly lost to view behind piles of paper, blotters, printing blocks, a whole battalion of old blue and gray bowls and brushes. He was supposed to carry out faithfully Miss Hyde's color scheme, but the Japanese art sense rebels against dull repetition. No one will repeat a thing he can possibly vary in the search for better results. So it was necessary for Miss Hyde to superintend each print—a tedious occupation.[27]

The mixture of respect for the craftsman and Hyde's need to oversee his work is reminiscent of the description of Lum's work with her Japanese artisans. Given that *ukiyo-e* printmaking in Japan was a highly gendered arena where male artists and artisans produced sexualized (many of them pornographic) images of actresses and courtesans of the "floating world," Hyde's transgression of such boundaries further highlight the way in which the racial, national, and economic status of a white, American woman in Asia often allowed her to break the gender conventions for herself as she recreated gender stereotypes for women of another race. Jaques's description of Hyde's relationship to her *jinrikisha* runner further underlines her relationship to Japanese men. According to Jaques, Shin, the runner, wrote long letters to Hyde while he was away fighting in the Russo-Japanese War, "giving details of his life in the army and very interesting comments on the famous men of the war, expressing himself with a freedom not usually employed by Japanese men to their own womenfolk."[28] These instances illustrate the relationship the American woman artist developed with her Japanese subjects based on both power and affect.

Lum and Hyde, working with the same medium and the similar subject matter in the same period, were both active producers of the visual culture of American Orientalism. In addition to their class privilege which offered them formal artistic training and ability to travel to Asia, their identity as white American women gave them access to the knowledge and connections needed for their exploration of Asian art that would not have been available to women of Asia. Both these social conditions and the gendered nature of artistic production—where women artists were compelled and geared to focus on "feminine" themes of women and children—shaped the two artists' portrayals of Asia in their works. On the one hand, they both depicted Asian subjects and scenes with warmth and sympathy and produced visual iconography for the mythic and folkloric Asia for the American audience. On the other hand, their work also inherited and reproduced the racialized and gendered language of popular Orientalism, creating exotic, feminized archetypes of Asia.

Women artists played an important role in the use of Asian—particularly Japanese—art in this period. According to historian William Hosley, "Japanese art conventions and decoration figured so prominently in [women's creative] activity that, unlike the fine and industrial arts where it was a sideline, women's art put Japan front and center. When critics and pundits referred to 'the Japan craze,' it was women's work they had in mind."[29] In addition to Japanese-style prints created by professional artists discussed above, media such as textile design, embroideries, and china painting became popular areas of artistic Orientalism among these new women artists. Through these activities, women were increasingly turning what was designated specifically as "feminine" and "amateur" occupations into more professionalized, market-oriented art forms. For example, textile artist Candace Wheeler, who founded the Associated Artists in 1879 and made significant contribution to the professionalization of middle-class women artists, was strongly influenced by Japanese art. For Wheeler, Japanese design expressed "elegance, refinement, and serenity of mind," "softness and harmony of coloring, and exquisite craftsmanship," while it showed no "profusion of costly and incongruous things," and "no false standards of display." Through her sensitivities that emphasized both art and economy—and her adoption of Asian design that accomplished both—she carved out a space for middle-class women's professional work in decorative arts.

Artistic Orientalism also gave birth to the career of Maria Longworth Nichols, founder of Rookwood Pottery in Cincinnati. Captivated by the Japanese exhibits at the Philadelphia Centennial Exposition of 1876, Nichols developed her highly idiosyncratic Japanese style in her own pottery. She painted dragons, gaping-mouthed fish with bulging eyes, crabs, frogs, leafy bamboo, swallows, and cranes; imitations of Japanese calligraphy enhanced her decorative scheme. In 1887, Nichols hired Japanese decorator Shirayamadani Kataro to be the principal decorator at Rookwood, and the company's Japanese design led a "Japanese mania" in Cincinnati. These examples show that the use of Asian design and methods offered an effective avenue for women artists to carve a niche for themselves in the field of art and to gaining new power both as women and as artists.[30]

Women's gendered role in the world of art shaped their relationship to artistic Orientalism—and what they did with it—in ways different from their male counterparts. Following the general tradition of the time, women artists tended to focus on subjects that were considered "feminine," such as the images of women and children. However, their embracing of Asian medium, style, and/or subject matter allowed each of them to make different interventions not only in aesthetics but also in gender and racial politics. For Cassatt, the use of Asian art form allowed her to express her gender politics without directly engaging in the racialized and gendered discourse about Asia itself. On the other hand, Lum and Hyde more directly inherited the racialized and gendered language of existing Orientalism and reproduced it through their power to learn and appropriate Asian art.

When analyzing those who were directly involved with Asian subjects in their work—such as Lum and Hyde—it is important to understand the relationship between the images they created and the conditions of their production. Women artists' engagement with Asian art was shaped by their class privilege—which gave them access to the artistic occupation as well as to Asia—and their white American identity, which placed them in the position of power vis-à-vis the Asian subjects they portrayed and Asian artists/craftsmen they hired. This class, racial, and national position allowed women artists to transgress the gender boundaries of both the United States and Asia, gaining artistic authorship while being dependent on Asian labor in the making of their art. Their artistic Orientalism was thus as much about racial, national, and economic power dynamics as it was about aesthetic creativity.

Performing Asia

"When I Don Your Silken Draperies"
New Women's Performances of Asian Heroines

O ne of the most popular icons of American Orientalism that emerged in this period is *Madame Butterfly*. The timing of publication of John Luther Long's original story in 1898 and subsequent stage and film productions of *Madame Butterfly* in the early twentieth century is significant. As critic James Moy demonstrates, the narrative of *Butterfly*—and many other texts representing Asians in this period—in which the Asian character dies at the end worked conveniently for America's nationalist ideology of the time. At the turn of the century, the United States was consolidating its imperialist power in Asia-Pacific. At the same time, the newly "opened" and supposedly subjugated Asian powers, such as Japan, was beginning to behave in a fashion not unlike its European mentors and thus posing a threat to the Eurocentric perception of the new world order. A popular American response to this phenomenon was simply to eliminate the threat, at least symbolically, by turning Asians into figures worthy of death and then killing them off.[1] While many critics have thus commented on the cultural politics of *Madame Butterfly* on the narrative level—that is, in the discussion of the plot—the meaning of *Madame Butterfly* was shaped on multiple levels beyond the written text. Far more Americans encountered *Madame Butterfly* through stage, opera, and later film productions than through the book, and the image of Cio-Cio-San was shaped tangibly by the white actresses who played the role on stage. Ironically, it was the white women performers that embodied the images and meanings of Asian femininity created by the white male author, playwright, and/or composer.

The popularity of Orientalist theater productions such as *Madame Butterfly* and white women's performance in them was part of a larger cultural phenomenon in this period. Japonisme and Chinoiserie were already in full vogue in America. European theater and opera during the eighteenth and nineteenth centuries, which many American dramatists studied and emulated, also used many "exotic" settings and explored imperialist and Orientalist themes in their productions.[2] There were other theatrical and musical productions, such as Gilbert and Sullivan's *The Mikado*, that preceded *Madame Butterfly* and provided performative tropes for American Orientalism. Given these factors, the proliferation of white women's Orientalist performance in this period is not particularly surprising. However, women's participation in Orientalist performances which proliferated in the early twentieth century marked a significant shift in the relationship of white women to the Orient in that these women literally became "actors" of Orientalism. It was not incidental that these Orientalist performances by white women took place at the same time that many white women were becoming New Women of the twentieth century, who challenged Victorian gender norms and the ideology of the separate spheres by participating in the women's suffrage movement, demanding birth control, engaging in socialism, expressing themselves in arts and letters, seeking "free love," cutting their hair and smoking cigarettes. The construction of such a new gender identity was closely linked to, and was articulated through, enacting roles and identities other than their own. The performance of Asian femininity thus provided an effective tool for white women's empowerment and pleasure as New Women. While not all white women who performed in these productions may have identified themselves as New Women, acting on stage and performing identities that were distinct from their own marked them as women of a new generation. Furthermore, both their roles as Asian heroines and their identities as professional performers appealed especially to the female audience, who saw them as liberating themselves from fixed categories while producing new, constructed identities for women. Focusing on white women's performances of Asian-ness in the first two decades of the twentieth century, this chapter analyzes the cultural politics of these performances by looking at the white actresses and singers who played the roles of Asian heroines on stage.

White women's performances of Asian femininity took place within the multilayered context consisting of: the *realpolitik* of U.S.-Asian relations; the producers' (author, playwright, composer, actress/singer, among others) construction of Asianness; the American audience's assumptions about Asian femininity; the actresses'/singers' identity as white, American women; the audience's notions of American womanhood; and the audience's understanding—"race" knowledge—of the performance as an act of racial-crossing.[3] White women's performances of alternative femininity—often in the form of subservient, tragic heroines of the East—served not only to advance their theatrical careers but to solidify their identities as modern American women. The performances and the debates around them demonstrate that these acts of racial-crossing were as much about performances of white American womanhood as they were about enactments of Asian femininity. Furthermore, their ability to perform the roles of Asian heroines was closely linked to the white women's material and representational power over real Asian women and men, the power they exercised both on and off stage.

David Belasco's dramatization of John Luther Long's *Madame Butterfly* was first performed at the Herald Square Theatre in New York in 1900, starring the actress Blanche Bates. Although Belasco's *Madame Butterfly* was a short, one-act play written as an after-piece to his play *Naughty Anthony*, it was immediately recognized as a "triumph of beauty and mastery of atmospheric detail."[4] Belasco created what he considered a "fully Japanese atmosphere" through careful attention to detail on stage sets and ingenious use of lighting, the effectiveness of which advanced his reputation as playwright and producer. Yet the significance of the play *Madame Butterfly* was much greater for the actress Blanche Bates. Although Bates had been performing for a number of years, she had had the reputation of being too temperamental.[5] However, her performance of tragic Japanese womanhood in the role of Cho-Cho-San won her the reputation as one of the most acclaimed American actresses.

The emotional power rendered by *Butterfly*'s dramatic plot and character was shaped by a unique relationship between the actress and her role. The audience appreciated Bates's Cho-Cho-San precisely for what it was: a performance. Just as it was apparent to any nineteenth-century audience that blackface minstrelsy was performed by white performers, and it was precisely this racial cross-dressing that made minstrelsy a truly popular culture form, the American audience in the 1900s knew fully well that Cho-Cho-San was a white actress's impersonation of a Japanese woman, and it was based on that "race knowledge" that the American audience applauded Bates's performance.[6] Thus, comments such as, "[Bates was] made up like a far more beautiful Japanese girl than any upon whom it has been the privilege of the writer to gaze," or "[Bates] looked pretty, too, which is no easy task for an Anglo-Saxon woman personating a Japanese maiden," repeatedly emphasized the actress's Anglo-Saxon identity and how she was *made up* as a Japanese character.[7] Rather than debating the authenticity or truthfulness of impersonation, the critics discussed the theatrical skills with which the actress "mastered" her "subject." The implications of this reception become clearer when one considers comments such as: "Physically she is too big and brainy a woman for a Geisha, but by the eloquence of her art and the sincerity of her emotion she speedily overcame this fault and carried the audience into interest and applause."[8] Commentaries like this, combined with the play itself, both capitalized on and reinforced the existing American notions about both Japanese femininity symbolized by Cho-Cho-San and modern American womanhood embodied by Bates.

The cultural politics of Bates's impersonation of Japanese woman was more elaborately enacted in the following years. The success of *Madame Butterfly* led Long and Belasco to collaborate on another "Japanese" performance, *The Darling of the Gods*, again starring Blanche Bates as the forlorn heroine, Yo-San (fig. 3.1). The play premiered in New York in December 1902, and after 200 performances, it traveled to Boston, Brooklyn, Newark, Philadelphia, Chicago, and Pittsburgh.[9] A five-act play with more than forty actors in the cast, *The Darling of the Gods* presented a much more elaborate narrative and lavish spectacle than *Madame Butterfly*. While both are set in Japan, the two plays constructed racial and gendered meanings in quite different ways.

In the fashion typical of Orientalist productions, the narrative of *The Darling of the Gods* takes bits of Japan's history and mixes them with heightened melodrama and distorted representations. The story takes place during the period of the "sword edict," when the Emperor took away the swords of the Samurai, and deals with a band of ten patriots who refused to obey the edict and were outlawed. The heroine, Yo-San, falls in love with Kara, the leader of the group, and protects him in her sanctuary from the pursuit of her father and Zakkuri, the Minister of War, as "It is better to lie—a little—than to be unhappy much."[10] When Kara is captured and Yo-San is outcast by her father, Yo-San makes a pact with Zakkuri to become his courtesan in exchange for Kara's life. When Zakkuri demands she reveal the whereabouts of Kara's fellow men, Yo-San gives out the information in order to set Kara free. Soon reunited with Kara, she is told that "before the betrayers of honor shall rise to the First White Heaven of Form, they shall sink down into the darkness of wandering souls, for the gods hold them back from heaven one thousand years."[11] Kara and the soldiers take their own lives, as does Yo-San. The play closes with the scene of the Celestial Heaven a thousand years later, where Yo-San and Kara are reunited.

While this romantic plot, in which the heroine pursues her love in the face of law and family obligations, led a critic to conclude that Yo-San "is a Japanese Juliet," the creation of the performance was founded on the material relations between the actress and real Asian men and women that were far less romantic than her performance.[12] According to the *Chicago Chronicle*, Bates began the task of collecting Japanese "atmosphere" when she was three years old. "That was at her home in California, and the effort was an unconscious one. The little Yo-San . . . to be had at the time a Japanese nurse and there were two Japanese 'boys' employed in the family."[13] Given the large percentage of Japanese women and men who made their living as domestic workers on both the West Coast and in eastern cities such as New York in this period, and the impact it had on gender and family relations within Asian im-

Figure 3.1 Blanche Bates as "Yo-San" in *The Darling of the Gods*. *Theatre* magazine (October 1903), front cover.

migrant communities as well as on gendered and class meanings assigned to Asians in white society, this foundation of Bates's "Japanese lesson" is significant.[14] Bates's performance as a form of American entertainment was not simply a matter of imaginative and creative art, but drew on her own experience of the relations between Asian immigrants in the United States and white households.

In an effort to authenticate her performance of Japanese womanhood in *Madame Butterfly* and *The Darling of the Gods*, Bates relied on her Japanese maid, Suki. Although the woman's background is unknown, Bates explains that Suki was "one of those California Japanese who was not coarse in her humility, like most of the lower class Japanese as we find them on the Coast." She was hired as a maid while Bates was performing another play in San Francisco, and she greatly helped Bates and Belasco in the production of the two plays with Japanese themes. Bates refers to Suki as "the original" of both her Butterfly and Yo-San. In an interview for the *Theatre* magazine, Bates recalls:

> From her I learned how to fan myself in true Japanese fashion and, more important still, how to walk "Japanesely." Suki also taught me the proper way to sit down and to get up, to hold a cup of tea in my hand and to sip the tea, and the hundred-and-one little things that Japanese women do that, all added together, make them the most fascinatingly interesting women on earth. She taught me how to gain a Japanese accent with English words, by certain little inflections of the voice, thereby giving a Japanese swing to the lines and showed me the A, B, C's of Geisha-girl coquetry. And she helped me in my makeup to such an extent, in the part of Yo-San, especially, that on more than one occasion I was mistaken for Suki by different members of the company while standing in the wings!

Bates claims that she copied Suki in every particular for her portrayal of Butterfly. Suki's manners were particularly effective for the role since, according to Bates, "She always had a frightened way about her that was sweetly pathetic, as though her head was always under a sword." Suki's influence was more than the coaching of mannerisms and speech. Bates also used Suki's real life and emotions. As Bates says,

> I will never forget her show of deep emotion and anguish when she received a letter from her brother telling her of the torture to death of her lover in far-away Japan on the eve of his departure to join her in San Francisco. She cried all that afternoon—it was a matinée day—and all during the evening performance crouched beside my trunk in the dressing room . . . . Later, in 'Madame Butterfly,' in the scene where poor little Butterfly kills herself, I tried my best to be poor Suki over again when she received that letter. At every performance Suki would watch me most carefully from the wings—she seemed to be made happy over having that sad memory brought back to her. Again, in 'The Darling of the Gods,' I made use of the same anguishing touch in the chamber of horrors scene. It was Suki that I was playing. Suki, Suki![15]

Bates's performance of the Japanese heroine was thus based not only on an actual Japanese woman but on the particular relationship Bates had with her. As a white, professional, American woman who put on many faces and embodied different roles on stage, Bates had both material and representational power over this Japanese immigrant woman whom she hired as the model of Japanese womanhood.

Bates's theatrical success in her Japanese roles was enabled, authenticated, and advanced by the real tragedy in the life of this Japanese woman.

As the power relations between Bates and the Japanese created her performance of the Japanese heroine, the performance in turn led to her more active role in U.S.-Japan relations. At the outset of the Russo-Japanese War in February 1904, Bates responded to the call for the organization of an ambulance corps to aid the Japanese army and sent over twelve volunteer nurses and personally paid for their services and equipment. The idea for this aid was initially suggested to Bates by Tingley Hudson, who played one of the geisha girls in *Darling of the Gods*, and like two other members of the company had been a trained nurse before going on the stage. The title of a newspaper article that reported Bates's aid vividly demonstrates the gendered and racialized ways in which it was understood by American readers: "Blanche Bates to Nurse Japs."[16]

It was in the context of the material relationship between Bates and real Japanese, and between the United States and Japan, that the "Japanese-ness" of *The Darling of the Gods* was constructed through both the narrative and the performance. The heroine's Juliet-like self-sacrifice may have triggered the sympathy of the audience in a manner similar to *Madame Butterfly*, but Bates's Yo-San was quite a different representation of Japanese womanhood from her Cho-Cho-San. Since all the characters in the play were Japanese, Belasco did not resort to the stunted English in order to emphasize the Japanese-ness of particular characters as he did in *Madame Butterfly*. Instead, feudal Japan is portrayed as excessively hierarchical and verbose through the characters' grammatically correct yet quaintly and strangely formalized English. This peculiar style of language effectively constructed, and confirmed, the audience's notions of Japanese-ness as expressed in speech. Numerous reviews commenting on the play's language indicate the assumptions about "Japanese speech" presumably shared by the producers, critics, and audiences. One Boston newspaper commented: "[Bates's] English speech, while in no way like the Japanese tongue supposed to be spoken by the woman she is impersonating, has about it certain tricks of intonation and inflection which are so absolutely un-English that the audience, by a sort of hypnotic influence and by force of imagination, thinks [it] is the real speech of Japan."[17] Another Boston paper wrote,

[*The Darling of the Gods*] is so thoroughly steeped in a Japanese atmosphere, that a foreign language seems totally incompetent to reckon with it. To be sure, the dialogue of the piece is all in English, but it is all so happily delivered with *the modulations and inflections we associate with the speaking Japanese voice*, that it seems it must be a masterly and literal translation from the works of a Japanese playwright. It has strange tricks and manners of speech that will fascinate you as you listen to them and haunt you for days later, and you will find the insistent "say so" that Yo San in particular uses so effectively creeping into your daily talk and establishing itself with you. [emphasis added][18]

These comments suggest that the critic and the readers shared knowledge of Japanese speech that are confirmed by Bates' performance and mimicked by the audience as well. Another article in a Boston paper comically illustrates the phenomenon of "Japanese speech" that was "creeping into" the daily life of Bostonians:

It is really too bad this latest fad for Japanese speech, but since David Belasco will persist in writing Japanese plays, and Blanche Bates will persist in acting their heroines, there is apparently no help for it. We hear it everywhere, not only at the Tremont Theater during the performance of "The Darling of the Gods," but in the lobbies, on the streets, in the hotels, and at home at all times of the day. The Japanese politeness is apparently with us always, since Blanche Bates has conquered Boston. During a short walk down Tremont street the other afternoon, one might have thought the entire town had gone Japanese mad.

One friend met another with this salutation: "And how is your most honorable health, excellency?" and was answered thus with great solemnity: "I humbly beg your august pardon, most noble sir. Would you deign to partake of a miserably inefficient drink with me?" Whereupon the friends presumably adjourned to the nearest hotel.[19]

At a time when many of the real Japanese immigrants' inability to speak English was seen as a sign of their unassimilability to the United States, the "Japanese speech" of Bates and the inspired Bostonians was seen as infectious humor. Enjoying the play as a performance allowed the American audience to deflect the political and social confrontation with the real Japan, while constructing and performing their own notions of "Japanese-ness."

Beyond Belasco's text, Bates exercised a great deal of agency in constructing Asian-ness, and more specifically, Japanese femininity. The actress was highly concerned with issues of authenticity in playing her lead roles. During the play's tour in Boston, a local paper described Bates's efforts in an article titled "How a Yankee Girl Becomes a Japanese Maiden." The writer described how Bates created an Oriental theme in her dressing room, with numerous Japanese cushions, little low bamboo tables, gaily colored fans, a huge Japanese parasol in gorgeous hues covering the ceiling, and paper lanterns hanging from every possible point. From this room she transformed herself into an Oriental character:

Clothed in Japanese style from head to foot, Miss Bates [gets] ready for the most exacting part of her task. So carefully, indeed, her head-dress and facial make-up are prepared that she is obliged to be at the theater over an hour before the curtain rises.

The making up of the face for the stage character requires both patience, but the preparation for the Japanese part needs to be especially skillful and in every way artistic, and entire contour and expression of the face must be compelled, by all the resources of the art of make-up, to take on those characteristics which are peculiar to the Japanese. To do this Miss Bates first of all deepens her complexion to the requisite Japanese hue, and then, by a clever manipulation of the eyebrows, she gives to her eyes the narrow look and upward tilt without which no oriental can be himself or herself.

She first covers her own eyebrows with flesh-colored grease-paint, and then by means of a pencil especially made for the purpose she replaces them with a heavy black and slanting line which at a short distance looks exactly like the Japanese eyebrow. This accomplishes wonders, and already Miss Bates has begun to look like a veritable Japanese. After that comes the head dress, with its rolls of coarse black hair, and then Miss Bates is ready to step upon the stage the actual embodiment of the romantic Yo San. With one task over, however, another begins.[20]

The article goes on to describe Bates's daily massage to round her muscular neck, throat, and arms into the full plumpness which a high-class Japanese woman would have considered ideal. At the same time, her athletic exercises enabled her to kneel on cushions or squat on the floor in a way "conforming to rigid Japanese custom." To do this, the article says, Bates "has had to unlearn for the time being all the movements which come most natural to her and to assume the artificial ways of the Japanese girl."

This lengthy and concrete description of Bates's mimesis reflects the writer's fascination with the material and the physical transformation of a white American woman into a "Japanese maiden," a transformation so fascinating to the American audience precisely because they found American womanhood and Japanese femininity so different from one another. The minute detailing of Bates's transformation into a Japanese maiden also serves as a reminder and confirmation that Bates really is a "Yankee girl." Bates's performance had such dramatic effect, not so much because of the "universal" appeal of the "Japanese" tragedy, but because Bates appeared to conquer the wide gap which the audience believed existed between white, middle-class womanhood and Japanese femininity.

The actress's own ideas about her performance demonstrate the paradox of her mimesis of and difference from her role. She is aware of her task of giving an impression to an American audience. Calling it in the end "only the story of the woman to be acted," Bates stresses in a newspaper interview that the universality of "the heart and the soul of a woman" is "very much alike everywhere" but at the same time recognizes the cultural distinctions between an American audience's response to her character's gendered behavior and that of a Japanese viewer.

"It is not possible to act as a Japanese woman would. She would not do at all as I, an American woman, would do under similar circumstances. If we were acting before a Japanese audience people who understood Japanese life, the stoical calmness of the Japanese woman might be shown, but it would never do before an American audience. They would only say of an actress who did that work: 'What a stick she has become.'"[21]

These cultural contradictions, instead of undermining her authenticity, increased Bates's performative power by demonstrating her ability to transform into an entirely different persona. In another article, she is even more explicit about her own distinction from her role: "Because as Yo San I depict the tiny mind, the tiny emotions and the tiny figure of the immature child-woman, it does not, by any means, presuppose that I have a half-formed mind."[22] Too close an identification between Bates and her characters would undermine her reputation as an intelligent and professional American woman. Successfully embodying the Japanese maiden on stage *and* carefully dis-embodying herself from her role off stage, Bates was able to both advance her theatrical career and reassert her identity as a white American woman.

Yet, the insistence on the distinction between the American actress and the Japanese character did not serve Bates alone but fit into contemporary American discourse about Japan. The *St. Louis Globe Democrat*'s comment on Bates's performance demonstrates the contemporary American view of Japan that was not entirely about admiration for a refined culture:

> Miss Blanche Bates' successful and deeply entertaining efforts to show St. Louis and her guests how a Japanese princess, anterior to the "discovery" of Japan by Commodore Perry, might have conducted herself, under highly dramatic circumstances, has resulted in the placing of some $300,000 to the credit of the box office; and it has been worth the money, if that is the way things really did go on in "old Japan." Because it is edifying to see something done on the stage to make us understand the Japanese . . . . But we can not quite believe that there was as much refinement of manners among the people of ancient Nippon as there is among the characters which Miss Bates and her players portray. *We ought to be thankful that everything has been veiled to suit Western ideals. . . . We don't want the Princess Yo San exactly as she might have been. We want her exactly like Blanche Bates.* [emphasis added][23]

To this critic, historical and cultural authenticity was by no means the point of the performance. In fact, he appreciated the very lack of authenticity in the play. Not only does the writer assume Japanese "semicivilization" as lacking in "refinement of manners," but he also clearly values Bates the American woman over Yo-San the Japanese princess. Because ideal models of womanhood were intricately connected to the racialized notions of civilization, the insistence on Bates's difference from her

Japanese role was important to upholding not only Bates's American womanhood but also American civilization itself.[24] The lack of authenticity thus served to confirm his belief in American superiority to the Japanese.

Bates was not just a white American woman, however; she was a symbol of New Woman. As historian Albert Auster demonstrates, the growth of the theater in America coincided with the revival of the women's movement between the 1890s and the 1920s. Theater was an important site where New Women were born, both on stage and in the audience. For those few who made it, a theatrical career offered economic opportunities, social recognition, and sexual independence enjoyed by few other women in society. For young women and girls who in growing numbers attended matinees unescorted, the theaters were "virtually unchallenged citadels of female attendance, sentiment, beauty, style, and fashion."[25] While Bates rarely expressed radical views on politics or culture and thus may not fit the strict definition of a New Woman, her very profession and her public role made her a model of New Woman to whom young women across the country looked in admiration. Thus, Bates's performance of both her Japanese role and her American identity—and the distinction between the two—had symbolic meanings for the making of New Women.

As influential as Bates's performances of Asian womanhood in the plays *Madame Butterfly* and *The Darling of the Gods* were in the United States, the character of Cio-Cio-San became the enduring representation of Asian womanhood through Puccini's opera production of *Madama Butterfly*.[26] First produced at La Scala, Milan, in 1904, where it was hooted and hissed, the opera was performed in a revised and shortened form a few months later to tumultuous applause. After its brilliant success at Covent Garden in 1905, *Madama Butterfly* became one of the most popular of Puccini's oeuvre.[27] The opera premiered in the United States at the Castle Square Opera Company in 1906, and a year later the New York Metropolitan Opera made its first production of the opera with the rising American soprano Geraldine Farrar in the lead part. As in the case of Blanche Bates, it was Cio-Cio-San's role that launched Farrar—a native of Melrose, Massachusetts, who had trained and performed in Germany—on her way to becoming the foremost American opera singer in the first two decades of the twentieth century. Although Farrar performed as prima donna in many famous operas, including *La Bohème*, *Tosca*, and *Carmen*, the role of Cio-Cio-San was her most popular. Only two years after her American début, she signed a contract with the Metropolitan Opera Company, which engaged her for the following five seasons and offered up to $1300 for each performance or concert, a figure only exceeded in America at the time by Enrico Caruso.[28]

Farrar and the character Cio-Cio-San came to be closely identified with one another in the minds of American audiences. "It will appear to many listeners that the popularity of 'Madame [sic] Butterfly' is largely bound up with the popularity of Miss Geraldine Farrar," wrote a critic.[29] Farrar's popularity as Cio-Cio-San only grew after she began recording for the Victor Talking Machine Company, which sold 4,663 copies of her record "Un bel dì vedremo" in one year, far outnumbering the sales of any other operatic records.[30]

The identification between the singer Farrar and the character Cio-Cio-San had much to do with Farrar's successful embodiment of the opera's narrative construction of the role. Whereas Long's and Belasco's one-act play began after the faithful Japanese wife had been awaiting her fickle American naval officer for nearly three years, the operatic libretto was expanded to include the marriage ceremony and wedding night of the naive young geisha. Blanche Bates never had to deal with her character's youth, but Farrar developed Cio-Cio-San from innocent joy to grim despair.

Although opera is, at least in the minds of traditional musicologists and opera fans, first and foremost a *musical* art, the analysis and appreciation of *Madama Butterfly* often focused on the specific narrative setting, going against the American operatic tradition which paid little attention to the histrionic elements of the performance.[31] Critics' comments about Farrar's Cio-Cio-San most often discussed non-vocal elements of her performance, highlighting aspects of her career she particularly focused on. Believing that music must always serve the drama and advocating the subservience of singing to acting, she claimed, "In my humble way I am an actress who happens to be appearing in opera."[32] In order to illuminate the librettist's and composer's intentions, the artist should, Farrar argued, "read books or look at pictures relating to the people, country, and era involved," become "familiar with the physical and mental mannerisms of every century and nation," and "know how these people dressed, walked, spoke, and thought in order to render a convincing portrayal."[33] Farrar followed these principles in her own performances of Cio-Cio-San. She wrote to her friend, "[W]hen I was studying 'Madame [sic] Butterfly,' I read everything I could find about the Japanese. I tried to imbue myself with their spirit. I bought up old prints, and pictures, and costumes; I learned how they eat, and sleep, and walk, and talk, and think, and feel. I read on the subject in French and German, as well as in English."[34] As the singer was responsible for furnishing her own costumes, she designed hers from the various prints she had studied.[35] Thus, Farrar's conception of her role inherited and perpetuated the existing Orientalist discourse in the form of literature, arts, and material culture.

Farrar's conception and performance of her Japanese role was a product not only of written and visual "texts" she studied but also of dynamics between the white American soprano and a real Japanese. Like Bates, Farrar hired a Japanese "maid" in order to observe her personality and manners. For weeks, she worked each day with a Japanese actress, Madame Fu-ji-Ko, "whose dainty personality and grace were her model for authentic gesture and carriage." The diva "padded about [the rooms] in gay kimonos, the heavy wig elaborately dressed, her feet in little one-toed canvas shoes used by the Japanese. She shuffled, posed, danced and gesticulated under the watchful eye of the Japanese artist, herself in native costume." Farrar incorporated into her portrayal of Cio-Cio-San much of her Japanese teacher's counsel—"the meekly bowed head, the modest composure, the small, shuffling steps, the serenity and grace characteristic of young Japanese women," and mastered "[how to] bow, kneel, [how to use] hand gesture, fan sleeves, head . . . and infused it with her own personality." In order to conform to the "correct physiognomy," she shaved her eyebrows and drew thin arches as substitutes well above her own. She also maintained the attitude of perpetual stooping, which she found most fatiguing[36] (fig. 3.2, cover).

Farrar's relationship to Fujiko bears a striking resemblance to Bates' relationship to Suki in that her performance of Japanese femininity was fraught with power dynamics based on racial, national, and class differences between herself and the Japanese woman she hired as a "maid." Even though as an actress, Fujiko probably belonged to a different class than Suki, she remains unidentified in history. Although Farrar mentions the role of Fujiko on several occasions, she is always referred to by her first name only if not simply as "a Japanese maid." As Farrar boasted,

> I took up the study of Japanese dress, costumes, and manners with Mme. Fujiko, a Japanese actress in New York. I went over every scene and situation with her

Figure 3.2 Geraldine Farrar as Cio-Cio-San. Music Division, The New York Public Library for the Performing Arts, Astor, Lenox and Tilden Foundations.

and had her advice on every detail of costuming and makeup. The result is that I believe I at least have presented a faithful stage representation of a Geisha. She assured me no Occidental woman could have more faithfully portrayed the exceedingly Oriental and foreign attributes.[37]

By emphasizing her Occidental identity which is extremely different from that of a Geisha, Farrar celebrates her own performative skills with which she bridged the gap between the two forms of womanhood. While she acknowledges Fujiko's role in the making of her performance, what is even more striking is that Fujiko is deliberately excised from the history of the opera. Later in her life, as Farrar was preparing her manuscript for her autobiography *Such Sweet Compulsion*, she apparently tried to insert Fujiko's photograph into the book. Although the attempt to place Fujiko in the text is striking, in the process of editing, the publisher noticed that the signature on the photograph did not match the name Fujiko attributed to the Japanese actress in Farrar's text. It is unclear how this "error" came about, but Farrar's and the publisher's solution to the problem was to simply take the photograph out and to replace it with the picture of Farrar's mother.[38] As in the case of Blanche Bates who performed her Japanese heroine on stage based on the hidden tragedy of a real Japanese woman who remained behind the curtains, the spotlight that shone on Farrar's Cio-Cio-San never shed light on the real Japanese woman who enabled the performance.

The reception of Farrar's performance was very much based on the American audience's notions of Japanese woman. At the same time, the audience response to the performance also rested on their ideas about American woman and the relationship between the singer and her role. As in the case of Blanche Bates, the discussions surrounding Farrar's performance of Cio-Cio-San say as much about Farrar's identity and role as an American woman as they do about her performance of Japanese femininity. On one level, the critics praised Farrar's oneness with her role, especially in terms of her racial and cultural crossing. One writer commented on how Farrar's histrionic and vocal performance allowed the audience to forget the distinction between the singer and the role: "It is a masterpiece, for it reveals its art by concealing it. One does not think of [Farrar] as the great singing actress. To every one of her hearers she is the little Japanese girl who approaches the mystery of love with such perfect trust and who grows to the knowledge of life and sorrow with such sweet womanliness."[39] Another review said:

> There are pretty girls in Japan, too! Her hands have the grace and eloquence of Sada Yacco [famous Japanese actress]'s; they are real Japanese hands, and she wears her kimono and obi, she walks and bows, and kneels and pleads, like one to the manner born. If she knew the language of Tokio, she might, as Burton did in Arabia, travel through the country without being recognized as a foreigner.[40]

Paradoxically, Farrar's performance authenticated the beauty of real Japanese women instead of being authenticated by it.

The relationship between Farrar's American identity and her Japanese role and the issues of authenticity and performativity that crossed the two triggered a heated debate among opera critics and Farrar's fans. The debate highlighted the fact that, beyond the issue of authenticity, the identity of Farrar as an American soprano was central to the American audience's understanding of the performance. Over the course of six months, an intriguing debate took place in the magazine *Musical America*, which revealed the audience's understanding of the opera's narrative, the notions about Japanese femininity symbolized by Cio-Cio-San, and the ideals of modern American womanhood embodied by Farrar. It started with a review of *Butterfly* in 1913 which argued that Farrar's performance revealed a misconception of the Japanese woman of the period:

> The Japanese woman has, for ages, been trained to absolute subservience, first to her parents, then to her husband. She has been taught practically to efface herself, but, with the infinite charm of womanhood, she has managed, at the same time to evolve a delicacy, a refinement and a graciousness of demeanor, which are captivating. If there is any eminent prima donna on the stage to-day who could represent the character, it is Miss Farrar herself, and so, the natural question arises, why does she exaggerate, particularly in much of her action and movement, when repression is within her own power and absolutely characteristic of the role itself?[41]

What is more interesting than the writer's assessment of Farrar's performance is his claims of authoritative knowledge about Japanese womanhood. Unlike many other commentaries which associated Cio-Cio-San's character with her lack of intelligence or the lesser level of Japan's civilization, the "absolute subservience" and the effacement of self which the writer assigns to Japanese womanhood is not invested with a negative judgment; rather it is associated with "captivating" qualities of "a delicacy, a refinement and a graciousness of demeanor." What is significant in the debate triggered by this commentary, however, is not so much the specific meanings attached to Japanese womanhood as the different claims made by the audience over an accurate understanding of it. The following April, the same magazine published a similar but more critical review of Farrar's performance:

> I have always thought that Miss Farrar never understood the character of the Japanese women of the period which *Madama Butterfly* is supposed to represent.
>
> For ages the Japanese woman had been nothing but man's slave, the mother of his children, who received no social recognition and who presented herself before her lord, on her knees, with her forehead to the ground. Out of this condition of servitude, the Japanese women developed a simplicity and sweetness of char-

acter. They were very gentle, and if there is anything which they did not have, it was the power of being self-assertive. That much had been drilled out of them carefully, in the course of time.

To represent, therefore, *Madama Butterfly*, as Miss Farrar does, was to get about as far from the reality as it was possible to get.[42]

If Japanese women were not self-assertive, this writer—who called himself Mephisto— certainly was. By seeming to be a sympathetic ally of Japanese women historically victimized by the country's patriarchy, the writer used his claimed understanding of Japanese womanhood to validate his authority on opera.

The ensuing debate over Farrar's Cio-Cio-San illustrated how the American audience claimed authority on Japanese womanhood in assessing Farrar's performance. The publication of Mephisto's review was followed by a series of exchange between Mephisto and the readers who argued against his criticism. All parties in the debate mustered their own knowledge of Japanese womanhood—based on their reading of the fictional story as well as other Orientalist texts—in justifying their assessment of Farrar's performance. For example, one "opera student" objected to Mephisto's argument by presenting her reading of Long's original story. According to this student, "under the influence of her American husband, [Cio-Cio-San] lost much of her Japanese sedateness and subservience," and Farrar successfully depicted "this American influence on the Japanese nature."[43] Mephisto himself elaborated his argument by explaining that the original story of *Madama Butterfly* derived from Pierre Loti's "Madame Chrysanthème," in which the heroine represented "absolute self-effacement" characteristic of Japanese women of the time. Yet another reader wrote to the editor of *Musical America* challenging Mephisto's reference to Loti in his criticism of Farrar. Pointing out the difference between Loti's story (in which the French naval officer leaves his Japanese wife and returns for a last look at her only to find her quietly counting the money she received from him) and the operatic libretto, this correspondent argued: "Miss Farrar is wholly justified in her presentation, for the reason that she is not endeavoring to present the character of Loti's novel, but the character as drawn by John Luther Long, and set to music by Puccini. Mephisto, therefore, it seems to me, is criticizing Miss Farrar from a point of view which is not justified."[44] These mobilizations of knowledge about Japanese womanhood indicate that the artistic assessment of Farrar's performance was inseparable from the issues of cultural authenticity and Orientalist authority.

However, the debate also demonstrated the centrality of Farrar's own American identity in the audience's response to her performance. In the midst of the debate, Mephisto made an acute observation that the fan's primary concern was Farrar rather than the opera. Furthermore, he identified the particular dynamics and the stakes of this debate when he pointed out that the reason "why the general public, and especially young girls, are so enthusiastic about Miss Farrar" was that "they see not *Madama Butterfly* but themselves represented. In other words, the bright, vital, intelligent, resourceful, self-assertive American girl sees herself represented on stage and promptly falls head over heels in love with Geraldine Farrar." He delineated the relationship between Cio-Cio-San the character and Farrar the singer, and between the opera and its audience, even more clearly in the statement:

> But, I say, in all deference, that the difference between the Japanese woman of the time depicted in the opera and the American girl of to-day is wider than the difference between the North and the South Pole. Indeed, it is the difference between *Butterfly* and Miss Farrar![45]

For those who praised Farrar's performance, the very difference between the modern American womanhood the singer embodied in real life and the quaint Japanese femininity she impersonated on stage served to *validate* her performative power; in contrast, in this argument the difference between Farrar's own personality and the qualities her role was supposed to represent was used to *dispute* the efficacy of the performance.

Both for those who praised and those who criticized Farrar's performance of Cio-Cio-San, the singer's Americanness was just as important, if not more important, as the Japaneseness of her performance. This issue of Americanness had much to do with the particular genre, the opera. As a cultural form so clearly associated with the European world of classical music, the opera had yet to produce many American-born stars. The American audience was thus particularly enthused about Farrar's rise to international stardom, as Farrar helped place the United States on the map of the classical music scene and consequently prove the maturity of America's "civilization." Many of the commentaries on Farrar conveyed patriotic pride by emphasizing her "American" identity. As one Chicago reviewer wrote,

> It is delightful to hail a new American star, a star who has gained the warmest praise in the world as well as in the new . . .
>
> Youth triumphant, strong, vibrant, confident, is expressed in her art in every detail. Great voices we have heard this week, but here is a voice girlish, fresh, new, marvelously sweet, under perfect control—such a voice as you will not hear again in many years in opera in America—because there will not come a Farrar again for long, and long, and long.[46]

The words used to describe Farrar, "youth triumphant, strong, vibrant, confident," and "fresh, new," are associated not only with the quality of her performance but also with her Americanness. There were a number of references to Farrar's "American beauty" in phrases such as: "Like its owner, that voice is an American beauty; it is a voice animated by the same sort of subtle expressiveness which has made American faces famous the world over as types of the highest feminine charm ever known."[47] Sometimes the press stressed Farrar's American identity by highlighting the rivalry between her and an "Old World" prima donna, Emmy Destinn.[48] Farrar herself appealed specifically to her American audience with comments such as, "It is very pleasant to be in America and to be received so kindly by American audiences, for I shall never forget that I was born in this country, though my first success were [sic] achieved in Berlin."[49] Given this appeal to the nationalist sentiment of America's operagoers, it is particularly interesting that Farrar's role of a Japanese heroine was what brought her fame as an "American" soprano. As demonstrated by the commentary, "proud we were as the strain of our national airs ran through the orchestra that the little Geisha girl was a yankee,"[50] Farrar's racial and cultural crossing served to boost America's patriotic pride.

Farrar's performance of Japanese femininity played a key factor in establishing her operatic career, a link she acknowledges in her autobiography:

Ah! Adorable, unforgettable blossom of Japan! Thanks to your gentle ways, that night I placed my foot on the rung of the ladder that lead to the firmament of stars! When I don your silken draperies and voice your sweet faith in the haunting melodies that envelop you, then are all eyes dim and hearts attune to your every appeal for sympathy![51]

Farrar's acclaimed performance of Cio-Cio-San had a larger meaning, however, than her personal success. Like Bates, Farrar's stardom was symbolic of her role as a New Woman. As Terry Castle argues, the opera house (along with the theater) in the early twentieth century was one of a few public spaces in which a woman could openly admire another woman's voice and body in an atmosphere of heightened emotion and powerful sensual arousal. The phenomenon of diva-worship, where young, anonymous female fans pursued their idols from opera house to opera house, was a unique terrain of potentially subversive gender norms and sexuality. From the outset of her career, she had appealed especially to the young generation of women who thought of her as "the great Glamour Girl of her era." The fandom for Farrar grew into a cult. Throughout America, young women formed fan clubs. In the teens and the twenties, these so-called Gerry-flappers waited every night at the stage door of the Met for Farrar, casting flowers and love notes in her direction when she emerged.[52] The flappers' worship of Farrar, whose career was established by her role of the Japanese heroine, suggests that the performances of alternative femininity, especially in the form of Asian heroines, were not only compatible with but solidified the identity of New Women in the early twentieth century.

After Farrar's retirement from the opera stage in 1922, *Madama Butterfly* remained one of the most popular performances at the Metropolitan Opera, with various singers playing the role of Cio-Cio-San and different directors interpreting the figure of the Japanese heroine. Florence Easton, for example, who was Farrar's colleague at the Met and took over the role of Cio-Cio-San upon Farrar's retirement, created a "cutesy" image that differed considerably from the one created by Farrar (fig. 3.3). Licia Alba-

Figure 3.3 Florence Easton as Cio-Cio-San. Music Division, The New York Public Library for the Performing Arts, Astor, Lenox and Tilden Foundations.

nese's performance of Cio-Cio-San, whose inaccurate uses of costume and accessories make the impersonation almost grotesque from the present perspective, also stressed the singer's performance rather than Japanese femininity. In fact, the diversity of styles with which the role of Cio-Cio-San (and Suzuki, Cio-Cio-San's maid) has been performed demonstrates that the image of the Asian feminine and ways of materializing it was far from static or monolithic. The range of the images reveals more about the white performers' identities, characters, and attitudes toward their Japanese roles than about the Japanese heroines they were supposed to embody (fig. 3.4).

White women's performances of Asian-ness in this period went well beyond the professional stage. For example, in the spring of 1898, an operetta entitled *The Orientals*

"MADAME BUTTERFLY"

Figure 3.4 *Madame Butterfly*. Music Division, The New York Public Library for the Performing Arts, Astor, Lenox and Tilden Foundations.

was performed at Radcliffe College. Its music and libretto were written by students Katharine Berry and Josephine Sherwood who later became a stage and screen actress. The plot follows the tradition of the eighteenth- and nineteenth-century comic opera: set in an "exotic" locale, it involves love interest, disguise, misunderstanding, heroic rescue of a woman in captivity, discovery of true identity and reconciliation. As in many Orientalist texts of the period, the setting conflates various unspecified Orients, with characters named Isrik, Tukiu, and Tuz, who are natives of Bamboozledum. The production was a big success, with the auditorium filled with excited crowds at all three performances. From the turn of the century through around 1930, women at Radcliffe produced several other performances with "Oriental" themes, such as *The Chinese Dummy* and *The Chinese Lantern*, some of which were original productions and some written by professional playwrights.[53]

White women's performances of Asian-ness did not take place only on stage but manifested themselves in tableaux vivants, Japanese-style bazaars, and costume parties across the country. A number of white, middle-class women enjoyed putting on Asian-ness and captured their performances visually in photo studios. Mabel Daniels, a Radcliffe class of 1900, for example, dressed in Japanese kimonos and posed to be photographed in the studio (fig. 3.5). As tableaux vivants became a popular medium of performative and visual spectacle, such practices came to be more elaborately staged. In 1908, some New York socialites hosted an evening of Japanese Tableaux at the Hotel Plaza, where scenes from famous Japanese historical narratives or generic scenes were performed by white women dressed in Japanese

Figure 3.5 Mabel Daniels, c.1898. Schelesinger Library.

Figure 3.6 *Luncheon under the Wisteria Blossoms*, in Drucker & Co., *Photographs [of] Japanese Tableaux*, [1909]. Harvard Theater Collection.

costumes (fig. 3.6).[54] As in "Asian" arts and artifacts that circulated in the American market as commodities, these settings and images are both de-contextualized and de-historicized. For the white women in these enactments, Asia was no longer an object which they gazed at or purchased; Asia was now a performance which the women themselves were part of. Rather than being owners or caretakers of Asian objects, or artists capturing the images of Asia, women now *embodied* Asian-ness.[55] Dressed in tight and elaborate kimonos and posing in formalized, often rigid postures, these women performed types of femininity that were clearly divergent from the models of womanhood many of them were living in their daily lives. Yet such performances of exotic, alternative femininity were very much congruent with their identity as "modern" American women.

These enactments testified to the relationship between the emerging gender politics of the New Women on the one hand and the racial, national, and economic dynamics of U.S.-Asian relations on the other. Such a relationship was vividly played out in the spectacular Orientalist performance put on by socialite and suffragist, Alva Erskind Smith Belmont.[56] In July 1914, Belmont opened her Chinese Teahouse on the grounds of Marble House in Newport, Rhode Island, at a tea in honor of an international conference of women reformers. Belmont had commissioned Richard and Joseph Howland Hunt, the prestigious architects and sons of Richard Morris Hunt, to design the teahouse. The Hunt brothers made extensive research trips to China to study architectural models, and made every effort to create an "authentic"

Chinese structure while accommodating their client's demands. The teahouse had a green-tiled roof with upswept eave-ends and was decorated with the stylized animal figures, characteristic of temples and dwellings of the Yangtze River Valley in southern China. For the top of the main entrance stairway, the Hunt Brothers designed a 20-foot gateway along traditional Chinese lines. The four-columned gateway was decorated with inscriptions inviting visitors to think of China, and the interior decoration included wooden panels painted in the style of the Ming Dynasty.[57]

Although the teahouse, being far too small to accommodate the number of guests invited to social events of Gilded Age Newport, served mostly a decorative purpose, Belmont carried out the Chinese theme more thoroughly by hosting a lavish Chinese costume ball. For weeks, the invited guests frantically sought appropriate costumes in the town of Newport. On the day before the ball, *Town Topics*, a New York magazine of social gossip, reported:

> From the appearance of the shop windows along Bellevue avenue, and even some in Thames street, one might imagine that Newport was preparing to receive a fleet of Chinese warships conveying thither all the highest dignitaries from the land of Confucius. But the display is only in preparation or anticipation of Mrs. Belmont's ball at Marble House tomorrow. The only wonder to me is that the streets are not hung with yellow flags emblazoned with the red dragon and that squads of Chinks are not selling chop suey and chow main at the entrance of the Casino. . . .[58]

According to the same magazine, "In order that the ball may be the success she has determined it shall be, Mrs. Belmont has ordered from a costumer in New York 100 Mandarin jackets, or coats, or camisoles, or whatever it is they call them, so that impecunious youths necessary to supply a fitting background may not be embarrassed by lack of costume."[59] On the evening of the ball, the Marble House terrace, a Chinese-style footbridge over an artificial pond, the path and the teahouse itself were illuminated by Chinese lanterns and banked with exotic plants and flowers. Many of the guests wore costumes imported from China. The hostess herself dressed in a heavily embroidered antique Chinese costume, the mauve tunic and skirt inset with jewels which she augmented with sapphires and diamonds, and an elaborate wig decorated with pearls and turquoise worn by aristocratic Chinese women. Her daughter, the Duchess of Marlborough, dressed as Lady Chang, consort of one of the greatest emperors of the Ming Dynasty, with a dainty costume of black velvet and gold cloth, gold earrings, and black serpentine bracelets. According to the *New York Times*, "Some of the women wore elaborate Oriental wigs but the majority were without these wigs, using Chinese caps or appearing in their natural hair arranged with flowers or ornaments of the Orient."[60]

Belmont's Chinese Teahouse and the costume ball illustrate the interconnectedness of the gender politics of New Women and the racial politics of Orientalist performance. That the Chinese Teahouse was built and the Chinese costume ball was given in honor of women's reform movement shows that Orientalism was not only compatible with, but gave expression to, the politics of the early twentieth-century American women's movement and the sensibilities of New Women. As Inderpal Grewal argues, nationalism, imperialism, and colonial discourses shaped the contexts in which Western feminist subjects became possible.[61] It is important to note that there was no Chinese representative at the "international" conference on women's reform movement for which the Chinese Teahouse was built. Many historians have shown that as New Women mobilized and celebrated their growing political and social power, they also maintained much of existing racial and class hierarchies, and that the women's movement of the early twentieth century was very much a white, middle-class women's movement. While white women's donning of Asian costumes and playing the roles of Asian women may not have directly addressed women's movement or explicitly made racist (or antiracist) statements, the performances and the discourse about them expressed contemporary American ideas about not only Asian femininity but New Women of America.

It was not coincidental that the proliferation of white women's performances of Asian heroines and the emergence of New Women overlapped. The freedom to cross racial, class, cultural lines—even if it was temporary "play"—was part of being "modern" American women, particularly New Women. Whether in the form of professional theater or private parties, the performance of Asian-ness allowed white women of the early twentieth century to enact alternative gender roles that were distinct from their own. Through performances of alternative femininity, white women enacted not only their assigned roles on stage but their "real" identities as New Women. Such performances both allowed and required the performers' physical and affective identification with their Asian roles, while they masked the material power relations between the performers' "real" identities as white women and the "real" Asian women they impersonated.

Racial Masquerade and Literary Orientalism
Amy Lowell's "Asian" Poetry

A s "Asia" came to occupy an increasingly visible and important place in America's cultural vocabulary, it became a representational tool with which to express not only American ideologies about U.S.-Asian relations but also changing cultural norms and social anxieties in the domestic context. The American engagement with Asian cultures manifested in material culture, visual arts, and performing arts also had a significant impact in American letters, particularly in literary modernism.

Literary modernism rebelled against the standard language and literature by tapping into, among other resources, dialect and the vernacular. This movement often employed racial masquerade and linguistic imitation, in which white modernists such as Joseph Conrad, Gertrude Stein, and T. S. Eliot reimagined themselves as "racial aliens" and mimicked the strategies of dialect speakers and blacks.[1] While literary Orientalism, which involved forms and subject matters in completely different languages and cultures, took somewhat different forms than straight importation or mimicry, it too bolstered the modernist movement's attempt to break from literary conventions and to invoke new representational forms. Just as Japanese *ukiyo-e* offered Mary Cassatt a new way of visually depicting "modern women," literary Orientalism provided modernist writers with tools to break from existing conventions and to express new literary aesthetics.

Orientalism in American literary modernism took two major forms. The first was the translations of Asian texts into English. For literary modernism, translation was an instrument for new aesthetics which urged writers to rigorously engage foreign literary forms. Thus, while there was already a significant corpus of English translations of Asian literature by the end of the nineteenth century—for example, those by professional Sinologists such as James Legge and Herbert Giles—it was during the height of modernism in the 1910s and 1920s that the Anglo-American literary world saw a burgeoning of translations of Chinese and Japanese texts. Ezra Pound's translations of classical Chinese poetry and Japanese plays and Amy Lowell's translations of Chinese poetry were part of this phenomenon. Since not all of these "translators" had working knowledge of these Asian languages, many of these "translations" were done in collaboration with scholars with the language skills (Ernest Fenollosa in the case of Pound, Florence Ayscough in the case of Lowell) and were, to varying degrees, adaptations of what the translators understood to be the qualities of Asian literature.

The proliferation of these translations of Asian literature inspired another form of literary Orientalism: new creative works, especially poetry, by American writers influenced by Asian forms and subject matter. The deployment of "the exotic" East in poetry challenged traditional assumptions of what constituted an appropriate stock of poetic images and expanded the scope of poetic references.[2] The brevity of Chinese and Japanese poetry and their use of images particularly inspired a new generation of American poets, particularly the advocates of the so-called Imagist movement. Ezra Pound and Amy Lowell, the two major figures in Imagism, were strongly influenced by Asian poetry. Pound came to be deeply interested in Chinese poetry, and in 1914 he declared that "It is possible that this century may find a new Greece in China."[3] Chinese and Japanese poetry, literature, and culture played a decisive role in the development of Pound's aesthetics and poetics, culminating in his works *Cathay* (1915), *Certain Noble Plays of Japan* (1916), and "The Chinese Written Character as a Medium for Poetry" (1919), all products of his intensive collaboration with Ernest Fenollosa. Literary Orientalism was popular beyond the Imagist circles, however. Chinese notions and methods inspired the early modernist works of William Carlos Williams, while Japanese forms like *tanka* and *hokku* inspired John Gould Fletcher. Marianne Moore used Chinese poetry to express her own dissatisfaction with contemporary trends in the writing of poetry and to resist the American habit of looking to Europe as a singular source of cultural tradition. Thus, by the time modernism became a full-blown movement in American letters, literary Orientalism was more than a trend. According to Lowell's biographer S. Foster Damon, "To ascribe the source of this interest to any one person or book would be impossible; it was simply in the air."[4]

Whereas Asian influences on Pound have been studied by many, the poetical exploration of Asia by Amy Lowell, the other key figure in the Imagist movement, has not received as much critical appreciation in recent years.[5] Although Lowell's poetry has had less lasting impact in American literary history, she was a key figure in American poetry in the 1910s and 1920s and contributed to the Imagist movement both through her textual productions and her cultural and intellectual network and financial resources. Understanding the role of Asia in Lowell's poetry offers an insight into the cultural work of Orientalism, particularly its politics of gender, in American literary modernism. This chapter examines the different ways in which Lowell's translations and compositions engaged Asia. Lowell's "Asian" works expressed diverse, multi-layered functions of Orientalism. On one level, her practice of translation reflected the hierarchical relations of knowledge and labor between her and her Asian subjects. Her relationship with her "native informant" on the one hand and her construction of classic Chinese poetry in her translations on the other together demonstrate the racialized and gendered notions that were at the base of her Orientalism. On another level, her constructions of an exoticized and antiquated gender and sexuality in her own "Asian" poems allowed a form of racial masquerade for her and her readers, which offered the freedom and play of performative gender. At the same time, the gendered constructions of the East and the West, established through specific uses of language and form, also allowed Lowell to address and critique the masculinist vision of U.S. imperialism. These different, and seemingly contradictory, engagements with Asia in Lowell's work demonstrate how the gendered constructions of Orientalism found their expressions in a complex mix of affect and power.

Amy Lowell was born in Brookline, Massachusetts, in 1874, the youngest of five children of Augustus and Katherine Lowell. Descendants of Percival Lowle, who settled in America in 1639, the Lowells made a fortune in the cotton industry in the early nineteenth century, and became one of the most prominent families in Boston. Amy Lowell's great-grandfather was one of the founders of the Boston Athenaeum; her grandfather was the first trustee of the Lowell Institute, which had been founded by his cousin. Another cousin of his was the poet James Russell Lowell. Four generations of Lowells served as fellows of Harvard College, and Amy Lowell's father was an officer in various learned societies.[6]

As a poet Lowell was mostly self-taught. She completed the manuscript of her first book, A Dome of Many-Coloured Glass, in 1912, which changed her life into that of a professional poet. At this time, the New Poetry movement began to take shape on the American literary scene. Ezra Pound's Ripostes appeared in London, with an appendix containing the works of T. E. Hulme, the founder of Imagism. A new generation of poets such as F. S. Flint, H. D., Richard Aldington, Robert Frost, and Vachel Lindsay published one book after another. Lowell discovered Imagism through Harriet Monroe's magazine *Poetry*, and it "suddenly. . . came over her: 'Why, I, too, am an Imagiste!'"[7] The philosophy and aesthetics propagated by Imagism were laid out in the March 1913 issue of *Poetry*, in which Flint explained its principles and Pound outlined "A Few Don'ts by an Imagiste." They called for precision, economy, definiteness, and direct treatment; they warned against abstractions, rhetoric, and dead-stop iambic lines. Inspired by these ideas and eager to learn more, Lowell went to London to meet Pound in the summer of 1913 and thereafter her poems increasingly appeared in poetry journals such as *Egoist* and *Poetry*. One of her poems was also included in the anthology *Des Imagistes* which Pound edited. Lowell thus quickly became a central figure in Imagism and in the literary scene of the period.

Lowell's friendship and collaboration with Pound ended abruptly and bitterly in 1914, however. Although at their first meeting Lowell was highly impressed with Pound's work and felt that she had made not only a "personal friend, but, through his kindness, a little wedge into the heart of English letters,"[8] Pound was organizing a new movement, vorticism, which was more radical than Imagism and more concerned with connections among all the arts. Not very interested in vorticism, Lowell wanted to discuss the future of Imagism and the possibility of a better organized Imagist anthology. After she gave her own party to celebrate the publication of *Des Imagistes*, a fierce battle began between the two domineering, quick-tempered personalities over the leadership of the New Poetry. Lowell and Pound quarreled over the editorial principles and management of the anthology, debated what Imagism was, and fought over who was entitled to the name Imagist. Lowell refused to support or submit to journals with which Pound was involved, and Pound derisively referred to Lowell's branch of the Imagist movement as Amygism.

The schism between the uncompromising, tyrannical expatriot and the ambitious, recognition-hungry Bostonian never ended, but the quarrel never deterred Lowell from her literary ambitions. She published her third book of poetry, *Men, Women and Ghosts* in 1916, followed by *Can Grande's Castle* two years later. While poems included in these books were still experimental, her Imagism was gradually taking its distinct shape. Lowell's interest in Asia as a literary theme and Asian poetry as a literary form began to occupy an important place in her aesthetics in this period.

The most important figure in Lowell's interest in Asia was her brother, Percival. Having made his name in the business world, Percival Lowell visited Japan in 1883. Shortly thereafter, he was appointed foreign secretary and counselor to the Korean special mission to the United States and lived in Korea for six months. He then spent the next ten years in Japan, associating with the contemporary Japanologists, such as Edward Morse and Ernest Fenollosa, as well as with English-speaking Japanese intellectuals, and rigorously studying Japanese culture, art, and history. His experience in Asia and the ideas he derived from the experience resulted in a series of books about history and culture: *Chosön: The Land of the Morning Calm* (1886); *The Soul of the Far East* (1888); *Noto* (1891); and *Occult Japan* (1895). These books evidence Percival Lowell's serious engagement with Asian cultures and the evolution of his ideas about Asia, although many of his views on the East-West binarism and his evolutionist framework reinforce the dominant racist and Orientalist stereotypes of his time.[9] During his residence in Japan, Percival wrote numerous letters about his experience to Amy. As a result of the strong influence by the images and ideas sent from the distant land by her brother, she began studying Japanese *haiku* and experimented with its use in her own poetry.

Another important source of Lowell's engagement with Asia was her friend Florence Ayscough, who introduced her to Chinese paintings and poetry in 1917. Ayscough, born and raised in China, lived there with her husband after attending school in Boston, and became one of the most important Sinologists of the period. Lowell was fascinated by Chinese ideograms and Ayscough's explanation that not only the meaning but also the composition of each ideogram constitutes an important element of the poetry. With Ayscough's help and translation, she started rigorously studying Chinese poetry, and after several years of intense and detailed correspondence across the Pacific, the two women published a collaborative translation of Chinese poetry, *Fir-Flower Tablets*.[10]

The making of *Fir-Flower Tablets* shows the structures of knowledge and relations of labor involved in the creation of Orientalism. Not knowing any Chinese, Lowell worked out a collaborative relationship with Ayscough, who worked with her Chinese mentor, Nung Chu. Like the relationships between white women printmakers and Asian craftsmen, and the ones between white actresses and singers and their Japanese "maids," Lowell's relationship with her "native informants"—both Ayscough and Nung—was one of unequal power. Lowell's preface to *Fir-Flower Tablets*, in which she describes how she and Ayscough worked on the translation, presents her version of the "collaboration" process:

> Let me state at the outset that I know no Chinese. My duty in Mrs. Ayscough's and my joint collaboration has been to turn her literal translations into poems as near to the spirit of the originals as it was my power to do. . . . The study of Chinese is so difficult that it is a life-work in itself, so is the study of poetry. A sinologue has no time to learn how to write poetry; a poet has no time to learn how to read Chinese. Since neither of us pretended to any knowledge of the other's craft, our association has been a continually augmenting pleasure. (v)

She thus acknowledges and justifies her lack of language skills by highlighting the mutually exclusive occupations of poetry and Sinology and underscoring her authority as a poet. In practice, however, it turned out to be less of "a continually augmenting pleasure" than a hierarchical division of labor, with power and decision-making authority concentrated at Lowell's end, and labor-intensive and mechanical aspects of literary translation placed upon Ayscough. Because Lowell refused to study the language but insisted on having multiple "approaches" to the original texts, Ayscough was burdened with the drudgery of producing the mountains of translations, cribs, ponies, glossaries, etymologies, and commentaries that Lowell demanded.[11]

Lowell's power and control over the production of her "translations" was exercised even more forcefully in relation to the true "native" informant, Nung Chu. In response to Nung's suggestion that they include some poems by Chinese women in *Fir-Flower Tablets*, Lowell wrote Ayscough: "Be firm with your teacher, hold him strongly between your finger and your thumb, and keep him to classics. Never mind his chivalrous affection for the ladies. The ladies—and I hate to have to say so—are seldom worth bothering with."[12] The commentary reveals a number of ideological foundations of Lowell's literary Orientalism. First, Lowell tried to protect her creative and interpretive authority by keeping the "native informant" in his place, between Ayscough's finger and her thumb. The Chinese teacher was deployed solely for the mechanical details of "local knowledge" and was never entrusted with the task of critical judgment about the art of poetry. While Lowell thus clarified the hierarchical relations between her and Nung, she did not hesitate to capitalize on his Chinese identity when the "native informant" was convenient for validating her work. While anticipating the reviews of *Fir-Flower Tablets*, she felt compelled to ask Ayscough for a biographical account of Nung and instructed her to "make it as grand as possible—to show that we have a native Chinaman behind us."[13] In addition to such relations of labor, Lowell's notions of what was "valuable" Chinese literature—as illustrated by her insistence on focusing on the "classics"—also typifies the Orientalist construction of Asia as a timeless, ethereal, utopic space removed from the reality of contemporary Asia. As a result, most of the poems in *Fir-Flower Tablets* are classic poems of the Tang dynasty, with the greatest space devoted to Li T'ai-Po's poetry. Finally, her striking comment about "the ladies" who were "seldom worth bothering with" exemplifies the gendered construction of her literary Orientalism. While Lowell resisted feminist politics, her own career as well as her relationships with her contemporary female writers engaged in the modernist movement demonstrate that she was certainly not categorically adverse to women writers. Her dismissal of "ladies," then, is implicitly directed at Chinese women.

The nature of Lowell's disregard for Chinese women poets becomes clearer when combined with her construction of gender in her translations. Many of the poems in *Fir-Flower Tablets* are narrated by women sighing after absent husbands. To be sure, poems about women's grief are highly common in Li Po's work and classic Chinese poetry in general, thus the featuring of such poems is not necessarily unnatural or reflective of specific gender politics. Yet given Lowell's creations of similar gender relations in her own poems, the cultural work of her "translations" of these poems of women's grief is noteworthy. In "The Lonely Wife," for example, Lowell depicts the suffering and grief of the woman who awaits her husband:

The mist is thick. On the wide river, the water-plants float smoothly.
No letters come; none go.
There is only the moon, shining through the clouds of a hard, jade-green sky,
Looking down at us so far divided, so anxiously apart.
All day, going about my affairs, I suffer and grieve, and press the thought of you
    closely to my heart.
My eyebrows are locked in sorrow, I cannot separate them.
Nightly, nightly, I keep ready half the quilt,
And wait for the return of the divine dream which is my Lord. . .[14]

Later in the poem, the female narrator refers to her self as "Unworthy One." In her notes to the poem, Ayscough explains that this term was "constantly used by wives and concubines in speaking of themselves to their husbands or to the men they love."[15] While terms such as "Unworthy One" and "my Lord" are translations of Chinese words in actual use rather than Ayscough's or Lowell's creation, the choice of such translations exoticizes and antiquates women's roles in the eyes of Anglo-American readers. The demarcation of foreign gender roles serves to heighten the exoticness of the overall setting and the narrative of the poem.

Gender relations are exoticized as well in her translation of "Cha'ang Kan," a famous poem by Li Po :

When the hair of your Unworthy One first began to cover her forehead,
She picked flowers and played in front of the door.
Then you, my Lover, came riding a bamboo horse.
We ran round and round the bed, and tossed about the sweetmeats of green
    plums.
We both lived in the village of Ch'ang Kan.
We were both very young, and knew neither jealousy nor suspicion.[16]

When we compare this first stanza with Pound's translation of the same poem, "The River-merchant's Wife: A Letter," one clearly sees the different effects, particularly in the construction of gender:

WHILE my hair was still cut straight across my forehead
I played about the front gate, pulling flowers.
You came by on bamboo stilts, playing horse,
You walked about my seat, playing with blue plums.
And we went on living the village of Chokan:
Two small people, without dislike or suspicion.[17]

Whereas Pound simply translates the first-person pronoun as "my" and "I," Lowell starts the poem by using the term, "your Unworthy One," and thereby accentuates the patriarchal relations whereby a woman is defined by her relation to her husband

and is considered "unworthy." By having the narrator use the third-person "[s]he" in referring to herself in the second line, Lowell's translation further distances the subject from the reader. Although the rest of the stanza depicts innocent, jovial scenes of childhood, Lowell uses "you, my Lover," in the first reference to the man, and thus prepares the reader for the remainder of the love poem. In contrast, Pound's translation simply refers to the object of narration as "you," and uses the word "dislike" where Lowell uses "jealousy." Consequently, from the outset, Lowell's translation bears a much more exoticized and sexualized tone.

In the third stanza, where the poem talks of the young woman's love for her husband, Lowell takes further measures to set the narrative in a locale foreign to her readers:

> At fifteen, I stopped frowning.
> I wanted to be with you, as dust with its ashes.
> I often thought that you were the faithful man who clung to the bridge-post,
> That I should never be obliged to ascend to the Looking-for-Husband Ledge.

While the expression of longing may bring the poem closer to the Western reader, the specific references used in the last two lines again place it in its cultural context. Ayscough's notes explain the legend behind the "bridge-post" reference: A certain Wei Shêng, with a great reputation for sincerity and reliability, had an engagement to meet a lady on a bridge. The lady did not come; despite the rising flood, he stood there clinging to the bridge-post, until the waves engulfed him. As for the "Looking-for-Husband Ledge," Ayscough explains the legend about a wife who went daily to the banks of the Yangze to watch for her husband's return until she was turned to stone.[18] Whether or not the readers actually referred to these notes as they read the poem, the specific expressions and translations such as the "man who clung to the bridge-post" and the "Looking-for-Husband Ledge" no doubt rendered the poetic narrative foreign and appealing to the Western readers. The effect of Lowell's translation in underlining the Chinese setting is obvious when we compare it to Pound's:

> At fifteen I stopped scowling,
> I desired my dust to be mingled with yours
> Forever and forever and forever.
> Why should I climb the look out?[19]

Pound thus does not bother with the specifics of the bridge-post legend, and although the reference to climbing the "look out" beckons explanation, it does not create the same degree of foreignness as Lowell's more literal translation.

A comparison of Lowell's and Pound's ending of the poem further demonstrates the different ways in which the translations construct gender. Lowell's translation reads:

It is the Eighth Month, the butterflies are yellow,
Two are flying among the plants in the West garden;
Seeing them, my heart is bitter with grief, they wound the heart of the
   Unworthy One.
The bloom of my face has faded, sitting with my sorrow.
From early morning until late in the evening, you descend the Three Serpent
   River.
Prepare me first with a letter, bringing me the news of when you will reach home.
I will not go far on the road to meet you,
I will go straight until I reach the Long Wind Sands.[20]

In contrast, Pound translates:

The paired butterflies are already yellow with August
Over the grass in the West garden;
They hurt me. I grow older.
If you are coming down through the narrows of the river Kiang,
Please let me know beforehand,
And I will come out to meet you
   As far as Cho-fu-Sa.

Whereas Pound expresses the woman's grief with the simple sentences, "They hurt me. I grow older," Lowell expounds on the gender-specific meanings of her grief by again using the reference, "Unworthy One," and making concrete the meaning of woman's aging by specifying, "The bloom of my face has faded, sitting with my sorrow." Finally, Lowell's mysterious last two lines would not make sense unless one reads Ayscough's note about the Long Wind Sands which implies "the end of the earth."[21] In contrast to Pound's phonetic transliteration, Lowell's literal translation of the place name and the final two sentences heighten the foreign quality of Lowell's translation.

   Through these devices, Lowell effectively emphasizes not only the exotic setting of the poem but the foreignness of the woman's subjectivity and gender relations, while simultaneously appealing to the Western readers by dramatizing the universalist sentiment of love and longing. This accentuation of alternative gender roles and sexuality, whereby both Lowell the writer and her Western readers can imagine or even temporarily assume the subjectivity of the Asian narrator, is further evidenced in Lowell's own compositions.

With the generally favorable reviews of *Fir-Flower Tablets*, Lowell secured her authority as a "translator" of Chinese poetry and Asia at large. While she was working with Ayscough on the translation, she was simultaneously composing a number of poems that came out in various literary journals and were later collected in her books, *Can Grande's Castle* (1918) and *Pictures of the Floating World* (1919). Although she continued to pursue her interest in Asian poetry after these publications, it was in these two collections that the intersection of her ideas about Asia and her Imagism produced the most distinct effect. Lowell's "Asian" poetry in these collections was unique in that she not only availed herself of Asian images, themes, and motifs, but she also appropriated Asian arts and letters *formalistically*. Lowell not only imported visual images and cultural icons from Asia into Western discourse, but brought Asian textual forms and structures into the American literary world. Lowell's literary Orientalism in both form and content allowed her to engage in a performance of alternative gender roles and sexuality through a racial masquerade whereby the author, the narrator, and the reader perform the roles of Asian narrators/characters.

Pictures of the Floating World, a collection of 174 short poems previously published in magazines and anthologies, represents Lowell's engagement with Asian art and poetry in her exploration of Imagism. The literal translation of *ukiyo-e*, a genre of Japanese woodblock prints, the book's title characterizes the Imagists' and other contemporary Western artists' interest in Japanese art. Her use of it illustrates her attempt to capture the aesthetic methods, forms, and themes of Japanese art.

The first section of the book is a series of fifty-nine "Lacquer Prints," written on Japanese subjects after the method of Japanese *hokku* (which juxtaposes two or three details which coalesce in the reader's mind and carry a dramatic effect through their association with one another), although they do not follow its strict syllabic rules (three phrases consisting of five, seven, and five syllables respectively). Lowell states, "I have made no attempt to observe the syllabic rules which are an integral part of all Japanese poetry. I have endeavoured only to keep the brevity and suggestion of the *hokku*, and to preserve it within its natural sphere."[22] Thus, Lowell's use of Japanese poems is, at least to a degree, conducted on both formalistic and content levels. On the other hand, the seven "Chinoiseries" which follow "Lacquer Prints" are longer, and rather than following the Chinese poetic form, they simply evoke images and events derived from China. The rest of the collection, "Planes of Personality," consists of lyrical poems, "deriving from everywhere and nowhere as is the case with all poetry" (viii), a few of which explicitly refer to Japanese or Chinese themes.

The brevity (some poems consist of merely eight or ten words; others are more than twenty-five lines long) and suggestiveness in the method of *hokku* used in "Lacquer Prints" give the poems an "exotic" flavor and seemingly Japanese aesthetic. The exoticism rendered through the formal structure is sustained by various elements which mark the poems as specifically Japanese. Some scenes or events take place in specific settings identified by proper place names, such as Kioto [*sic*], Yoshiwara, Uji River, Asama Yama, and Matsue. Some portray specific individuals, such as Hokusai or the Emperor. Many poems refer to flora and fauna that are used as markers of the Japanese setting, such as the maple, lotus, chrysanthemum, iris, camellia, and bamboo. Others make references to Japanese material life and social practices, such as lanterns, the paper carp (hung outside Japanese houses in the spring for the Boys' Festival), shôji (Japanese sliding doors with paper screens), the New Year festival, processions of geisha, and a temple ceremony.

The exoticism furnished by these cultural clues is further heightened by the atemporality of the poems' settings. All fifty-nine poems sketch miscellaneous scenes in Japanese life, but they are frozen in a historical past. As Lowell notes in her foreword, "[s]ome of the subjects are purely imaginary, some are taken from legends or historical events, others owe their inception to the vivid, realistic colour-prints of the Japanese masters, but all alike are peculiar to one corner of the globe and, for the most part, to one epoch—the eighteenth century." (viii) Given that these poems are meant to emulate the visual effects of *ukiyo-e* prints and to capture the portentous meanings in ephemeral occurrences, the snapshot method and its effects are plausible. Setting the scenes in the eighteenth century, on the other hand, carries more significant implications and results. Although Lowell's knowledge of Japanese life and culture came from her brother Percival's descriptions and her own reading, she grasped the general conditions of contemporary Japanese life and many of the social and cultural issues in post-Perry Japan. Lowell's decision to depict scenes set exclusively in the past century was, therefore, her deliberate aesthetic choice rather than a result of her limited knowledge of Japanese culture. By being set either in a historically unspecified, timeless scene or in a social and cultural landscape of the past century—when, in the era when Japan had closed its doors to foreign trade, distinct Japanese culture was peacefully in place—the poems signify the pure, traditional Japanese aesthetics safe from the action, conflict, and instability of "modern" society. Even when there is a specific historical and cultural reference, the effect is not so much to convey some particular content as to evoke the exotic quality of the setting. For example, "One of the 'Hundred Views of Fuji' by Hokusai" is specific in its temporal and cultural setting. It verbally depicts a famous image by the eighteenth-century master woodblock artist:

Being thirsty,
I filled a cup with water,
And, behold! Fuji-yama lay upon the water
Like a dropped leaf! (11)

While the poem's title identifies the setting, the image it portrays is more of a static, timeless landscape than the temporally and spatially specific action of an individual. Other poems likewise hint at the historical and cultural context through their setting, but the effect is never more than an exotic flavor. Similarly, the seven poems in "Chinoiserie" depict miscellaneous scenes suggestive of an unspecified past. The structure and style of the poems in this section are more loosely "Chinese" than the poems in "Lacquer Prints" are "Japanese." They do not follow the conventions of Chinese poetry in any apparent way besides evoking the exotic setting. Even in the last piece in the section, "Li T'ai Po," the focus is more on the narrator's admiration for Li Po than on the poet's life or work.

More importantly, the foreignness of the setting is codified by the forms of gender relations and sexuality depicted in the poems. In the same way that Lowell's translations in *Fir-Flower Tablets* emphasized the patriarchal gender relations in Li Po's China, many of her poems portray the types of courtship that are marked as distant in time and space from her Western readers. For example, the poems "By Messenger," "A Lover," and "A Burnt Offering" portray scenes and sentiments around the epistolary affection, which was a central mode of communication in romantic relationships in Japan, particularly among men and women in court.

By Messenger

One night
When there was a clear moon,
I sat down
To write a poem
About maple-trees.
But the dazzle of moonlight
In the ink
Blinded me,
And I could only write
What I remembered.
Therefore, on the wrapping of my poem
I have inscribed your name. (4)

A Lover

If I could catch the green lantern of the firefly
I could see to write you a letter. (8)

A Burnt Offering

Because there was no wind,
The smoke of your letters hung in the air
For a long time;
And its shape
Was the shape of your face,
My Beloved. (23)

These poems make no references to any specific historical context but rather depict portentous moments of timeless romance. While the poems may express romantic

sentiments that transcend cultures, the premodernness of their material surroundings—such as writing under the moonlight or the light of the firefly and burning letters outdoors—codifies the foreignness of not only the setting but the gender and
sexual relations depicted.

In these poems, the author, the narrator, and the reader all participate in a racial
masquerade—assuming the role of an Asian narrator/character—which in turn fa-
cilitates a performance of alternative gender and sexuality. In the discursive context
of Orientalism in which the trope of Madame Butterfly was circulating widely, the
qualities embodied in the Japanese narrators and characters in the poems—for example, faithfulness, romantic idealism, self-restraint, patience—had specifically
gendered and racialized meanings, and for white women to identify with and perform that role had both liberating and eroticizing effect. Lowell's literary performance of racial masquerade is achieved through the poems' form and content. As in
these poems, many in the collection are written in the first-person, and often include the second-person subject to whom the narrator speaks. Although first-person
speech is common in both Western and Asian poetry, its use in this particular form
of poetry serves unique functions. As the settings are Japan or China of the past and
the poetical structure is presumably Japanese or Chinese, the narrative "I" assumes
the role of a Japanese or Chinese character even though Lowell's intended readers
are English-speaking Westerners who know the author's Western identity. In this
process, the author, the narrator, and the reader all engage in the performance of
racial crossing through identification and fantasy, in the same way that both the performers and the audience of Orientalist stage took part in the construction of Asian
femininity.

Once the presumed racial and cultural identity of the narrator is thus established,
the next step in performing and authenticating the cross-dressing is the literal donning of the "Asian" garb. By making clear that one is dressed in authentic clothing,
the narrator "becomes" Japanese. For example, in the poem "Vicarious," the narrator's clothing is critical in authenticating her "Asian" performance:

When I stand under the willow-tree
Above the river,
In my straw-coloured silken garment
Embroidered with purple chrysanthemums,
It is not at the bright water
That I am gazing,
But at your portrait,
Which I have caused to be painted
On my fan. (5)

Just as the white actresses' donning of the kimono and "Asian" makeup simultaneously authenticated the performance and confirmed the performer's white identity,

the kimono and the fan the narrator of this poem carries invite the reader to appreciate both the authenticity and the performativity of literary Orientalism. The title of the poem, "Vicarious," explicitly foregrounds the performative cross-dressing the narrator engages in.

When the characters are rendered sufficiently Japanese by their clothing, they also "do" things Japanese. Significantly, much of "acting Japanese" is done through the performance of "Japanese" gender relations and romantic courtship. For example, in both "By Messenger" and "A Lover," the reader sees a Japanese character, presumably dressed in kimono, sitting at night in the yard outside a Japanese vernacular house, composing a poem for the loved one. The loved one, who is also presumably Japanese, is a partner in this enactment. The gender of both the narrator and his/her lover is uncertain. Yet, regardless of whether the reader assumes the narrator to be female or male, the racial and cultural cross-dressing allows her/him to engage in an alternative gender and sexuality. If the narrator is assumed to be a Japanese woman, the poems create a highly "traditional" Japanese woman and gender/sexual dynamics—a woman longing for the absent lover, similar to the narrators in Li Po's poems. By assuming this particular Japanese womanhood, the narrator and the reader fictively and temporarily perform a gender role that is distinct from the role of the modern American woman in both time and space. On the other hand, if the narrator is assumed to be a Japanese male, the poems reinforce existing Orientalist stereotypes of feminized Japanese men, as they are depicted as being so fragile as to have their eyes blinded by the moonlight in the ink or so delicate as to long for the firefly for the light. In this scenario, the narrator and the reader would perform a form of masculinity that is quite distant from the one valued in the modern West yet that also has a sensual appeal similar to aestheticism's fervor for Oscar Wilde.

Not all narrative voices are indeterminate of gender, however. "Road to the Yoshiwara" and "A Daimio's Oiran" (21), respectively, portray the red-light district that flourished in the eighteenth century and a feudal lord visiting a courtesan, both of which are scenes from a distinctly Japanese social and cultural landscape. Both poems evoke exoticism through the specifically sexualized narrative setting. The particular selection of these extramarital sexual relationships that would not be openly condoned in Lowell's and her readers' social world illustrates how, by setting the poems in a foreign locale and using foreign forms for expression, the writer could engage in alternative forms of gender and sexuality as an imaginative performance. In "A Daimio's Oiran," the narrator is a courtesan in the red-light district waiting for the arrival of her samurai client:

> When I hear your runners shouting:
> "Get down! Get down!"
> Then I dress my hair
> With the little chrysanthemums. (21)

The racial and cultural cross-dressing allows the author, the narrator, and the reader to perform the role of an exoticized female sexuality. The samurai status of the narrator's client implied by "your runners" demanding the people to honor him by getting down, the narrator's commodified sexuality indicated by the title "oiran" (courtesan), and her dressing of the hair with chrysanthemums all combine to create a form of sexuality that is outside the Western conventions of propriety, culturally foreign, and exotically appealing and sensuous. On the other hand, in "The Return," the narrator of the poem is a Japanese man returning from a journey, possibly from his obligatory service for the shogunate at the capital while his family waits at his hometown:

> Coming up from my boat
> In haste to lighten your anxiety,
> I saw, reflected in the circular metal mirror,
> The face and hands of a woman
> Arranging her hair. (15)

Here, in assuming the role of a Japanese man expressing his love for his Japanese wife or lover, the author engages in a gender as well as racial cross-dressing. By playing the role of a Japanese male, the poem engages in alternative gender and sexuality not only in the form of the woman who prepares herself physically and emotionally for the man she awaits, but also by assuming the role of the man who avails himself of that womanhood.

The politics and poetics of cross-dressing are most vividly represented in "Free Fantasia on Japanese Themes," which appears in a later section of *Pictures of the Floating World*. In this poem, the narrator foregrounds the act of cross-dressing, making explicit her Western identity and the fact that this is an imaginary act. The poem opens and closes with the depiction of the room where the narrator sits with an open book. It is unclear whether this setting is in Japan or in the West. However, the passages at the beginning and the end of the poem, "And my heart is still and alert, / Passive with sunshine/ Avid of adventure" (105) and "I would anything/ Rather than this cold paper, / With, outside, the quiet sun on the sides of burgeoning branches, / And inside, only my books" (108) are clearly juxtaposed against the middle section of the poem illustrating the imaginary Japanese settings and roles she plays. This suggests that regardless of setting, the reader is supposed to identify with this frame as a familiar site from which one escapes into the adventure and fantasy of "going native" in Japan. Even as the narrator immerses herself in her fantasy, she makes clear that this is an imaginary performance. Each stanza begins with the phrase "I would . . . ," each sentence is written in hypothetical past tense, and is sometimes further qualified with the word "perhaps." In addition, the second stanza, where she sets herself up for the imaginary adventure, is filled with words that signify the object of fantasy as the Other:

I would experience new emotions—
Submit to strange enchantments—
Bend to influences,
Bizarre, exotic,
Fresh with burgeoning. (105–106)

Once she foregrounds the "new," "strange," "bizarre," "exotic," "fresh" nature of the object of her fantasy, the narrator travels to one Japanese scene after another, dressed as a Japanese character. First she would "climb a Sacred Mountain," struggling with other pilgrims up a steep path and prostrate herself before a painted shrine. Whereas here the "other pilgrims" are presumed to be the "real" Japanese among whom the narrator disguises her Western identity, in the next scene she sets up the reader to perform with her. The "you" in the following passages is made to participate in the racial and cultural cross-dressing:

I would recline upon a balcony
In purple curving folds of silk,
And my dress should be silvered with a pattern
Of butterflies and swallows,
And the black band of my *obi*
Should flash with gold, circular threads,
And glitter when I moved.
I would lean against the railing
While you sang to me of wars—
Past, and to come—
Sang and played the *samisen*.
Perhaps I would beat a little hand drum
In time to your singing;
Perhaps I would only watch the play of light
On the hilts of your two swords. (106–107)

While the narrator enacts the luxurious Japanese femininity by dressing in the colorful and shining kimono and obi and indulging in their glitter, the "you" is made to join the performance of exotic gender and sexuality by playing Japanese lyric music and wearing swords. By playing the role of Japanese lovers, the narrator and her partner engage in an exoticized romance and sexuality.

In all of these poems, the cross-dressing is supported by the poems' formal structures. Their brevity and the suggestiveness and associations evoked by the scenes render the author's and the narrator's voice credibly "Japanese," and provide a formalistic stage for the content of literary performance. They allowed Lowell and her Western readers to cross not only the boundaries of race and culture but also of gender and sexuality. In the cultural context where modernist identity and aesthetics were often expressed through performative self-fashioning and the donning and changing of masks, these narrative and formal compositions of gender relations and sexuality of Japan's past articulated sensibilities that were particularly liberating for white women who had the power and freedom to play with such disguises. Like white women's performances of Asian heroines on stage, Lowell's literary Orientalism made it possible for her and her Western readers to "put on" Asian-ness and imaginatively place themselves in the historic past of exotic Japan.

While Lowell's "translations" in *Fir-Flower Tablets* and her own "Asian" poems in *Pictures of the Floating World* constructed an exoticized gender relations and sexuality and engaged the reader to perform in a racial masquerade, the mode of Lowell's Orientalism was not consistent. Lowell's poem, "Guns as Keys: and the Great Gate Swings," first published in the journal *Seven Arts* (1917) and included in her collection *Can Grande's Castle* (1918), shows an engagement with the Asian subject that is quite different from her other "Asian" work. In many ways, the poem's narrative voice is much more self-conscious about its relation to the existing Orientalist discourse and addresses the theme of East-West contact in a way that is more self-referential than Lowell's poems in *Pictures of the Floating World*.

"Guns as Keys" depicts the arrival of Commodore Matthew Perry's squadron in Japan and the cultural meaning of the first contact between the United States and Japan for both countries. While the poem is set up as a historical narrative portraying the encounter from both American and Japanese perspectives, Lowell's voice historicizes the setting and sheds a critical perspective on the masculinist visions of American expansionism. The content of such a critical representation is effectively achieved by the form she deploys to both heighten and problematize the binary between the United States and Japan.

"Guns as Keys" consists of two parts and a postlude, each of which shows different formal and linguistic strategies. Part One stresses the contrast between the two worlds depicted by alternating between "polyphonic prose" to represent the United States and "free verse" for scenes in Japan. This juxtaposition of form seems to reflect, at first glance, the Orientalist binary which constructs the West as free and democratic and the East as more rigidly constrained. Lowell's own statement about polyphonic prose indicates the ideas behind its use:

> "Polyphonic prose" is perhaps a misleading title, as it tends to make the layman think that this is a prose form. Nothing could be farther from the truth. The word 'prose' in its title simply refers to the manner in which the words are printed; "polyphonic"—many-voiced—giving the real key. "Polyphonic prose" is the freest, the most elastic, of all forms, for it follows at will any, and all, of the rules which guide other forms. Metrical verse has one set of laws, cadenced verse

another; "polyphonic prose" can go from one to the other in the same poem with no sense of incongruity. Its only touchstone is the taste and feeling of its author.[23]

While her definition of polyphonic prose may seem vague, especially given that the "free verse" aimed to accomplish quite similar goals, the effect of the juxtaposition becomes clear when seen in conjunction with the content of the poem. Besides the juxtaposition of form, the language also shifts between the colloquial American speech and the subdued and almost stately diction of the free verse representing the Japanese scenes. For example, in the opening scene, Perry's squadron is just leaving the United States, while the Japanese live a bucolic, "premodern" life, unaware of the impending arrival of the foreign power:

> My! How she throws the water off from her bows, and how those paddle-wheels churn her along at the rate of seven good knots! You are a proud lady, Mrs. *Mississippi*, curtseying down Chesapeake Bay, all a-flutter with red white and blue ribbons.

> At Mishima in the Province of Kai,
> Three men are trying to measure a pine tree
> By the length of their outstretched arms.
> Trying to span the bole of a huge pine tree
> By the spread of their lifted arms.
> Attempting to compress its girth
> Within the limit of their extended arms.
> Beyond, Fuji,
> Majestic, inevitable,
> Wreathed over by wisps of cloud.
> The clouds draw about the mountain,
> But there are gaps.
> The men reach about the pine tree,
> But their hands break apart;
> The rough bark escapes their hand-clasps;
> The tree is unencircled.
> Three men are trying to measure the stem of a gigantic pine tree,
> With their arms,
> At Mishima in the Province of Kai.[24]

Language and action in these stanzas function as an index to national characters. While the Americans, with daring enterprise, circle the globe with modern technologies such as paddle-wheels (terms such as "key-guns," "furnaces," and "stem frigate" are used as signifiers of the American scene throughout the poem), the Japanese are attempting a far more local and primitive act of joining hands around a tree. The phrase "pine tree" is repeated four times, stressing the specificity of the Japanese landscape. Likewise, the word "arms" is repeated at the end of four lines in the stanza, combined with the adjectives "outstretched," "lifted," "extended" in the first three and no adjective in the final one, suggesting that the arduous effort is destined to fail. The use of the same description of the three men trying to measure a pine tree at the beginning and the end of the stanza heightens the sense of circularity and closure in the Japanese scene. Furthermore, the Japanese failure to complete the enclosure as symbolized by the gaps in the clouds above Mt. Fuji and the breaking apart of the men's hand-clasps suggest the anticipated "opening" of Japan by Perry's arrival.[25]

Lowell further stresses the juxtaposition of the progress of the American frigate and the stasis of the Japanese landscape by the narrative structure of the poem's first section. The American scene moves progressively as Perry's squadron on the *Mississippi* "noses her way through a wallowing sea; foots it, bit by bit, over the slanting wave slopes" (53). The ship circles the globe, starting from the Chesapeake Bay and stopping at the "stepping stones" of Madeira, Cape Town, Mauritius, and Singapore. On the other hand, the Japanese scenes are sketches of miscellaneous images and episodes with no apparent linear narrative or relation to one another. Men measure a tree in the Province of Kai, an insect-seller carries cicadas in the cage in an anonymous place, a silk merchant is entertained by a celebrated geisha, a colorful and lively parade of women promenades in the Sanno quarter, women visit Asakusa to gaze at peonies, and so on.

The contrast between the American scene and the Japanese scene is also gendered. The world and the culture aboard the *Mississippi* is a very masculine one, and Lowell's language heightens the effect. The robust, loud, and rough nature of the sailors' life is represented by their colloquial and plain dialogue:

Across the equator and panting down to Saint Helena, trailing smoke like a mourning veil. Jamestown jetty, and all the officers in the ship making at once for Longwood. Napoleon! Ah, tales—tales—with nobody to tell them. A bronze eagle caged by floating woodwork. A heart burst with beating on a flat drop-curtain of sea and sky. Nothing now but pigs in a sty. Pigs rooting in the Emperor's bedroom. God be praised, we have a plumed smoking ship to take us away from this desolation.

"Boney was a warrior
    Away-i-oh;
Boney was a warrior,
    John François."
"Oh, shut up, Jack, you make me sick. Those pigs are like worms eating a corpse. Bah!" (60–61)

Even in scenes where there is no actual dialogue among the sailors, the narrative assumes the voice of a male subject:

> The Gate! The Gate! The far-shining Gate! Pat your guns and thank your stars you have not come too late. The Orient's a sleepy place, as all globe-trotters say. We'll get there soon enough, my lads, and carry it away. That's a good enough song to round the Cape with, and there's the Table Cloth on Table Mountain and we've drawn a bead over half the curving world. Three cheers for Old Glory, fellows. (62)

Unlike the language of machismo used in American scenes, the free verse in Japanese scenes is much more delicate and feminine. Such language and style, combined with the depiction of women as a part of the landscape, feminize the whole Japanese scene. For example,

> The ladies,
> Wisteria Blossom, Cloth-of-Silk, and Deep Snow,
> With their ten attendants,
> Are come to Asakusa
> To gaze at peonies.
> To admire crimson-carmine peonies,
> To stare in admiration at bomb-shaped, white and sulphur peonies,
> To caress with a soft finger
> Single, rose-flat peonies,
> Tight, incurved, red-edged peonies,
> Spin-wheel circle, amaranth peonies.
> To smell the acrid pungence of peony blossoms,
> And dream for months afterwards
> Of the temple garden at Asakusa,
> Where they walked together
> Looking at peonies. (61–62)

This picturesque feminine scene comes immediately after the "pigs in the sty" scene, juxtaposing between the vulgar masculine world of the American squadron with the delicate femininity of Japan. Like the use of the phrase "pine tree" in the earlier stanza, the pertinacious repetition of the word "peonies" not only stresses the specific Japanese locale and its feminine associations but also contrasts formalistically with the polyphonic prose of the American scene by giving the stanza a more versified structure and tone.

The gendered contrast between the cultures is made more explicit in the portrayal of gender and sexual relations in the two countries. In one scene, Commodore Perry writes to his wife at his table aboard the *Mississippi*, to be posted at the next stopping place. The short passage, ending with the sentence, "Two years is a long time to be upon the sea," implies a marital and family relations where husband

and wife are bonded by love and trust. Thus, while all of the American scenes in the poem are extremely masculine and contain only male characters, the United States' expansionist project of opening the Gate of Japan is upheld by white American women back home. The poem marks the gender dimension of the U.S.-Japan encounter through the constitutive absence of American women in the scene, just as Mrs. Pinkerton's absence and final appearance do in *Madame Butterfly*. In a striking contrast, immediately after this passage, Lowell depicts a Japanese scene where a wealthy silk merchant is being entertained by a geisha at a teahouse:

Nigi-oi of Matsuba-ya
Celebrated oiran,
Courtesan of unrivalled beauty,
The great silk mercer, Mitsui,
Counts himself a fortunate man
As he watches her parade in front of him
In her robes of glazed blue silk
Embroidered with singing nightingales.
He puffs his little silver pipe
And arranges a fold of her dress.
He parts it at the neck
And laughs when the falling plum-blossoms
Tickle her naked breasts.
The next morning he makes out a bill
To the Director of the Dutch Factory at Nagasaki
For three times the amount of the goods
Forwarded that day in two small junks
In the care of a trusted clerk. (56–57)

The portrayal of the commodified sexual relationship depicted with colorful and vivid detail and a highly sensuous language contrasts sharply with the brief and restrained passage about Perry's correspondence with his wife. The association between the merchant's extramarital sexual relations and his suspicious business presents Japan's impenetrable underworld in gendered and sexualized terms, contrasted with the practical, commercial trade to be initiated by the American power.

Although the carefully constructed binary between the United States and Japan in the first section of the poem neatly fits the Orientalist binary drawn between the West and the East, Lowell's narrative is more complex than it appears. As the poem moves from one scene to another along Perry's progress en route to Japan, Lowell occasionally inserts the voice of a third party viewing the American penetration into the Japanese market. These commentaries render Lowell's narrative specifically historicized—she is writing from the perspective of an American living fifty years after Perry's travel—and present a critical and cynical perspective on the American enterprise and its masculinist visions. For example, at the outset of the poem, Lowell describes the American scene where Perry's squadron is preparing to depart. "On shore, all the papers are running to press with huge headlines: 'Commodore Perry Sails.' Dining-tables buzz with travellers' tales of old Japan culled from Dutch writers. But we are not like the Dutch. No shutting the stars and stripes up on an island. Pooh! We must trade wherever we have a mind. Naturally!" (49–50). The reference to the Dutch (who were the only Western nationals to be given the privilege of trading with Japan on a small island off Nagasaki during the seventeenth and eighteenth centuries when Japan closed its doors to foreign trade) lays out the politics of Western imperialism, which is often represented in terms of the dynamics between the Western metropolitan powers rather than those between the metropole and the colonial periphery.[26] Lowell's depiction of Americans comparing themselves to the Dutch demonstrates her critical perspective on American expansionism in Asia in relation to the larger global politics. Later in the poem, in a scene where the ship has moved into the doldrums, Lowell inserts a cynical voice:

> The North-east trades have smoothed away into hot, blue doldrums. Paddle-wheels to the rescue. Thank God, we live in an age of invention. What air there is, is dead ahead. The deck is a bed of cinders, we wear a smoke cloud like a funeral plume. Funeral—of whom? Of the little heathens inside the Gate? Wait! Wait! These monkey-men have got to trade, Uncle Sam has laid his plans with care, see those black guns sizzling there. "It's deuced hot," says a lieutenant, "I wish I could look in at a hop in Newport this evening." (57)

The representative speech—instead of third-person narrative—justifying American expansionism and the trade with the heathen "monkey-men" highlights Lowell's critical perspective on U.S. imperialism, rather than an uncritical and purely aesthetic portrayal of an historical event. While the reader is invited to identify with the "we" of the American scene, he/she is made to feel uncomfortable with that identification. Finally, Lowell showcases another American voice:

> Down, down, down, to the bottom of the map; but we must up again, high on the other side. America, sailing the seas of a planet to stock the shop counters at home. Commerce-raiding a nation; pulling apart the curtains of a temple and calling it trade. Magnificent mission! Every shop-till in every bye-street will bless you. Force the shut gate with the muzzles of your black cannon. Then wait—wait for fifty years—and see who has conquered. (63–64)

The explicit remark about the historical changes to take place in the fifty years after Perry's opening of Japan and its consequences may disrupt the poem's aesthetic effect as a historical narrative, but it makes Lowell's discursive location more complex than the one that simply replicates the dominant Orientalist narrative. Rather than simply setting the poem at the time of Perry's expedition, Lowell locates the reader in his/her time, when Japan itself has become an imperial power and is making its territorial expansion in Korea, Taiwan, and China as well as sending immigrants to the United States. By bringing the reader back to the present and reminding him/her of the sociopolitical and cultural conditions that followed Perry's expedition, Lowell implicitly critiques the masculinist visions of American expansionism and the ideological binary between the East and the West created by the latter. This historicization sets the stage for Lowell's more explicit critique of U.S. imperialism in the later parts of the poem.

Whereas in Part I of the poem Lowell heightened the binary and the contrast between the American and the Japanese scenes through the juxtaposition of polyphonic prose and free verse, Part II foregrounds the merging of two cultures through both content and form. Formalistically, Part II is written entirely in polyphonic prose. The use of polyphonic prose for Japan illustrates Lowell's view that once Perry arrives, Japan becomes increasingly modernized and Westernized and takes on the voice of the West, both literally and figuratively. The Japanese, who had lived in peace for two centuries and for whom "war [was] an old wives' tale, a frail beautiful embroidery of other ages" (75) with their weapons rusted unused in arsenals, degenerate into chaos and lose their dignified postures and aesthetic charm they represented in the previous part. The panicked Japanese now use the Americans' vulgar and masculine/masculinist colloquial speech. The use of this type of language to represent the political, social, and cultural confusion that followed Perry's arrival suggests Lowell's critique of the process of the U.S.-Japan encounter. For example, the *daimios* [chiefs of samurai], who were making dignified processions in Part I, have now lost their authority:

Daimios smoke innumerable pipes, and drink unnumbered cups of tea, discussing — discussing — "What is to be done?" The Shôgun is no Emperor. What shall they do if the "hairy devils" take a notion to go to Kiôto! Then indeed would the Tokugawa fall. The prisons are crammed with those who advise opening the Gate. Open the Gate, and let the State scatter like dust to the winds! Absurd! Unthinkable! Suppress the "brocade pictures" of the floating monsters with which book-sellers and picture-shop keepers are delighting and affrighting the populace. Place a ban on speech. Preach, inert Daimios — the Commodore will *not* go to Nagasaki, and the roar of his guns will drown the clattering fall of your Dragon Doors if you do not open them in time. East and West, and trade shaded by heroism. Hokusai is dead, but his pupils are lampooning your carpet soldiers. Spare the dynasty — parley, procrastinate. Appoint two Princes to receive the Commodore, at once, since he will not wait over long. At Kurihama, for he must not come to Yedo. (81–82)

The apparent disorder and ineptness of the Japanese response to Perry's arrival is accompanied by Lowell's cynical voice. Whereas Lowell's critical eye was directed primarily at American imperialists in Part I, it is now pointed to the Japanese as well.

> A locomotive in pay for a Whistler; telegraph wires buying a revolution; weights and measures and Audubon's birds in exchange for fear. Yellow monkey-men leaping out of Pandora's box, shaking the rocks of the Western coastline. Golden California bartering panic for prints. The dressing-gowns of a continent won at the cost of security. Artists and philosophers lost in the hour-glass sand pouring through an open Gate. (94)

Here Lowell not only sheds a critical perspective on the Americans who forced themselves through Japan's closed gate but also on the Japanese who sold out to the West. She also presents the view that Japan in a sense "took over" the West, and that the opening of Japan has led to a certain permeability of racial and cultural lines. Whereas many poems in *The Pictures of the Floating World* use such permeability as a source for cross-racial performance on the part of the Western author, narrator, and reader, here Lowell problematizes the blurring of boundaries as manifested in "yellow monkey-men" shaking the rocks of the Western coastline, people buying Japanese prints, and admiring Whistler's Japonisme paintings.

Lowell's view on the consequences of cultural contact and permeability of cultural boundaries frames the entire poem. "Guns as Keys" ends with a postlude depicting two scenes, one Japanese and one American, set in 1903, fifty years after Perry's trip. In Japan, a young man kills himself by jumping off the cliff of the Kegon waterfall after carving on the trunk of a tree his belief that the universe is "unknowable" (96–97). In the United States, crowds gather around the paintings by Whistler which are strongly influenced by Japanese art (97). This juxtaposition symbolizes Lowell's critical view of the historical, cultural, and ideological consequences of the East-West contact. Lowell herself has explained her ideas behind these scenes as follows:

> What I meant to give in both those postludes was the effect that each country had upon the other. In the Japanese section, how difficult it was for the Oriental to assimilate the Occidental habits of thought, how he broke in the effort; in the American part, how, in conquering Japan for our commerce, as we thought, we had ourselves been conquered on the aesthetic plane, and our habits of thought insensibly modified by contact with the Japanese.[27]

Thus, in "Guns as Keys" Lowell both depicts and problematizes the binary and cultural contact between the United States and Japan, and the poem's formal structures and language reinforce the content of its representations. On the surface, the juxtaposition of polyphonic prose and free verse to represent the two nations seems to reproduce a simplistic binary between the two cultures and to reify the gendered notions about the East and the West. Lowell herself stated that she "wanted to place in juxtaposition the delicacy and artistic clarity of Japan and the artistic ignorance and gallant self-confidence of America."[27] The idea replicates the existing Orientalist view which essentializes Japan into the category of delicacy, simplicity, and aesthetics and posits it in opposition to the modern West. However, Lowell's strategic use of polyphonic prose also allowed her to expose the complexities of the cultural encounter she depicted and to interject her critical perspective on American expansionism and the Japanese response. Lowell's implicit critique of the masculinist discourse of U.S. imperialism and her perspective on the permeability of racial and cultural boundaries are effectively expressed through her manipulation of language and form.

Lowell's modes of Orientalism in her "Asian" works appear to be internally at odds. Her translations in *Fir-Flower Tablets* and her "Asian" poems in *Pictures of the Floating World* seem to be based on an Orientalist practice whereby Lowell—the wealthy, white, American woman writer—constructs an exoticized and antiquated gender and sexuality for the Orient and embraces it by performing a racial masquerade. On the other hand, "Guns as Keys" presents a much more nuanced, self-referential, critical look at American expansionism and the consequences of East-West contact.

These seeming contradictions in Lowell's engagements with Asia exemplify the multiple ideologies, expressions, and functions of Orientalism, especially the gendered nature of the discourse. The gendered constructions of Asia reflected and shaped U.S. domestic racial and gender ideology on the one hand and the unequal power relations between the United States and Asia on the other. The gendered language functioned sometimes to endorse and at other times to challenge U.S. imperialism, while constituting a mix of exoticism, desire, control, and domination for the East. In this context, Orientalism served several functions for women such as Lowell. First, it provided new ideas, themes, and forms for expression, as we see in her "Asian" poetry. Secondly, as evidenced by her status in the Imagist movement and her relationship to her "native informant," Orientalism bestowed her with authority and power, both in relation to American society and culture and to the Asian subjects. Finally, like the performances of Asian heroines on stage, Lowell's racial masquerade and performance of alternative gender and sexuality illustrate that through Orientalism women gained freedom from the conventions of Western gender and sexual relations, enabling them to engage in a play that enhanced their own identities as modern American women. Lowell's gendered constructions of Asia were both reflections and shapers of these mixed interests.

"Side by Side with These Men I Lie at Night"
Sexuality and Agnes Smedley's Radicalism

*W*hether on stage or in letters, the racial cross-dressing and performance of the role of Asian persona offered liberating and expressive power for many white American women in the early twentieth century. However, white women's engagement with Asia and their performance of "alternative" gender and sexuality did not always take place in the form of theatrical or textual work; it was also not always a temporary "play" that one chose to put on or off at one's will. For some, Asia was not a symbolic place that offered new tools for expression, but a physical space to live in with real people. For some, Asia became less a vehicle for expanding their horizons in their Western home than their adopted home and lifetime commitment. Some chose to "explore" Asia, not to exercise their freedom and power but rather to escape from oppression at home. Gender and sexual relations of Asia were appealing to some not so much because of their presumed exoticness or antiquatedness as because it presented a potential for equal relations between men and women. In other words, some women performed "Asian" identity not just temporarily and imaginatively, but adopted it for their real lives. Such an alternative vision that saw Asia less as an object of consumption or appropriation than as a living model of human relations superior to American society adds a new meaning to white women's "performances" of Asian-ness and their relationship to Orientalism.

Agnes Smedley was such a woman. During her commitment to the Chinese Revolution in the 1930s, she deliberately crafted a role for herself that was distinct from what she knew of women's role in the West, and she persistently performed that role in China. As a result, in China she was able to attain a relationship with men as equals and as comrades, something she could not achieve in America and Europe. To be sure, the role she chose for herself and the relationship she forged with the Chinese did not solve all of her personal problems or entirely erase the issue of power in her relationship to China. One cannot conclude that she successfully transcended the boundaries of race, class, and nation, nor that she indeed found in China fulfillment and happiness for herself. Furthermore, her conscious "adoption" of Asia as her home and her choice to make the Chinese Revolution her "project" may be characterized as Orientalist in its assumption of her "responsibility" to Asian people. Nevertheless, the path that brought Smedley to Asia and what she did there were distinct from the modes of white women's engagement with Asia discussed in previous chapters.

This chapter explores the politics of gender and sexuality in Smedley's relationship to China, as manifested both in her personal life and her writing. For Smedley—whose experience of gender and sexual oppression of women, of the harshness of working-class life, and of the interference of sexuality into politics had shaped her radicalism prior to her involvement with China—Asia was a site where she could shape her own gender and sexual identity in ways she could not in the West. Putting on the uniforms of the Chinese Communists and playing the role of a de-sexualized being, Smedley was able to pursue the political goals of the Communist Revolution and her personal quest for equality and freedom. While such construction of her own identity as well as the actual position she occupied in China were not without contradictions, through her performance of her self-defined role, Smedley was able to forge a tie with the Chinese that was defined less by Orientalism than by nationalist struggle and, at least to a degree, transcended race, class, and nation.

The role Smedley created for herself in China was greatly shaped by her experience and ideas about gender and sexuality prior to her involvement in the Chinese Revolution. Growing up in the harsh, impoverished, and violent environment of a Missouri farming country and witnessing the misery of working-class women who had one child after another, Smedley saw marriage and childbearing as enslavement. Raised with a Puritanical view that sexual desire and expression were sins, for a long time she could not come to terms with her own desire or emotions or accept sex as part of male-female relationships. Smedley left her family to educate herself and to become economically independent. Yet even after she married Ernest Brundin, a sensitive, educated, and sophisticated man, she was unable to envision a happy marriage based on freedom and equality, and she had two abortions and then a divorce.

She then moved to New York, where she became a committed leftist working for the Socialist press as well as Margaret Sanger's birth-control movement and was arrested for her involvement in the Indian nationalist movement. She spent the 1920s in Germany among Indian expatriates. She finally found a man she could love and respect in Virendranath Chattopadhyaya, one of the leading figures in the Indian nationalist movement, and the two began their married life and worked together in the underground political activity in Berlin. However, the meanings assigned to her sexuality became entangled with her political activities: the sexism of the exclusively male cohort of the Indian nationalist movement used Smedley's sexuality as a political weapon. A man with whom Smedley had slept before she met Chatto disclosed the affair, leading to the end of her marriage and ostracism by the movement. At this point she went to Asia. She arrived in China in 1929, after writing an autobiographical novel, *Daughter of Earth*. Deeply committed to the Chinese Communist movement, Smedley became the only American woman who marched with the Chinese Communists throughout the 1930s, and wrote prolifically and vividly what she had witnessed until she left China in 1941.

Smedley's rendition of her life prior to going to China in *Daughter of Earth* gives an excruciating account of the intersecting forces of class, race, and sexuality in shaping the protagonist Marie Rogers's consciousness.[1] The fragments of Marie Rogers's life include a childhood tainted by poverty and ignorance; desperate attempts to educate herself while struggling with the feeling that she had deserted her family; dismissal from college for her political activities; marriage broken by her inability to handle love and tenderness; involvement in the Indian nationalist movement; marriage to a prominent leader of the movement which collapses because of the husband's inability to accept her previous relationships with men; and her decision to end the relationship. Rogers is a woman who is extremely sensitive and tender, yet hardened by the harshness of life, the selfishness of men, the double standards of gender and sexuality, and the impossibility of negotiating love and freedom.

In Smedley's construction of Marie Rogers's quest for knowledge, freedom, and love, Rogers's encounter with Asia and her involvement with the anti-colonialist movement plays a pivotal role. The involvement with a non-white, colonized people and their nationalist movement offers Rogers the arena and the tools with which to fight the oppression of her youth. In Rogers's voice, Smedley writes of her own commitment to, and the sense of mission she found in, the Indian nationalist movement. "To me the Indians became a symbol of my duty and responsibility. They took the place of my father, of my brother who was dead and of the brother of whose destiny I was yet uncertain."[2] It is significant that here Rogers sees the Indians in specifically gendered terms, as replacing her "father" and her "brothers." One could see this as a result of Freudian psychoanalysis which she was undertaking at the time of her writing. Or one could see it as an example of Smedley's antifeminist attitude, that because "she wanted to be like a man, she could only admire men," as writer Marge Piercy argues.[3] Yet, it is more useful to see Smedley's gendered reference to Indian men in the larger context of the formation of her radical politics.

Rogers's/Smedley's realization that her sexuality was indeed an issue among Indian men and that it undermined her political commitment was devastating. Her marriage collapsed as she realized Indian men's unwillingness to see her as anything other than a woman, and her husband's inability to grant her the freedom and independence which he was struggling to gain for his country. As described by Smedley, Rogers's husband Anand claimed: "I care only for political reasons! So many western women have nothing but an erotic interest in Indians. I have not married such a woman, and I don't want such things used against us politically."[4] Under the guise of anti-Orientalist and anticolonialist rhetoric, her husband justifies and imposes patriarchal ideas about women's sexuality and conflates sexualized racial dynamics with women's sexual freedom. Later, Juan Diaz uses Rogers's sexuality as a political weapon by disclosing his affair with her to others, including Anand. They later discover that Diaz was a spy; but the mistrust, jealousy, and fear that had already developed between Anand and Rogers could not be repaired, and at the end of the novel Rogers leaves her husband.

As can be seen in Smedley's construction of Rogers's gender and sexual identity and her struggle to free herself from it, these issues had a central place in the formation of Smedley's radical politics. Outside the United States, Smedley sought a freer, more egalitarian relationship with men, and hoped that the cross-racial solidarity for a common political goal of liberation would transcend gender and sexuality.

Smedley's views on gender and sexuality, as expressed in both her writing and in her personal life, were dramatically different in China than from her earlier stance. Her works on China—documentaries, journalistic reports, and short stories, many of them based on the real lives of the Chinese—do not use gender and sexuality as her central focus or organizing thread. This seemingly sudden change in her writing reflects the way in which she crafted her own gender and sexual identity in the Chinese setting. To establish a relationship with the Chinese Communists that was consistent and compatible with her and their political goals, Smedley deliberately created a role for herself that was de-sexualized and persistently performed that role to varying success.

Smedley arrived in China by way of Soviet Union in 1928. As a newspaper correspondent for *Frankfurter Zeitung*, she spent her first winter in Manchuria, an area then ruled by a combination of warlords and foreign powers. The Japanese, intent on turning the region into a semi-colony, were the most threatening force. Political and cultural turmoil spread in the region as Chiang Kai-shek's Kuomintang and the Communists split, leading to a massive execution of the Communists in 1927. Smedley supported the Communists and sympathized and worked with the rural peasants. She soon moved south, from Port Arthur, Beijing, Nanjing, and then to Shanghai where she based herself for the next seven years, working with the Communists and sending prolific reports to American and European presses. As China's most populous city and largest treaty port, Shanghai was thriving economically, politically, and culturally. While foreign powers owned and governed more than half of the city as concession areas, it also served as a haven for Chinese intellectuals and political dissenters fleeing Kuomintang jurisdiction and as the underground headquarters of the Chinese Communist Party. In such a political climate and intellectual atmosphere, Smedley found her new cause and identity.

Smedley's crafting of her role in China in part derived from her alienation and self-drawn distinction from other Western views of China. Although Americans generally viewed China as heroically fighting Japan's military aggression in the 1930s, popular American discourse about China employed highly racialized language, which shaped the way the American public saw Smedley. When she became an international celebrity with her broadcasting of the Xian Incident in 1937, American newspapers gave her front-page coverage under sensational headlines such as "Huge Army at Her Back," "U.S. Girl a Red Peril," and "American Woman Aids Chinese Rising." A background story by Associated Press described her as "the one-time American farm girl who may become a virtual 'white empress' over yellow-skinned millions."[5] Clearly, these expressions inscribed specific meanings of race and gender onto both the Chinese and Smedley—the emasculated mass of Chinese men led by a defeminized American woman.

Working directly with the Chinese in the revolutionary army rather than through more "respectable" avenues of evangelical activity or reform movements, she threatened not only the gender ideology of the separate spheres but also the racial ideology which used the rhetoric of white women's purity and difference from men as a sign of civilization.[6] Smedley consciously distanced herself from such Western ideology. In *China Fights Back*, a book consisting of a mixture of Smedley's reportage of her travel with the Eighth Route Army, her autobiographical reflections, and her contemplations on the conditions of China, she writes:

My experience with American officials in China had not been enviable. Most of them thought of the Chinese as "Chinamen" who took in washing for a living; I didn't like their religion, so to speak. Because I regarded the Red Army as a revolutionary organization of the poor, some Americans considered me a glorified streetwalker; and after the Japanese invasion their women in particular had looked on me as a camp follower, a creature who lowered the prestige of the white race.[7]

Smedley's aversion to the condescending racial attitude of many Westerners in China is clear in her writings. She wrote to Margaret Sanger how she was "boycotted" by the foreigners in Shanghai because she left the Country Club upon learning that "no Chinese could tread the sacred precincts of that club house, even as a guest."[8] While such a racial attitude undoubtedly prevailed among many Western men as well as women in China, Smedley's critique of the women was particularly strong.

> Almost all foreign wives and children, and the wives and children of Chinese officials and the well-to-do, had been evacuated from Hankow. An occasional American woman, well groomed and wearing a hat, would arrive to write feature articles about women—it was amazing that American women had not advanced beyond that stage. A few serious foreign writers flew in and out in the course of gathering information . . . . Both then as before and later many freebooters in the journalistic and camera world arrived and used the China war as a background for their own personal glory. They were as filled with physical energy and as empty of ethics or social consciousness as, let us say, an American steel or oil magnate busily making a fortune by supplying Japan with war materials.[9]

She was also impatient with the sentimental idealism to which many Americans in China, especially women, were prone. In a letter to Margaret Sanger, she wrote:

> I am living with an American girl in Shanghai . . . But in her, a radical, I see the inability of even many American radicals to give help where help is needed. All she can do is to weep when she sees a miserable beggar in the street—as if this were a personal business instead of a colossal social movement. She is horrified by the misery of China; so was I at first and I nearly went insane when I was in the north. But I have come through it, as one seems to pass through a dark night of horror. Perhaps one looses [sic] much on the way and becomes hardened; I seem to have. But I know that I am better able to be of service to China because of it. I can look at all the beggars of China now and see beyond them to the thing that has made them like this.[10]

Thus, Smedley was able to move beyond emotional empathy with the Chinese to work for a structural revolution in the social and political realms.

Smedley's self-drawn distance from the Western racial discourse about the Chinese and middle-class gender ideology led her to construct a specifically de-sexualized role for herself in China. Her political activity allowed her to renounce sexuality as a controlling force in her life and to live for political principles. In 1930, she wrote to her friend Karin Michaelis, "I live now only for an idea. This surprises me more than anything else. More and more I become political [and] intellectual, with emotions being crowded completely or nearly completely out of my life—I mean any emotions of personal love."[11] A few months later, she wrote to her again:

China has done me much good. It has made me a sane woman; sane and clear-headed and hard in mind. . . . No man will ever get his hooks in me again. I shall have men friends and I shall now and then live with a man whom I admire intellectually and who appeals to me physically; and the basis of our union must be a broad and generous friendship. But I am now a sane woman. There is always a little tendency in me to long for the old kind of love that is senseless and dependent and cruel. But I try to analyze that out of my mind and heart. . . . But all this does not mean I am or ever will be a hardboiled woman. I can tell that by the response of the Chinese to me: I have countless friends whose devotion to me knows no limit . . . The thing is that I love the Chinese and all Asiatics, and they feel that.[12]

Her claim of her love for the Chinese "and all Asiatics" seems to reproduce the Orientalist vision which sees all Asians as a monolith. On the other hand, it is significant that Smedley sees China as enabling healthy, respectful male-female relationships and making her "a sane woman." It is also ironic that such ideal gender relations were, in Smedley's view, possible only through her own deliberate de-sexualizing of self. In the sense that she links Asia with her de-sexualized identity, one could argue that she replicates the Orientalist discourse that associates Asia with lack of proper sexuality. Yet, the sexual meaning Smedley finds in China serves to empower herself, less vis-à-vis the Chinese than the dominant gender and sexual relations she has known.

Smedley believed that the Chinese considered her an asexual being, or that they considered her sexuality to be irrelevant. She later wrote of her Shanghai years:

For a time I was a companion of the patricians; and with a few I remained good friends. To them I was not a man, woman, concubine, or courtesan. I was a foreigner who was no longer young, was not beautiful, earned her own living, and associated with men as an equal. Neither wifehood nor love was my profession.[13]

Despite her protests, she was seen as sexually as well as intellectually attractive by individual Chinese men. She had an affair with Xu Zhimo—China's leading romantic poet, educated at Oxford, and a disciple of the Indian poet Rabinandrath Tagore—whose high point was a two-week boat trip down the Yangzi to the Xu family country estate.[14] She was also intimately involved with another Chinese writer, Hu Shih.[15] Nevertheless, Smedley did not consider the sexual dimension of her relationship with Chinese men to be very important.

Smedley's construction of her relationship with Chinese men is vividly seen in her portrayal of her life and work among the Chinese Communists. In *China Fights Back*, she makes remarks about her gender and sexuality among the Chinese soldiers.

I lie and watch them and think. In no other country, I believe, could I live the life I live in China—living and sleeping side by side with men, without one thought of doubt about my safety. I feel far safer than if I were in closed Western rooms. Some of these men have carried me on their backs over streams. Others have put their arms about me and carried me down hills. As we go along, others gather wild flowers and stick them in my stretcher or give them to me. They come up and tuck in the blankets about me. When I must ride a horse they lift me in and put me on the horse so that my back may not be strained. If they have a bit of food, they share it with me . . . .

Side by side with these men I lie at night. And never have I known such impersonal love and affection as that shown me. I know that if I should ever speak to middle-class, conventional people anywhere about these experiences of mine, they would smirk and titter or look at me with cold, hostile eyes. To each other they will say, "She has been sleeping with bunches of coolies and *mafoos!*"

Yes, I *have* been sleeping with coolies and *mafoos*, with Chinese workers and peasants. They have lain on all sides of me. And I know that they are my protection and my strength and that on them I can depend to the very end.[16]

By deliberately manipulating the racialized vocabulary used by Westerners for Chinese and daring the reader by asserting that she has been "sleeping with" them, she exposes not only American racism toward the Chinese but American patriarchy that does not allow its women the freedom and safety Smedley enjoys in China. By stressing that she has been sleeping with Chinese men without being sexually threatened, she seems to affirm the popular American notion of the emasculated Chinese. Yet, by declaring that she depends on them as her protection and strength, she reverses the rhetoric of the masculine West as the guardian of women's purity. Rather than viewing the Chinese men as emasculated, she sees their masculinity in their ability to control their sexuality.

However, Smedley is aware that the issue of sexuality is not entirely nonexistent among the Chinese. As she talks frankly about sexuality in the Eighth Route Army, Smedley draws a connection between revolutionary politics and sexuality. She explains that the majority of soldiers have entered the army in their adolescence and are virgins, and "men who have never known sex experience and who live the rugged, active life of this army, do not find the need for sex expression as do other men."[17] Smedley uses the lack of the need for a physical outlet for sexual desires among the Chinese soldiers as a critique of an American society filled with unhealthy sexual expression.

Although her self-crafted role as a desexualized being was liberating for Smedley, her actual relationships with the Chinese were not without contradictions, nor were they uncontested by the Chinese. Although both her class and ideological positions set her apart from many other white women and men in China, Smedley's own identity in China was implicated in and shaped by the reality of U.S.-China relations. During her twelve years' work with the Chinese Communists, Smedley increasingly realized her position not just as an outsider but as an embodiment of white female privilege.

In certain instances, it became painfully clear that some Chinese saw Smedley as a threat to their sexual economy and ideology. Smedley's teaching of Western-style social dancing to the Chinese while stationed in Yanan (the mountain citadel of the Communist Party after the Xian Incident) precipitated a series of events that illustrated the Chinese view of Smedley. Believing that the grim survivors of the Long March needed some recreation and that dancing might help break down the rigid social code imposed by the wives of leading cadres, Smedley held dance classes in the old Catholic church. The soldiers came without their wives, but were accompanied by young women and men who had recently joined the united front from campuses in Beijing and Shanghai. In Smedley's biographers MacKinnon and MacKinnon's words, "Smedley was playing with dynamite but didn't seem to know it."[18] One evening, Mao Zedung was talking with Lily Wu, a young, attractive, and progressive woman serving as Smedley's interpreter, when Mao's wife walked in and yelled at her husband, "You idiot! How dare you fool me and sneak into the home of this little bourgeois dance hall strumpet." Not listening to Mao's quiet and severe order to quiet down, she cried to Wu, "Dance-hall bitch! You'd probably take up with any man. You've even fooled the Chairman." Then, turning to Smedley who came in, she shouted, "Imperialist! You're the cause of all this," and struck the "foreign devil" with her flashlight. Smedley flattened Mrs. Mao with a single punch. As Mrs. Mao reproached her husband for remaining silent while she was "being struck by this imperialist right before [his] eyes," Mao rebuked his wife, saying, "Didn't you strike her even though she had done nothing to you? She has a right to protect herself. You're the one who has shamed us. You're acting like a rich woman in a bad American movie."[19]

The dancing continued after the scandal and became popular beyond Yanan to the villages and cities of northern China. Smedley considered this a significant victory, a step toward removing the vestiges of feudal thinking from Chinese society. Yet the tension played out in this incident was representative of the chasm between Smedley's ideas about gender and sexuality and those of the Chinese. Along with social dancing, Smedley in fact introduced her own ideas about love and marriage, which were distinctly Western even if they diverged from conventional white, middle-class gender ideology. The Chinese did not approve of the notions of "free love" associated with social dancing. While Smedley saw marriage as nothing but an oppressive institution, the Chinese considered monogamous marriage a great victory for Chinese women, a cultural advance to be protected and strengthened.[20] Thus, even as she consciously distanced herself from the dominant racial and gender ideology of the white, middle-class America, her own presence and work resonated with the evangelist missions that exported Western bourgeois gender ideology to China.[21]

Far from being irrelevant, Smedley's gender and sexuality—as well as her race, nationality, and class in relation to the Chinese—were indeed important elements of her identity among the Chinese Communists. It was precisely the difference between Smedley and her Chinese surroundings that allowed her to live out her radical ideology in ways that were difficult or impossible in the United States. While the Chinese were sometimes stunned by her ideas, because she was so alien they did not try to make her conform to their culture or traditions. Furthermore, her gender allowed her to act and be accepted by the Chinese soldiers in ways that may not have been possible if Smedley had been a white man.

Racial and national differences between her and the Chinese, and the power relations shaping those differences, also prohibited her from completely transcending the gender division. Despite her political and emotional identification with the Chinese, she was also painfully aware of her outsider status:

> Tonight, as these hungry men sang, and then as they marched away to their beds of straw or cornstalks spread on mud floors, their singing had more meaning to me than ever before. Their voices were like a string orchestra in the night. I, who had had food this day, realized that I can never know fully the meaning, the essence of the Chinese struggle for liberation which lies embedded in the hearts of these workers and peasants. I am still an onlooker and my position is privileged. I will always have food though these men hunger. I will have clothing and a warm bed though they freeze. They will fight and many of them will lie on frozen battlefields. I will be an onlooker. I watched them blend with the darkness of the street; they still sang. And I hungered for the spark of vision that would enable me to see into their minds and hearts and picture their convictions about the great struggle for which they give more than their lives.[22]

Furthermore, when she tried to go with the Red Army to the front in Wutaishan, a heated controversy took place at the headquarters about it. She delineates what was at stake for the Army and how she came to her decision:

> The argument came down to this—that headquarters did not want me to go because of two things: I was a foreigner, and I was a woman. At least this was my challenge to them. But I could give a written statement to the American Ambassador that in case of my death only the Japanese should be held responsible. If I could not go because I was a woman, then that was an injustice unparalleled. Headquarters denied that this was the reason. Chu Teh said they wanted me to live and work, and not go to Wutaishan and die. Chinese are dying in Wutaishan, I argued, but Chu Teh replied with justice, "That cannot be helped."
>
> At last Jen Peh-si gave way and said, "All right, go!" And Chu Teh added, "We will give a very strong force to protect you."

Well, at that I backed down. I could see that if I went, a strong force of men would have to be withdrawn from other necessary duties just to guard me. I did not want that. With mingled misery and resentment I gave up the plan. In Wu-taishan one of the most decisive campaigns of China is being waged by the Eighth Route Army and thousands of armed peasants. I wanted to live through that campaign. Captain Carlson promised to give me a full account when he returned. It will not be the same as if I lived through it, but it will help. With heavy heart I have agreed to remain behind and go to another front a little later.[23]

Despite her intentions, Smedley embodied white female privilege. Her decision shows, however, that her commitment to the class and national revolution was more important to her than her personal aspirations to transcend gender and racial boundaries. While earlier in her China years she negated the centrality of gender and sexuality, here she does so by subsuming her own desires to a larger political goal.

The contradictions in Smedley's self-defined sexual identity manifested themselves not only in her relationship with the Chinese but also in her own emotions. Although Smedley's distancing of herself from the Western middle-class gender ideology helped her gain a more empowering identity in China, she was not always comfortable or happy with the total renouncement of the kind of male-female relationship which earlier had proved so tortuous. Being a woman with as much tenderness and affection as high-powered energy, she remained ambivalent about her own relationship to men. While she lived up to her political goals, she confessed her emotional ambivalence in her personal correspondence. In June 1939, she wrote to Freda Utley, a close friend and confidant:

Though I have never liked to be treated as bourgeois women are treated, still the foreign men from England, America, and perhaps France, have a deep and unconscious attitude of respect for women; a little feeling of protection for women; of helping a woman; and a kind of gentleness toward her. Often [their] kindness blended a bit with tenderness or a breath of romance. It is difficult to explain, because it is there as an atmosphere. In the Chinese man this is totally lacking in all respects. There is not even friendship and comradeship between man and woman in China. The foreign word "romance" has been taken into the Chinese language and means promiscuous sexual relations. And "love" means sexual intercourse in its usual use in China. For a Chinese man to even touch a woman's arm or hand means something sexual and arouses shock.[24]

The confession of her longing for the Western notions of a romantic, and even chivalric, relationship between men and women suggests that Smedley's decision to separate her sexuality from her politics was not without pain or struggle. And although she rationally tried to obliterate the former, emotionally she often fluctuated between the two forces.

Smedley tried to compensate for her rejection of "womanhood" through a sort of surrogate motherhood to a Chinese boy, Shen Kuo-hwa, whom everyone called the "little devil." Kuo-hwa was assigned to serve Smedley as an orderly when she joined the Storm Guerrilla Detachment of the New Fourth Army. Although Smedley initially felt uneasy not only about having a child serve her but also about exposing children to battle, she became attached to Kuo-hwa and played a parental role for him, physically and emotionally. She wrote of him as her son in a section of her *Battle Hymn of China* called "My Chinese Son." In describing Kuo-hwa's life and her relationship with him, Smedley illustrates an incident where the young boy defiantly defends Smedley in front of suspicious Chinese villagers:

> They came back and gathered about us in joy, but their excitement was greatest when they saw me. They gathered about me in crowds and I heard men trying to decide whether I was a man or a woman, American, German, or English. One woman pulled back her little child in fear and declared: "She has eyes like a cat!"
>
> My little Kuo-hwa could not endure this. He stood up before them and cried: "She does *not* have eyes like a cat! She is a woman and our American friend! She helps our wounded! In Tingjiachun she found a wounded man and fed him and gave him a bath. She even helped him do all his business."
>
> The people turned their eyes on me in amazement. My "son" would not stop. "Look at her bandaged hand!" he demanded, taking my hand in his. "She got this when she picked up a pan of hot water while she was bathing a wounded soldier. She is both my father and my mother! If any of you are sick, she will cure you."[25]

The depiction of the scene illustrates the gendered dimension of Smedley's relationship with the boy. Kuo-hwa's assertion of Smedley's gender—followed by his description of her helping the wounded—seems to be a way of declaring that she is not a threat. His claim that she was "both [his] father and [his] mother" simultaneously masculinizes and feminizes Smedley. Struggling to transcend the conventional gender and sexual identity, Smedley, in playing both parental roles, was able to fulfill her maternal instincts and to be a role model for the boy. She actualized what was missing from her own childhood: a role model, constant care and affection, a sense of protection and emotional security.

Smedley's affection for Kuo-hwa culminated when she made a decision to leave the Storm Guerrillas because of her deteriorating health and worsening battle situations. She decided to adopt Kuo-hwa, take him away from the front, and to send him to school. She describes her ideas and emotions in *Battle Hymn*:

> I questioned very much the desirability of having a foreigner bringing up a Chinese child and perhaps thereby isolating him from his own people. Yet I allowed

my mind to stray to some far-off time when I might even be able to send Kuo-hwa to a foreign country for advanced scientific studies. But my own life was so dreadfully insecure and uncertain, dare I undertake such a project? I would try.[26]

Although the commander of the detachment gave her permission to adopt Kuo-hwa, the boy decided that he was going to stay at the front. He told her, "You can adopt me after the final victory."[27] In the final paragraphs describing her arrangement for the boy to join the Children's Dramatic Corps of the Storm Guerrillas and their last parting, Smedley puts the word *son* in quotation marks and uses a restrained voice in illustrating the scene. As she had always done in viewing and describing her relationship to the Chinese, she keeps a critical and detached eye on her own commitment and feelings.

By seeing herself as de-sexualized, renouncing conventional Western gender norms, and distancing herself from many Western women in China, Smedley was able to identify with the people who were separated from her by race and nationality. But such a conscious positioning of her self in relation to matters of sexuality and gender also brought her loneliness. She sometimes longed for the security of a definition of womanhood into which she could fit. While struggling with such emotional vulnerability, she prioritized her political goals and fought for the liberation and independence of the Chinese poor.

Smedley's self-defined role in China and her relationship to the Chinese were reflected not only in her personal life but also in her mode of writing, especially her fictionalized short stories about Chinese lives. In these works, rather than putting on the voice of the Chinese (i.e. speaking through the voice of a Chinese narrator) or speaking *for* the Chinese (i.e. representing the Chinese on their behalf), Smedley's writing delivers Chinese voices to the American readers while making clear the mediated nature of such delivery. While Smedley disclaimed her objectivity by saying, "I always forgot that I was not a Chinese myself," in her writing she was quite conscious of her own narrative position and her relationship with her subjects.[28] Just as in her life in China she deliberately played the self-defined role of a de-sexualized being, in her writing she consciously took on the role of a deliverer of the Chinese voice. While such self-awareness sometimes rendered her writing structurally clumsy, it enabled a narrative of Chinese lives written by a white American woman that was based more on a dialogue between the author and her subjects than on her one-directional assuming of the Chinese voice.

Smedley's first two books on China, *Chinese Destinies* (1933) and *China's Red Army Marches* (1934), consist mostly of journalistic articles and essays, some of which had already appeared in magazines such as *New Republic* or *New Masses*. In many of these works, Smedley used some unique narrative strategies to deliver the voice of the subject and to let the subject speak in his/her own voice. In "The Dedicated," for example, Smedley portrays Chang Siao-hung, a young woman born and raised in a wealthy Hong Kong family involved in the slave trade. After having the privilege of going to school for several years in Canton, she decides to become a physician and leaves to study at Peking National University without telling her parents. She becomes an active member of the Communist Party, fighting against the White Terror. Smedley opens the narrative by describing her appearance, and then says: "The woman may speak for herself, as do many actors on the old feudal stage of China, who often step forward to explain what rôle they are playing. It is best that the woman speak quickly, lest tragedy overtake her and silence her tongue forever. So, let her speak."[29] Then she presents an autobiographical narrative of Chang Siao-hung. The narrative is put in quotation marks, told in first-person, sometimes addressing the audience and suggesting Smedley's presence as the interviewer. In the middle of the narrative, the speaker says, "But I have wandered from my own personal story. I thought this story of human slavery would interest you; for it is one of the countless facts of human subjection that awakened me to my duty that showed me the face of the ruling class."[30] At the closing of the story, she says:

> You wished to know the rôle I play in China. It is enough to say that I am a Communist, for that means I am fighting in the ranks for a new world. It means that I may one day cease to appear on this stage of historical events—but it means also that all that I work for now will be carried to fruition by the revolution of which I am but a part. Now I will be on my way, for there is much to do and I never know how much longer I have to do the share allotted to me.[31]

There is no evidence that Smedley's presentation of the story reflected Chang's story in the exact manner she narrated it, and it is likely that Smedley framed and tailored the narrative to have a theatrical and dramatic effect, as suggested by her reference to the feudal Chinese stage. Yet, the presence of "you"—presumably Smedley—in the narrative reminds the reader of this mediated, performative nature of the text itself, rather than hiding the relationship between the author and the subject and thereby naturalizing the author's representation of the Chinese subject.

In "Yu-kung Speaks of Battle," Smedley uses the direct voice of the subject without inserting her own narrative voice.[32] The narrative starts and ends with a young soldier's rendering of his life and his experiences in the Red Army, told in the first person with no quotation marks. Still, Smedley makes clear her own presence in the construction and presentation of the narrative, by having the narrator address her in the second-person. Yu-kung begins by saying, "You think I am very young to be a soldier in the Red Army? No! For I am a worker. I was a worker in the mines when I was only seven years old, and we workers have no childhood. We have the responsibilities of men when we are children."[33] Thus, the narrator's speech directed at the "you" is also directed at the American reader through Smedley's narrative construction. Rather than creating an illusion of identification between the American reader and the Chinese subjects, Smedley's writing underscores the difference in their positions.

Smedley's challenges to dominant American discourse about China were also seen in her depictions of the real lives of contemporary Chinese people. Far from portraying the Chinese as an undifferentiated mass or creating an archetype, Smedley captured the diversity of identities and issues among the Chinese, including their explicit political and class positions. Smedley's uncompromised commitment to class struggle and her seeming marginalization of the issues of gender and sexuality in that struggle—both in her political agenda and in her own life—led some feminists to critique Smedley for privileging class issues.[34] It is true that Smedley did not view women's issues as the single most important agenda in the revolutionary movement. Nor did she devote the majority of her writing to portraying women. Smedley focused mainly on male subjects in portraying China's class revolution, growing nationalism, and its challenge to imperialism, and her final and the largest project was a biography of Chu Teh, a leader of the Chinese Communist Party.[35] It is also true that Smedley's view of gender and sexuality, shaped by a specifically white, working-class American context, led her to a particular kind of radical feminism which was often inapplicable to the Chinese context.

Smedley did not subordinate women's causes to class or national struggles, however. Nor did her idealized view of gender relations among the Chinese Communists blind her to the patriarchal oppression of women in China. In fact, she saw women's issues as one arena where class and national struggles were most distinctly played out. Unlike the popular Orientalist tendency to construct a monolithic view of Asian women as oppressed victims of the patriarchal order or to portray them as heroic rebels overthrowing such an order, Smedley's depictions of Chinese women captured the various ways in which women's bodies became the sites of ideological and cultural contestations, and illustrated the women's attempts to become historical actors and to regain control over their lives. Through these portrayals, Smedley showed how women's struggles against patriarchy were national struggles.

The connection between nationalist revolution and fight against patriarchy is portrayed in the story, "Hsu Mei-ling" (1930). In the figure of Hsu Mei-ling, Smedley presents a tragic story of an "old-fashioned girl, with the faults and virtues of an old-fashioned girl."[36] The protagonist embodies Chinese history through her unbound feet, which give her as much pain as when they were bound. As in many Western texts about Chinese women in this period, Chinese women's "freedom" from foot-binding is used as a metaphor for China's modernization. However, instead of presenting unbound feet simply as progress, Smedley's story shows that, for ordinary Chinese women, modernization and revolution entailed pain just as great as the suffering brought by feudalism and patriarchy. Smedley scornfully describes how Mei-ling's husband, who worships modernity and mimics Western lifestyle,

brought suffering to Mei-ling, who fails to adapt herself to the "modern" life he es-
pouses in Shanghai.[37] Dissatisfied and impatient with Mei-ling, her husband has
an affair with a "White Russian dancing girl." Mei-ling then decides to make herself
a "modern" woman, bobbing and waving her hair, shortening her gown almost to
the knees: "Below were her heavy, awkward ankles, tightly wrapped with bandages,
which one had not noticed before unless she walked."[38] She asks Smedley to teach
her to dance, "[b]ut to dance there must be joy in the heart and the feet must be
elastic, and light. And Mei-ling's heart was as heavy as lead and her feet had been
crippled while she was still a child. After taking a few lame steps, she stopped suddenly in the middle of the floor and wept like a little girl, holding the sleeve of her
gown before her face."[39] Smedley thus critiques the superficial importation of
Western culture (cheap upholstered furniture, gaudily colored prints of moonlight
on German and Swiss landscapes, a huge photograph of the Grand Central Station
in New York City, and a phonograph with American jazz records) which leads not
to freedom and equality but to another form of imperialism and patriarchy.
Through her portrayal of Mei-ling's and her husband's view of modernity and Westernization, Smedley critiques the imprints of Western imperialism as well as Chinese patriarchy.

Smedley also depicts a Chinese woman's failure to fully comprehend the political situation in "Martyr's Widow." The protagonist of the story is Hwa-chuan, the
wife of Deng Yin-chu, a Communist martyr. Being uneducated and materialistic,
Hwa-chuan fails to understand her husband's commitment to Communism, and
Den Yin-chu is executed partly because of her pettiness (she tries to bargain with
the officials and refuses to pay the sum they propose as a bribe). After his death, she
is celebrated as the martyr's widow, and eventually marries a high Kuomintang official and pledges to "be of more service than ever to the revolution."[40] The cynical
tone of the narrative and its portrayal of Hwa-chan's vulgarity underscores Smedley's consistent support of the Communist Party and her critique of the Kuomintang. What is more significant, however, is Smedley's construction of the relationship between gender and revolutionary politics. Through the character of
Hwa-chan, Smedley critiques not the women who are unable to see the meaning of
revolution but the patriarchal system that deprives women of political consciousness and manipulates them as tools of male-defined politics and revolution.

In contrast to the above two stories in which the women protagonists were unable
to comprehend and control their political circumstances, in "Shan-Fei, Communist," Smedley portrays Chinese women who have a clear sense of their historical
and political condition and actively exercise their agency as historical actors. The
protagonist, Shan-fei, is a daughter of a rich landowner in Hunan. She is given a
modern education by the determination and intrigues of her mother, who had sub-
missively endured and "appeared to bow her head to every wish of her husband who
held by all that was old and feudal."[41] Shan-fei grows up to think independently,

leads a student's strike against the corrupt administration of her school, and rebels against her betrothal to the son of a rich neighboring landlord by going on a hunger strike. Saved from the match by the landlord's first wife, Shan-fei becomes an active Communist and announces her unarranged marriage to a man she loves. She carries on propaganda among peasants and workers, works as a spy among the Kuomintang, undertakes the technical work of the party, is imprisoned and emerges diseased, and finally studies Marxist theory while in the hospital. Smedley concludes the story:

> There are those who will ask: "Is Shan-fei young and beautiful?"
> Shan-fei is twenty-five years of age. Her skin is dark and her face broad; her cheek bones are high. Her eyes midnight, but they glisten and seem to see through a darkness that is darker than the midnight in China. She is squarely built like a peasant and it seems that it would be very difficult to push her off the earth—so elemental is she, so firmly rooted to the earth. Beautiful? I do not know—is the earth beautiful?[42]

Readers find the story compelling not only for the courageous and committed life of Shan-fei and other young Communists, but also for the actions of women who belong to the generation oppressed by feudalism and patriarchy: her mother and the landlord's first wife. While they themselves lived within patriarchal gender ideologies, obeying their husbands who have many concubines, they have a clear view of history and high hopes for Shan-fei and manage to empower her. The life of Shan-fei as a revolutionary contrasts sharply with that of the two women, yet they each exercise historical agency in spite of the strictures of gender and class.

As these examples demonstrate, Smedley had a sophisticated understanding of women's relationship to history and the specificity of issues Chinese women faced. Just as she herself was struggling to negotiate between her political commitment and emotional needs and to challenge the sociocultural contexts which circumscribed her, she saw that Chinese women were fighting to find and assert their places amidst the historical transformation then taking place. Smedley recognized that the search for freedom and independence caused Chinese women great pain, and that China's historical, political, and ideological conflicts and change were most often played out in the issues of women and gender.

In 1941 Smedley left China because of her worsening health and the difficulties of carrying out her advocacy work during the war between Communist and Kuomintang units. After twenty-one years of living abroad, Smedley made a bittersweet homecoming to the United States, whose political climate was now very foreign to her. *Battle Hymn of China* was written during her residence in California and was published in 1943. Physically detached from China and trying to synthesize what she saw and found there, in *Battle Hymn of China* Smedley integrates her autobiographical recollections and her portrayals of the Red Army. Written in the context of World War II and the increasingly severe Japanese aggression in China, the book speaks eloquently to the American public of the Chinese struggle. As she did in *China Fights Back,* Smedley reflects on her self-positioning vis-à-vis China in terms of class, race, and gender. More than twelve years after she first landed in China, she articulates what she did not realize while she was fully absorbed in her self-assigned mission. Early in the narrative, she writes:

> Some people called me an idealist, others a fool; some called me both. Within my heart was some vague conviction that love and understanding begot love and understanding. For a long time I did not understand that most Chinese believe that all foreigners are rich. Nor did I realize how well dressed and well fed I seemed to the Chinese poor. To them I was nothing but a source of money. Once, when I fell while crossing a ditch in Peiping and lay unconscious, a crowd of Chinese, including a policeman, gathered around me, staring curiously—perhaps watching to see how a foreigner died. Not one offered to help, until by chance a student came by; he directed a ricksha coolie to take me to a hospital. Never had I felt so alone and deserted.
>
> From that time on I began to seek out men and women who were socially aware, to wait in patience until they learned to trust me. Live apart from the Chinese people I would not. The road to an understanding of them and their country led only into their ranks; nor did there seem any other way to justify my own existence among them.[43]

Her realization of not only her outsider status but also her racial and class privilege in China is particularly forceful since this passage comes after the first section of the book, "Glimpses of the Past," in which she reflects on her poor childhood and her quest for a free, independent life as a working woman.

For Smedley, the intersections of race, nationality, gender, sexuality, and class and the power dynamics that shaped those intersections were simultaneously a political and personal issue. Whereas in the West Smedley was unable to find an identity or life in which her gender or sexuality did not interfere with her class or racial politics, in Asia she saw a possibility of establishing a life in which she could put her sexuality aside and detach the personal from the political. After her involvement in the Indian nationalist movement ended precisely because her sexuality was used as a political weapon, Smedley chose to shape her gender and sexual identity in China in such a way that minimized its significance in her relationship with the Chinese. But despite her often painful struggle to detach her sexual and emotional desires from her political pursuits, she was also aware that her gender and sexuality, as well as her race and nationality, were distinct markers of the difference between her and the Chinese Communists with whom she identified.

Smedley also performed the role of a deliverer of the Chinese voice and conveyed to American readers Chinese women's—and men's—nationalist struggle for liberation. Conscious of being an onlooker, she became increasingly aware of her relative position of privilege as a white American woman in China. That bittersweet recognition and her application of that awareness to her writing enabled a narrative that neither presumed to speak for the subjects nor used the subjects' voice for the writer's own expressive purposes. The role Smedley performed in China made a clear break from the tradition of Orientalist performances.

Authorizing Asia

"Popular Expert on China"
Authority and Gender in Pearl S. Buck's
The Good Earth

*I*n 1931, two years after Agnes Smedley's *Daughter of Earth* came out, Pearl Buck's novel, *The Good Earth*, was published and became a best-seller. That two female American writers published novels using the Earth as central motifs within a two-year period was not simply coincidental. The motif reflected the social awareness shared by many writers of the Depression period concerned with the relationship between individuals and the capitalist society. For many women writers, the earth was an effective metaphor to interrogate not only the capitalist economy but also the issues of gender and sexuality. Both *Daughter of Earth* and *The Good Earth* strikingly captured the relationship between humanity and the earth.

The earths they portrayed were geographically and culturally distant from one another, however: Smedley's earth was the American West, Buck's was that of rural China. Yet in their personal lives, Smedley and Buck shared their dedication to the same earth distant from their American home—China. Both women became outspoken advocates for China and wrote prolifically about China for American readers. When the two women got acquainted upon Smedley's return to the United States in 1941, they found they had more in common than they had expected. At different times, each had had an affair with a romantic Shanghai poet Xu Zhimo.[1] The women liked each other: Buck, who had achieved a world-class reputation, offered to help Smedley in arranging speaking engagements. Smedley was impressed by Buck's energy and courage in addressing issues of racism.

In addition to their dedication to China, Smedley and Buck shared another concern and commitment. Both had troubled relationships with the dominant ideology of gender and sexuality that shaped the early part of their lives. Buck's father embraced religious fundamentalism and consistently displayed a misogynist attitude toward his wife and his daughters. Buck's first husband, John Lossing Buck, did not provide her with the emotional and sexual intimacy she needed. Moreover, having spent the first half of her life in China, Buck was also highly exposed to the patriarchal structure and misogynistic culture of Chinese society. Thus, Buck shared with Smedley a deep concern with the causes of women and gender equality in China as well as in the United States.

Despite their shared commitment to China and to issues of gender and sexuality, the two women's relationships to China also differed greatly from one another. Smedley arrived in China in 1929, after writing *Daughter of Earth*. She spent all of the 1930s there and aligned herself explicitly and consistently with the Communists. On the other hand, by the time Buck wrote *The Good Earth*, she had already spent the first half of her life in China as a daughter of Presbyterian missionaries and later as the wife of an agricultural economist conducting research in rural villages across North China. Her upbringing was therefore bicultural and bilingual. After returning to the United States in 1934 and becoming a civil rights activist and a leader in promoting cross-cultural understanding between the United States and Asia, however, she never set foot on the Chinese soil again. While a strong advocate of progressive politics, Buck, unlike Smedley, had a deep skepticism for the Communists. Her work and rhetoric were less political or ideological than moral and humanitarian.[2]

The American public responded very differently to the lives and works of the two women. Although Smedley was the only American woman who worked with the Chinese Communists throughout the 1930s and had a first-hand experience of the revolution, her impact on American public opinion was relatively small, and she never became as well-known as Buck. While Communist sympathizers and radicals welcomed Smedley's writings, her work never reached far beyond the leftist community.[3] On the other hand, Buck's writings, speeches, and various political and social activities captured the attention of mainstream America.

Indeed, Pearl S. Buck became the most influential figure in constructing China in the American mind during the first half of the twentieth century. Historian Michael Hunt's characterization of Buck as "Popular Expert on China" was quite appropriate.[4] Her most acclaimed novel, *The Good Earth*, was a best-seller in 1931 and 1932 and was awarded the Pulitzer Prize and the Howells Medal of the American Academy of Arts and Letters. The book was adapted into a Broadway play in 1932 and made into a motion picture in 1936, which attracted 23 million Americans to movie theaters. Juvenile editions of *The Good Earth* were published, and students at all levels were assigned to read the book as an introduction to Chinese culture. In 1938, Buck became the first American woman to win the Nobel Prize for Literature. As of 1970, her work had been translated into 145 different languages and dialects. In a study of American views of China, historian Harold Isaacs stated: "It can almost be said that for a whole generation of Americans she 'created' the Chinese, in the same sense that Dickens 'created' for so many of us the people who lived in the slums of Victorian England."[5]

The Good Earth contributed to the "favorable" image of the Chinese as hard-working, land-loving people engaged in the same economic struggle as Americans were during the Depression. Buck re-created and re-presented China for the American public for whom China could only be imagined as a remote Oriental land. The public reception of Buck's work marked a major shift in American views of China, which had previously been dominated by visions of a mythic and timeless past or the blatant racism manifested in the Heathen Chinee, Fu Manchu, and Charlie Chan stereotypes.[6]

While the book raised popular interest in Asia, intellectuals' opinions on its literary or social value were quite mixed. In particular, Buck's receiving the Nobel Prize in 1938 sent most of the literary elite into an orbit of rage. "It should have gone to Theodore Dreiser, Sherwood Anderson, or some other . . . but not to this upstart missionary woman from China," they argued.[7] The debate over *The Good Earth* often centered around the novel's political, social, and moral standing rather than its literary or artistic merit. Some critics praised the novel on the basis of its "universal" appeal and its contribution to the understanding of China. For example, critic Carl Van Doren asserted that in "the United States, which had a special friendly liking for China, *The Good Earth* for the first time made the Chinese seem as familiar as neighbors."[8] Another commentator noted that *The Good Earth* made "American readers aware, in the lives of a completely alien people, of universal human bonds."[9]

On the other hand, critics who disapproved of the novel critiqued it for the lack of "authenticity" and "accuracy" in its portrayal of China. Claims of inaccuracy came mostly from Chinese critics who declared that Buck depicted the lowliest members of Chinese society and that she caricatured the Chinese by emphasizing "a few special points and [she] makes things appear queer and unnatural to both Western and Chinese eyes."[10] One critic commented that the novel fell short because Buck failed to achieve true sisterhood with the Chinese and to create a meaningful bond between China and the West:

Unfortunately, Mrs. Buck's substance stops with mere observations. In spite of her abundant sympathy, the native reader cannot but feel that the author of "The Good Earth" is, after all, a foreigner, who has never mixed with the Chinese more than what is permitted by the relation between the mistress and the amah, or between a student and a tutor. There cannot have been any intimate association of minds and hearts such as could be obtained only from the free and frank comradeship of everyday life. In spite of her long residence in China, Mrs. Buck seems to have held faithfully to her Teutonic tradition: she always keeps herself apart from the nation of which she writes, and never becomes a part of it. The result of this aloofness is that nearly all her characters in "The Good Earth" are types, and not individuals.[11]

Yet another group of critics considered much of Buck's writing excessively sentimental, moralistic, and artistically immature, and characterized it as "woman's fiction" rather than a "serious" work of literature.

This chapter analyzes the cultural politics of *The Good Earth* and examines the meaning of Buck's position as the "Popular Expert" on China—in other words, how her popularity and expertise were constructed in relation to both her Western readers and her Chinese subjects. The key to Buck's popularity lay in her discursive strategy, which engaged both the discourse of Orientalism and the discourse of gender. She employed the tools of two distinct genres—ethnography and domestic fiction—in order to reorganize the history of China's modernization into a coherent and comprehensible narrative without fundamentally challenging or altering the constructs of American Orientalism. By skillfully employing the discursive techniques of ethnography, she secured her own authority. Through her mastery and display of ethnographic details and her construction of an authorial narrative voice, she simultaneously established her position of expertise vis-à-vis her Western readers and gained authority over her Chinese subjects. Buck used gender to explain China, employing it as a category of analysis and domestic fiction as a narrative genre to both universalize and racialize her Chinese subjects. In doing so, she constructed a "universal" narrative that transcended the historical and cultural specificities of the Chinese setting, while simultaneously naturalizing the link between Chinese culture and particular gender relations and sexuality.

The establishment of Buck's authority and the canonization of *The Good Earth* emerged out of the existing discourse of Orientalism and contributed to the increasingly systematized and institutionalized body of knowledge and representation of Asia. Buck and her second husband Richard Walsh played a role in the institutionalization of Orientalist knowledge in the United States through their founding of the East and West Association, an organization for educational exchange, and their publication of the magazine *Asia*, which had a substantial influence on American opinion about East Asia. Buck's authority as a China expert demonstrates that, by the 1930s, white, middle-class American women were not only integral participants in Orientalism but could also serve as authorities.

The Good Earth is a Horatio Alger-like story of Wang Lung and his family, who rise from humble peasant origins to become a family of great wealth during the period when China transformed itself into a modern nation. Wang Lung marries O-lan, a kitchen slave in a wealthy family, who gives birth to three sons and a mentally retarded daughter. The family is struck by a famine and forced to leave the land to live as beggars in the city. They regain their land amidst the chaos of political uprising and come to accumulate great wealth through hard work in the fields. At the end of the story, Wang Lung's sons grow up and leave the land.

As she constructs this narrative combining personal drama with historical and cultural interest, Buck carefully employs the discursive modes and structures of ethnography. Buck's ethnographic knowledge and its textual display do not simply provide the basis for the plausibility of the plot and characters. Her mastery of ethnographic detail of Chinese life and society as well as her mode of narration clearly separates the author/narrator from the subjects, placing Buck in a position of superiority over her Chinese subjects.[12] Buck's ability to present a vision of China's social structure and culture, which neither Wang Lung nor any other character has, is a manifestation of her cultural and discursive authority over China.

The novel opens with Wang Lung, the protagonist, waking up on the morning of his marriage.

He hurried out to the middle room, drawing on his blue outer trousers as he went, and knotting about the fullness at his waist his girdle of blue cotton cloth. He left his upper body bare until he had heated water to bathe himself. He went into the shed which was the kitchen, leaning against the house, and out of its dusk an ox twisted its head from behind the corner next the door and lowed at him deeply. The kitchen was made of earthen bricks as the house was, great squares of earth dug from their own fields, and thatched with straw from their own wheat. Out of their own earth had his grandfather in his youth fashioned also the oven, baked and black with many years of meal preparing. On top of this earthen structure stood a deep, round, iron cauldron.

This cauldron he filled partly full of water, dipping it with a half gourd from an earthen jar that stood near, but he dipped cautiously, for water was precious. Then, after a hesitation, he suddenly lifted the jar and emptied all the water into the cauldron. This day he would bathe his whole body. Not since he was a child upon his mother's knee had anyone looked upon his body. Today one would, and he would have it clean.[13]

The elements illustrated here show a striking resemblance to the materials commonly described in ethnographies: the physical features of the dwelling, the economic condition of the environment and the character's status, rules and expectations governing the marriage system, ways of dressing, ways of making fire and cooking, and so on. Significantly, the text does not specifically state that the story is set in rural China, yet the Other-ness of the setting is clear to American readers.

The opening chapters also describe the gradually changing social climate in rural China. Wang Lung's conversation with the barber about cutting his braid suggests the modern lifestyle overtaking traditional Chinese customs. The impudence of merchants and the presence of beggars on the commercial street expose the increasing penetration of the market economy and the growing class stratification in the area. The prevalence of bribery, overflowing wealth, and opium addiction in the House of Hwang reveal the corruption of the dominant class.

While Buck considered herself a friend of the Chinese people and distinguished herself from the notions of racial and cultural supremacy commonly held by Western missionaries in China, her authority as a writer was nonetheless embedded in and emerged out of the unequal power relations between the West and China. However, the discursive functions of *The Good Earth* are too complex to be dismissed simply as Orientalist. The uniqueness of the book lies in Buck's narrative techniques, which allow her to simultaneously maintain the basic power structure in the relationship between the author and her subject and to mask the novel's Orientalist bent by presenting the story as a sympathetic portrayal of the Chinese.

The first of such techniques is the erasure of the author's subjectivity. In *The Good Earth*, the presence and subjectivity of Buck as the American woman author is skillfully erased, on the levels of both narrative style and content. An outsider looking in from above, the author does not impinge upon the story's action, but presents and frames the entire text in the third person. The narrative does not make visible the author's racial or gender identity. Except for the scenes of Wang Lung's brief encounters with the missionaries, there are no foreign characters in the novel, and the issue of the Western impact on China's modernization is referred to only indirectly. In addition, by using representative speech, as shown in the above quotations, Buck presents Chinese social structure through the voice of Chinese characters and avoids judgment from a Western perspective. Particularly in the context of ethnography, the erasure of the author's subjectivity was a crucial element during the period when anthropologists sought to establish their field as a scientific and systematized discipline. To be recognized as "valid," "objective," and "scientific," the modern ethnographer needed to purify the narrative of his/her subjectivity and write "degree zero." For that purpose, the presence of the author in the text was minimized or managed so that he/she did not interfere with the facticity of the reality reported in the text.[14] The text thus maintained the distinction between the writing subject and the written object by making the former invisible and focusing on the presumably neutral description of the observed.

Buck's second technique is the annihilation of geographical and historical specificity. Throughout the novel, she never mentions any proper place names. Instead, she uses more vague and symbolic references such as "the country," "the South," "the coastal city," and "the land." Similarly, the historical events that occur during the course of the novel are left elusive. Nowhere in the book does she mention the years during which the story takes place. Although the narrative refers to the contemporary social climate and events such as the penetration by Western powers, antiforeign rebellions, and nationalist movements, Buck negates such historical specificity by constructing Wang Lung as an ignorant farmer who does not comprehend the social changes taking place around him. Instead of directly engaging with current events, Buck centers the story around the presumably ahistorical, timeless, and universal relationship between the man and the land. The narrative repeatedly underscores Wang Lung's rootedness in the land and the farming life, and evokes a sense of unchanging landscape in which people work the earth. In such a landscape, unstable forces such as class conflict, economic dislocation, political and military struggles, and the confrontations with the foreign, are rendered secondary to the more pressing issue of the family's life on the land. By annihilating geographical and historical specificity, the narrative denies the temporal coevalness of the land and people being described and turns them into static, ahistorical objects, turning the tale into a sort of allegory that generates another—more "universal"— level of meaning beyond the specifics of the narrative.[15] The technique also functions to evade positioning the novel in relation to the political and ideological debate over China's modernization, a subject Buck was more than qualified to discuss and addressed in her numerous articles and lectures.

The third technique is the use of a unique language style that functions to infantalize the characters. With the frequent use of inversion and the repetition of short, simple sentences, Buck's language in *The Good Earth* has an archaic and austere tone similar to that of the Bible or, seen from another perspective, to that of children's literature. This style could be a product of Buck's missionary background and/or her immersion in the Chinese language which made English prose somewhat foreign to her. Such a style functions to construct Wang Lung and other Chinese characters as childlike figures who do not think beyond the simple matters of life. Buck's use of the literal translation of certain Chinese words, instead of the equivalent words in English, functions in a similar vein. For example, instead of "train," she uses the expression, "firewagon"; "flying boat" instead of "airplane"; "electric letter" for "telegram."[16] Such a technique not only evokes the exotic atmosphere of the setting but also stresses that Wang Lung is childlike, ignorant, and premodern. By doing so, the novel suggests the politico-economic, technological, and intellectual level of the Chinese as embodied in the figure of Wang Lung.

The erasure of the author's subjectivity, annihilation of historical and geographic specificity, and infantalization of characters—all of these techniques are embedded in the discursive functions of modern ethnography. They convert the narrative from a work of pure fiction into an enabling code of Orientalist knowledge and grant Buck the authority of an expert. The way in which the author is presented to the readers reveals the importance of her authority to the text. The first sentence of her biography in the first edition of *The Good Earth* reads: "Pearl S. Buck has always lived in China." The experience of living in China for over twenty years and witnessing China's vast social changes during that period presumably gives her a unique knowledge and power.

The significance of Buck's ethnographic authority is also seen in the extensive response Buck gave to the *New York Times* review of *The Good Earth* written by a Chinese critic. She declares:

> In the first place let me say that [Kiang Kang-Hu] is distinctly right in saying that I have painted a picture of Chinese that is not the ordinary portrait, and not like those portraits which are usually not completed until after the death of the subject. Any one who knows those portraits must realize how far from the truth of life they are; the set pose, the arranged fold, the solemn, stately countenance, the official button. I have dealt in lights and shades, I have purposely omitted the official button, I do not ask the subject if he recognizes himself—lest he prefers the portrait with the official button! I only picture him as he is to me. Nor do I apologize.[17]

Then Buck goes on to claim that every detail which the reviewer decried as being "false" was actually "real" and that she had seen it with her own eyes. Acknowledging that China is after all a huge country with varied local customs, she states that "[f]or this reason I have deliberately chosen to localize my customs fairly closely, in order to be accurate at least to one region. In addition, I verify my accounts by reading them to Chinese friends of that region."[18] Buck's effort to defend her ethnographic expertise demonstrates the importance of perceptions of accuracy and authenticity in the making of her narrative.[19]

Buck's reliance on ethnographic narrativization becomes particularly important when one considers the significance of anthropology as a growing body of social science in this period and the role of missionaries and women in relation to this development. In the decade preceding the publication of *The Good Earth*, anthropology came to be established as a systematized and scientific branch of knowledge. As methodological values and structures became standardized in newly-founded anthropology departments in research-oriented institutions such as Columbia University and the University of Chicago, fieldwork-based ethnography became the conventional procedure for recording the observations of foreign cultures. Believing in fieldwork, a holistic approach, and relativistic valuation, academic anthropology replaced the works of travelers, missionaries, and government officials who recorded their observations for their specific purposes and audience. Prior to the development of modern anthropology, missionaries were the chief providers of information about the land and the people they endeavored to convert. Missionaries' reports were generally considered more reliable than those of "naturalists" who resided in the area only for a short period of time and never learned the language. However, as emergent anthropology focused its interest on the culture and social structure of a certain area, and as religious beliefs came to be considered a central component of culture and society, the reports of missionaries whose primary concern was to convert "heathens" to Christianity gradually lost their credibility in the face of observations of academically-trained fieldworkers.[20] At the same time, the objectives of mission work and anthropology also dovetailed, with missionaries and former missionaries with language skills and local knowledge playing an indispensable role in the institutionalization of Orientalism in the 1920s.[21]

In this context of the development of anthropological discourse, Buck was positioned at a transitional juncture. Being a daughter of Presbyterian missionaries to China, she inherited many of the Victorian and evangelical ideals of her parents. On the other hand, spending her childhood with Chinese amahs and Chinese children, she became keenly aware and critical of Western missionaries in China who, in her view, were comfortably stationed within the walls of their quarters and knew little of the China they were trying to save.[22] In the transition from Victorian evangelism and Progressive reform to relativist social science, Buck had the advantage of understanding the values and paradigms of both forms of knowledge and later came to play an important role in institutionalized forms of Orientalist expertise.

Gender also shaped Buck's relationship to anthropological discourse and an ethnographic mode of writing. Coming of age at the turn of the century, Buck lived during the period when white, middle-class women's lives went through a vast transformation in America, demanding equal rights and opportunities. Women's role in the understanding of foreign cultures reflected this transformation. During the height of the missionary enterprise, women played important roles despite their exclusion from actual religious work, by exercising the power of intimacy and preaching what historian Jane Hunter has called "the gospel of gentility."[23] Women missionaries generally mastered the language more quickly than men, had access to women's quarters, gained intimate, personal relationships with native men and women, and engaged in moral and intellectual instruction. However biased by their religious beliefs and racial thinking, their reports to the home missions and their letters to families and friends were a rich source of information about the culture and peoples of foreign nations. Then, with the emergence of modern anthropology, women entered the academic enterprise of understanding other cultures, with the most prominent contributions made by Margaret Mead and Ruth Benedict. Because anthropologists viewed gender norms and kin network as central factors in cultural and social structure, women's access to family life advanced that knowledge. Anthropology, like emerging academic disciplines of sociology and psychology, offered a means for educated white American women to expand their sphere of life, enter the male-dominated world of academia, and participate and intervene in the masculinist discourse of imperialism, colonialism, and/or Orientalism.[24]

While ethnographic narrativization offered Buck an Orientalist authority, that alone does not explain the enormous popularity she and her work gained. Orientalist discourse was produced and consumed in the United States long before Buck's time, and there were many writings about China available in the 1930s. Yet none gained the popularity or impact of Buck's work. What marked *The Good Earth* as uniquely different from other forms of writing about China was the second genre and discourse from which the novel derived its essence: domestic fiction and gender. Buck's use of domestic fiction, with emphasis on themes of gender, sexuality, family, and domesticity, enabled her both to universalize the narrative and to racialize her Chinese subject. The use of domestic narrative supported, rather than subverted, the Orientalist framework she established through her ethnographic narrativization.

Rather than positioning the domestic site as a retreat from the "public" sphere, the novel demonstrates the domestic site as the embodiment of historical and political contestations. Using domesticity as an organizing thread, *The Good Earth* translates "public" issues into common language, making China's historical, social, or cultural specificities accessible to American readers. Through various incidents that befall Wang Lung, *The Good Earth* explains to the reader the vast social changes and ideological issues involved in China's clash with modernity—namely, the growth of the commercial economy and the greater stratification of class; the disparity between life in the city and on the farm; imperialism and the penetration of Western powers; and the rise of nationalism and military unrest.

Yet *The Good Earth* is also different from most domestic fiction, first because it does not construct women as agents of political power who ultimately take control over social reality through their sentimental power. The protagonist of the novel is the patriarch, Wang Lung, and O-lan remains an impressive yet marginalized figure throughout the novel. And although O-lan embodies self-sacrifice which ultimately leads to her death, it does not have a critical impact on the plot. Although many reviews of the novel have framed O-lan as the heroine, her heroism lay in the power of her silence and perseverance, rather than in her agency to change the world around her. Secondly, the novel differs from other domestic fiction because it does not highlight the emotional and sentimental intensity of the characters. On the contrary, the novel stresses the lack of, or repression of, emotions in the characters: O-lan does not cry or complain as Wang Lung mistreats her and indulges in his extra-marital affair, and Wang Lung does not shed a tear in facing his wife's death.

Despite these differences from typical domestic fiction, *The Good Earth* reconstructs and rewrites the "public" issues of Chinese history by envisioning them as issues of family, gender, and domesticity. For example, the meaning of social class is embodied in male-female relations, as manifested in Wang Lung's relationship with women. In the first chapter, this poor, timid farmer goes to the great House of Hwang to receive his bride. He encounters the gateman who contemptuously demands a bribe to let him in the estate; then he receives his wife from the satin-robed Old Mistress who sits on a splendidly carved dais and indulges in opium-smoking. During this visit, Wang Lung is repeatedly made aware of what appears, at this point in the novel, to be the insurmountable class difference between himself and the Hwangs. This is underscored most forcefully by the meaning of his marriage. His wife, O-lan, is one of the kitchen slaves in the House of Hwang, and Wang Lung's father has "purchased" her from her owner with "two silver rings, washed with gold, and silver earrings" (10). She was selected for the work she could carry out for the household and not for her beauty, as a conversation between the groom and his father shows:

> Wang Lung had suffered that she must not be pretty. . . . His father, seeing his mutinous face, had cried out at him,
> "And what will we do with a pretty woman? We must have a woman who will tend the house and bear children as she works in the fields, and will a pretty woman do these things? She will be forever thinking about clothes to go with her face! No, not a pretty woman in our house. We are farmers. Moreover, who has heard of a pretty slave who was virgin in a wealthy house? All the young lords have had their fill of her. It is better to be first with an ugly woman than the hundredth with a beauty. . ." (9–10)

The passage demonstrates not only the objectification and commodification of women as laborers and reproductive tools but also that a man's wealth determined the sexual relations he practiced and a woman's sexuality determined her economic value in the market.

The interdependence of class and gender as well as domesticity becomes clearer as Wang Lung's relationship with O-lan and other women evolves along with his class status. In the initial stage of their marriage, when Wang Lung is a poor farmer, he is satisfied with his hard-working wife who toils in the field and gives birth to his sons. But once he becomes wealthy, "O-lan he would not allow to work in the fields for he was no longer a poor man, but a man who could hire his labor done" (140). As he attains wealth, the reconstruction of his domestic life and his ideas about sexuality play a key role in his emulation of middle-class and upper-class life. Wang Lung is increasingly irritated by O-lan's appearance only after he becomes rich:

"I mean, cannot you buy a little oil for your hair as other women do and make yourself a new coat of black cloth? And those shoes you wear are not fit for a land proprietor's wife, such as you now are."

But she answered nothing, only looked at him humbly and without knowing what she did, and she hid her feet one over the other under the bench on which she sat. Then, although in his heart he was ashamed that he reproached this creature who through all these years had followed him faithfully as a dog, and although he remembered that when he was poor and labored in the fields himself she left her bed even after a child was born and came to help him in the harvest fields, yet he could not stem the irritation in his breast and he went on ruthlessly. . . (150)

The contrast between Wang Lung's modest hope at the beginning of the novel that his wife not be pock-marked and his later disgust with his wife for not being sexually attractive demonstrates how the transformation of his class status affected his ideas about women. Through a repeated emphasis on O-lan's self-sacrificing devotion and on Wang Lung's sense of guilt for reproaching her about her appearance, the narrative underscores that the change in Wang Lung's perception of his wife is brought about by the change in his class status rather than a simple change of heart. Later in the novel, Wang Lung obtains a concubine, Lotus. The contrast between the status of Lotus (a former prostitute purchased for concubinage) and that of O-lan (a former slave purchased for marriage), the very practice of concubinage, and Wang Lung's neglect of O-lan after buying Lotus all demonstrate the ways in which Buck uses gender, sexuality, and domesticity to highlight the issues of class.

The economy—both agrarian and commercial—is also rewritten as a narrative of domesticity. Stricken by a famine, the Wangs are forced to leave the land and to live in the city practically as beggars. The urban economy, of which the Wangs constitute the basest stratum, threatens the integrity of the family's domesticity. Being forced to leave the land on which they had built their self-sufficiency and patriarchal family order, the Wangs face the loss of autonomy. Wang Lung's need to make O-lan and his children beg for money threatens his masculine authority as provider for the family. While he labors as a rickshaw-puller to earn a meager sum, O-lan reverts to her earlier life as a beggar in order to support her family. Wang Lung becomes aware that he is beginning to lose his authority over his children as his son starts to steal food. While O-lan is tolerant of her son's action, Wang Lung concludes, "We must get back to the land" (100), the only place where he can sustain his patriarchal authority and the domestic order.

The narrative of domesticity also allows the text to engage larger political and ideological issues, such as Western imperialism and Chinese nationalism. The city setting gives the reader a glimpse of the Western presence in China and the forces and implications of Western imperialism, but these are rendered from the perspective of

Wang Lung's domestic life. As a novice rickshaw-puller untrained to negotiate with the customer over the fee, Wang Lung is scorned by his peers, "Know this, idiot, only white foreigners can be taken without argument! Their tempers are like quick lime, but when they say 'Come' you may come and trust them, for they are such fools they do not know the proper price of anything, but let the silver run out of their pockets like water" (92). Although this phrase expresses the Chinese manipulation of foreigners, it is clear that they are simultaneously dependent on and controlled by the economic power of the Westerners. Given such power relations between the "white foreigners" and the Chinese poor in the modernizing/Westernizing city, it is significant that the first white foreigner whom Wang Lung ever encounters is a female missionary.

> It was only one day when he was on the street of the silk markets looking for a passenger that he learned better than he had known, and that there were those who were more foreign than he in this city. He happened on this day to pass by the door of a shop from whence ladies sometimes came after purchasing silks within, and sometimes thus he secured one who paid him better than most. And on this day someone did come out on him suddenly, a creature the like of whom he had never seen before. He had no idea of whether it was male or female, but it was tall and dressed in a straight black robe of some rough harsh material and there was the skin of a dead animal wrapped about its neck. As he passed, the person, whether male or female, motioned to him sharply to lower the shafts and he did so, and when he stood erect again, dazed at what had befallen him, the person in broken accents directed that he was to go to the Street of Bridges. He began to run hurriedly, scarcely knowing what he did, and once he called to another puller whom he knew casually in the day's work,
> "Look at this—what is this I pull?"
> And the man shouted back at him,
> "A foreigner—a female from America—you are rich—"
> But Wang Lung ran as fast as he could for fear of the strange creature behind him, and when he reached the Street of Bridges he was exhausted and dripping with his sweat.
> This female stepped out then and said in the same broken accents, "You need not have run yourself to death," and left him with two silver pieces in his palm, which was double the usual fare. (95–96)

Wang Lung's inability to tell the sex of the customer shows that the ideas about gender and sexuality developed through his peasant Chinese upbringing are completely useless in the face of Western culture. Furthermore, the female white missionary serves as a generous provider for Wang Lung, who is now unable to financially support his family, thus undermining his masculine authority. This scene emasculates China and the powerless Chinese man in the face of the West by drawing a link between gender dynamics, on the one hand, and the vast economic and political power imbalance between China and the West, on the other.

Wang Lung's encounter with the white female missionary is also significant in that it causes him to recognize his own Chinese identity in relation to other races. He realizes that the missionary woman was "indeed a foreigner and more foreign yet than he in this city, and that after all people of black hair and black eyes are one sort and people of light hair and light eyes of another sort, and he was no longer after that wholly foreign in the city," but in fact "belonged to his own kind, who have black hair and black eyes" (96). The encounter with the white woman thus marks Wang Lung as both emasculated and as Chinese/Asian/non-white in the eyes of both Wang Lung himself and the Western readers.

Chinese peasants' encounters with the West is also rendered from a domestic per-spective. Shortly after serving the white female missionary, Wang Lung sees another white foreigner, this time a male missionary who hands him a drawing of Christ. Wang Lung, being illiterate and ignorant, cannot make sense of the paper.

> He carried the picture home at night and showed it to the old man. But he also could not read and they discussed its possible meaning, Wang Lung and the old man and the two boys. The two boys cried out in delight and horror,
> "And see the blood streaming out of his side!"
> And the old man said,
> "Surely this was a very evil man to be thus hung."
> But Wang Lung was fearful of the picture and pondered as to why a foreigner had given it to him, whether or not some brother of this foreigner's had not been so treated and the other brethren seeking revenge. He avoided, therefore, the street on which he had met the man and after a few days, when the paper was forgotten, O-lan took it and sewed it into a shoe sole together with other bits of paper she picked up here and there to make the soles firm. (109–110)

Instead of directly engaging in the debate over the effects and implications of im-porting Christianity into China, Buck stresses the distance between such an ideo-logical debate and the everyday lives of the common Chinese family, for whom a picture of Christ means nothing more than paper to support shoe soles.

The rise of nationalism, militarism, and warlordism is also told in terms of what they mean to Wang Lung's family. Wang Lung—whose ignorance distanced from the political forces outside of his world and to whom "war was a thing like earth and sky and water and why it was no one knew but only that it was" (232)—witnesses the rise of nationalist militarism when his nephew, a soldier, comes with his fellow sol-diers to the wealthy Wang Lung's estate. To him, the soldiers are nothing but a horde of invaders of his peaceful life on the estate, as they tear at the trees and the flowers in the garden, ruin the furniture, and kill the golden fish in the pond. Most significantly, the sojourning soldiers threaten the purity of the women in the family.

Fearing that unless he provides his nephew with a slave he would take any woman in the house, Wang Lung arranges for one of the female slaves to cater to the soldier's sexual needs. Upon leaving Wang Lung's estate after a month and a half long visit, the soldier boasts of having made the slave pregnant: "Well, and if I come not back to you I have left you my second self and a grandson for my mother, and it is not every man who can leave a son where he stops for a moon or two, and it is one of the benefits of the soldier's life—his seed springs up behind him and others must tend it!" (293). The rise of nationalism and militarism symbolized by the soldiers' tour thus functions in the narrative not as a political event or issue but as a threat to domesticity. If the slave conceived the nephew's son, she could claim a place in the family, but the baby being a girl, "it was only a slave bearing a slave, and she was no more than before" (294). The soldiers' visit also has an impact on Wang Lung's domesticity because during this incident Wang Lung notices a pale, delicate slave called Pear Blossom who begs not to be mated with the soldier. Feeling pity for the child, Wang Lung arranges for another slave to do the service. Later in the novel, he takes Pear Blossom as his second concubine. Therefore, the soldiers' visit brings another change in the structure of the gender/sexual roles in the family.

All of these issues—class, the economy of the city, Western imperialism, and Chinese nationalism and militarism—are tied together by the metaphor of the land that runs throughout the novel. Buck had a strong faith in the strength of farmers in rural China, and the novel refers to the land and the farming life as the backbone of China. The vision of the land in the novel is constructed in specifically gendered terms. Man achieves and sustains identity and integrity by owning and cultivating the fertile land. The land unites the family, educates the children, and helps reconstitute traditional mores in times of crises. On the other hand, woman's fate parallels that of the land: both are purchased and worked on by man, with their primary function to reproduce. The vivid imagery of O-lan's hard labor on the land, even on the day of her childbirth, underlines the analogy between the heroic female figure and the land and symbolizes China's ever-lasting strength. Like the land which always remains the same despite vast social upheavals, O-lan's image never changes throughout the novel. While Wang Lung experiences the rise and fall in his fortunes that are reflected in changes in his own character and behavior, O-lan remains an obedient yet strong-willed, hard-working woman even as a vast historical and socioeconomic transformation surrounds her. The inscription of such gendered meanings of the land, which ties the man and the woman together, is symbolized by the impressive image of the couple toiling together:

The sun beat down upon them, for it was early summer, and her face was soon dripping with her sweat. Wang Lung had his coat off and his back bare, but she worked with her thin garment covering her shoulders and it grew wet and clung to her like skin. Moving together in a perfect rhythm, without a word, hour after hour, he fell into a union with her which took the pain from his labor. He had no articulate thought of anything; there was only this perfect sympathy of movement, of turning this earth of theirs over and over to the sun, this earth which formed their home and fed their bodies and made their gods. The earth lay rich and dark, and fell apart lightly under the points of their hoes. Sometimes they turned up a bit of brick, a splinter of wood. It was nothing. Some time, in some age, bodies of men and women had been buried there, houses had stood there, had fallen, and gone back into the earth. So would also their house, some time, return into the earth, their bodies also. Each had his turn at this earth. They worked on, moving together—together—producing the fruit of this earth. . . . (28–29)

When O-lan confesses to Wang Lung that she is pregnant, Wang Lung rejoices with the thought: "Well, it was their turn at this earth!" (29).

The gendered symbolism of the land epitomizes the way in which Buck rewrites the history of China's modernization in terms of a domestic narrative. Gender and domesticity in the text function as the site where historical conflicts between tradition and modernity get played out in personal and tangible forms. In this sense, using gender as a category of analysis and domestic fiction as a narrative genre enables Buck to eliminate or dissolve the Chinese specificities of the tale, and to "universalize" and "popularize" the narrative. The novel constructs a universalized landscape which subsumes other issues and categories—such as class, race, and nation—under a unified narrative about gender and domesticity.

However, gender also serves to reinforce cultural differences, particularly between white, middle-class gender norms and Chinese ones. The text naturalizes the link between Chinese culture and a particular gender ideology (i. e. patriarchy) and sexual relations (represented by Wang Lung's extramarital relationships). Consequently, it reproduces the dominant Orientalist discourse that uses gender and sexual ideology to codify the East-West binary.

At the core of Buck's descriptions of the Chinese setting is its patriarchal family structure and gender ideology. It is not Chinese history but non-historicized ideas about gender, family, and domesticity that mark the Chinese-ness, Asian-ness, or non-Western-ness of the setting most vividly. Buck begins to delineate this quite clearly early in the novel, by recounting Wang Lung's thoughts :

This was the last morning he would have to light the fire. He had lit it every morning since his mother died six years before. He had lit the fire, boiled water, and poured the water into a bowl and taken it into the room where his father sat upon his bed, coughing and fumbling for his shoes upon the floor. Every morning for these six years the old man had waited for his son to bring in hot water to ease him of his morning coughing. Now father and son could rest. There was a woman coming to the house. Never again would Wang Lung have to rise summer and winter at dawn to light the fire. He could lie in his bed and wait, and he also would have a bowl of water brought to him, and if the earth were fruitful there would be tea leaves in the water. Once in some years it was so. (4–5)

Here, the reader is informed of the patriarchal family mores which bind the son in obedience to his father and which takes for granted that the woman in the house will serve both the father and the son. The patriarchal and patrilineal family structure is further underscored by Wang Lung's and his father's expectations for children yet to be born: "Now the grandsons were coming, grandsons upon grandsons!" (5).

By repeatedly stressing that patriarchal gender relations and family structure are central factors of Chinese life, the narrative makes patriarchy—which of course is an issue in the West as well—into a marker of Chinese-ness that is distinct from Western traditions and practices. The first few chapters not only delineate the gender ideology that becomes the basis of the novel's plot of family crisis, rebirth, and regeneration, but they also naturalize patriarchy as an essential element of Chinese-ness. Through Wang Lung's daily practices and beliefs, Buck attributes patriarchal and misogynistic thoughts and behavior to the "Chinese way of things" or the "Chinese way of thinking." On the morning of his marriage, Wang Lung washes his body before he goes to meet O-lan for the first time, but "[h]e was ashamed to say to his father that he wished his body to be clean for a woman to see"(6). Once married, Wang Lung develops affection for her, but he is "ashamed of his own curiosity and of his interest in her. She was, after all, only a woman" (28). Such uses of representative speech, which Buck employs extensively throughout the novel, serve to stress that patriarchal gender ideology is at the core of Chinese social structure.

In this sense, the category of gender and the genre of domestic narrative stress the distinction between the Western writer/reader and the Chinese subject in the way that the dominant imperialist discourse rhetorically elevated the status of Western women to distinguish the West from the rest of the world. Given that Buck had a clear understanding of gender inequities in both China and the United States and was a strong spokesperson for women's issues, her textual reliance on these gendered constructs all the more highlights the effectiveness and appeal of the domestic narrative. Both the genre and analysis allowed Buck to gloss over the historical specificities of the Chinese setting and to turn the story into a "universal" narrative, while simultaneously underscoring the non-Western nature of the Chinese. By using the dual effects of domestic fiction, Buck successfully constructed an accessible, popular narrative which supports, rather than destabilizes, the Orientalist authority she established through her ethnographic narrativization.

The discourses of ethnography and domestic fiction offered Buck both authority and popularity. Although the assumptions and frameworks of the two discourses are quite different and often contradictory, Buck used those differences to her advantage. Their importance to the commercial success of *The Good Earth* becomes clearer when one contrasts the novel to its two sequels, *Sons* and *A House Divided*, which trace the lives of Wang Lung's son and grandson respectively. In these two novels, the historical and social settings undergo major transformations, and the development of the characters depends heavily on their relationship to the specificities of those social transformations. Although the issues of gender and sexuality are significantly featured to illustrate larger political and ideological issues, they operate quite differently from the way they do in *The Good Earth*.

Set in the age of warlordism, *Sons* is a narrative about Wang Lung's youngest son, Wang the Tiger, who struggles to attain power and authority in a world whose system he doesn't completely comprehend. Wang the Tiger becomes the leader of an independent band of soldiers who establish themselves as the official troop contingent for a section of northern China. However, Wang the Tiger proves to be too tender-hearted and naïve to be a successful military leader. When he falls in love with the sensuous mistress of a rival bandit leader, he is so blinded by his love that he kills the robber chief and takes the woman for his wife, not realizing that she is a traitress scheming a revenge for her former lover. He is excessively devoted to his son and is so engrossed in his education that he fails to grasp his own social circumstances and to increase his military and political influence, which eventually leads to his demise. It becomes apparent later in the novel that his area of control was limited to only a small part of a large province, and that he was no more than a puissant and arrogant bandit.[25]

Through the story of Wang the Tiger's son, Yuan, *A House Divided* deals directly with the conflict between China and the West, between tradition and modernity. A sensitive youth who has a love-hate relationship with his father, Yuan rebels against Wang the Tiger's domineering attitude and narrow, short-sighted vision, and joins the revolutionary army in Shanghai. After being jailed for his political activities, he is smuggled aboard a ship bound for America. During his six years of residence in the United States, Yuan studies diligently and learns what propelled America's prosperity and material accomplishments. However, dismayed by the racial prejudice and discrimination he encounters, Yuan becomes a chauvinistic defender of the China which he has embellished and idealized in his mind. Upon returning to his country, which has undergone another revolution while he was away, he is disillusioned by the stark social inequality and the self-indulgence of the new generation embracing a Western lifestyle. At the end of the novel, Yuan comes to terms with both China's past and present, and finds his role in shaping the nation's future.[26]

In both novels, authority and authenticity are established through Buck's historical rather than ethnographic mastery. Instead of describing the details of daily life, Buck devotes much of her text to describing historical events and context, such as the rise of warlordism and banditry in rural China, the nationalist movement in the city and subsequent revolutions, and the increasing penetration of Western ideas and lifestyle. The central focus of both novels is the protagonists' struggles to find their identity in the vast historical transformation and turbulent society. The novels are much more concretely historicized than *The Good Earth*, which depicts a symbolic landscape transcending time and space.

Although Buck effectively uses debates over gender and sexuality to frame the political, cultural, and ideological issues that the novels address, the domestic narrative is not the central thread organizing the texts. In *A House Divided*, the issues of gender, sexuality, and domesticity are tropes for the ideological conflicts with which Yuan struggles. What drives Yuan to join the revolutionary army is the realization that "he is not free" under Wang the Tiger, who pressures him to marry the woman he picked for his son. During his life in the United States, Yuan sees that racism is expressed most clearly in white women's attitude toward him and understands that racial and national power dynamics manifest themselves most explicitly in male-female relations. But gender relations and sexuality provoke racial feelings not only on the part of Americans but also in Yuan himself. What incites his distaste for the white race and his racialized sense of identity is his relationship with Mary, the daughter of a professor whom he befriends. Yuan and Mary develop a trustful friendship until Yuan suddenly becomes aware of the distance between himself and Mary when kissing her for the first time: "In that instant he drew back. Why he must draw back he could not tell, for there was that in him, too, which wanted to press on and on, deeper and long. But stranger than that desire was a distaste he could not understand, except it was the distaste of flesh for flesh that was not its own kind" (209). The introduction of a sexual dimension to their relationship makes him equate his sense of physical alienation from Mary with his sense of racialized identity.

The links between gender and sexuality and modernization and Westernization confront Yuan back in China as well. Later, he sees Western women and Westernized Chinese women in his own country and laments:

> "It is these foreign ways that set our women to all this stubbornness and talk of freedom, so that they set nature aside and live like nuns or courtesans!" And he remembered with especial hatred that landlady's daughter and her lewdness and Mary, whose lips had been too ready, and he blamed even them. At last he looked at every foreign female that he passed with such hatred that he could not bear them and he muttered, "I will get out of this city somehow. I will go away where I shall see nothing foreign and nothing new and live and find my life there in my own country. I wish I had not gone abroad! I wish I had never left the earthen house!" (281–282)

At the end of the novel, it is by marrying Mei-ling, an intelligent woman who carries herself with a perfect balance between Chinese tradition and Western modernity, that Yuan finds his place in the present and the future of his country. However, these instances are episodic manifestations of historical conflicts and do not constitute a sustained domestic narrative as in *The Good Earth*.

These characteristics make the two sequels quite different from *The Good Earth*. The protagonists show more emotional complexity than Wang Lung and are depicted as individual "characters" rather than "types." Historical and ideological conflicts in periods of vast social transformation are represented with complexity, and the reader hears competing voices rather than a coherent narrative. From the present perspective, the two sequels seem to be much more artistically and ideologically sophisticated than *The Good Earth*, but these complexities were exactly what made the novels commercially less successful than *The Good Earth*. Although the reputation gained by the best-seller helped the sales of its sequels, they were nowhere near as popular or as well received. Malcom Cowley observed that the material in *A House Divided* is too scattered and does not progress to any significant conclusion; he critiqued that the China the novel describes is separated into different groups and lingers between past and present conditions with the future unknown and uncertain.[27] Critic Paul Doyle argued that "*Sons* falls short of *The Good Earth* because it does not have the same universal quality of timelessness, the same inevitable moment of birth and death, of success and failure, of tragedy and joy."[28] These views indicate that it was the unified and universalized, de-specified and non-historicized nature of the text that made *The Good Earth* so popular and well-received by American readers.

Buck's tactful use of discursive structures and genres as well as her use of gender and domesticity brought her high acclaim as "the popular expert" on China, a term which itself carried specifically gendered connotations. As a "popular" writer, her work was continually regarded as "women's literature" which supposedly used the language of moral suasion and sentimentality, unlike the works of male Great Authors. Buck tried to overcome her continuous identification as a "woman writing about China" and published several of her later novels, set in America, under the male pseudonym "John Sedges."[29] None of these works was anywhere near as successful as *The Good Earth* or Buck's other China stories, suggesting the importance of Buck's identity as "popular expert on China" to her authorial position. However, her career extended far beyond her fiction writing. She published nonfiction works and was also passionately committed to the cause of social justice. An advocate for American civil rights and women's rights movements, Buck's activities led to an FBI file of nearly three hundred pages. She also founded the first international adoption agency. An outspoken promoter of international and cross-cultural understanding, she served as a cultural ambassador between the United States and China and as president of the East and West Association.[30]

Throughout her career, Buck's stance on her political, cultural, and ideological work was consistent. She was, and opted to remain, a "popular" expert on China. Although she did not necessarily see her role in U.S.-Asian relations as specifically gendered, she clearly did see herself in opposition to the predominantly male group of intellectuals committed to the causes she was advocating. Buck's objective in founding the East and West Association in 1941 was "to help ordinary people on one side of the world to know and understand ordinary people on the other side."[31] When Edward Carter of the Institute of Pacific Relations (IPR) proposed the possibility of the East and West Association becoming the educational, cultural, and promotion department within the IPR in order to avoid duplication and conflict between the work of the two organizations, Buck replied as follows:

> We are just too totally different. I want to get down to the level of the comic strip if I can. And I cannot imagine the Institute [of Pacific Relations] there! But you know as well as I do that there is a wide area which the Institute does not reach and cannot reach. That is the area where we propose to work. Consider the small scale of your publications, for instance. They are excellent books—you know how frequently I have said so. We do not propose to publish any such material, but to work out ways of using the material you and other organizations have on your shelves. Our meetings will not be meetings of experts nor will our radio programs be discussions on economic or political or social matters. They will be on a level which frankly I doubt the Institute of Pacific Relations would want to sponsor. But that is where I want to work. I want somehow to get down into the level of people who don't and won't listen to your programs or read your books. The experts who distinguish your work, the high record which you hold for scholarship and research, the standing you have among intelligent and intellectual people—all these are invaluable and you will know how I value them myself. But the sort of people I want to interest, and who I believe must be interested—simply cannot and will not be interested by the sort of thing you do. You do a work we can't and don't want to do, and we plan a work that you can't and don't want to do—or you would have done it during these twenty-five years you have been going.[32]

As this statement demonstrates, Buck's position in the U.S. discourse about Asia was consistently populist. And her authority as the "popular expert" was most manifested in the skillful narrative strategies she employed in *The Good Earth*.

Re-gendering the Enemy
Culture and Gender in Ruth Benedict's
The Chrysanthemum and the Sword

*T*he international rivalries in the Pacific, incited by Japan's aggression in Manchuria in 1931 and the subsequent Sino-Japanese War, prompted Americans to refine their understanding of Asians as an undifferentiated alien race. As the attack on Pearl Harbor in 1941 made the United States' enmity toward Japan and support of China unquestionable, Americans needed to distinguish between the "evil" Japanese and the Chinese "heroes risen" against the Japanese.[1] The media put out sensational and propagandistic calls for people to make a distinction between the two groups, exemplified by articles like "How to Tell Your Friends from the Japs."[2] On a more strategic level, government agencies and the military mobilized academics and professionals to gather information about and analyze enemy behavior for the purposes of accurate military planning, psychological warfare, and policy-making for the postwar period. The projects of these specialists — mostly anthropologists, sociologists, and psychiatrists — in developing what later came to be called "culture and personality studies" or "national character studies" differed from the earlier American efforts to understand Asia in that they were avowedly "scientific," although wartime circumstances and political objectives inevitably shaped the nature of these studies.[3] It was also significant that the first institution-alized attempts to understand a "modern" culture—as opposed to the dominant anthropological tradition of studying "primitive" cultures—emerged out of wartime imperatives.

The Chrysanthemum and the Sword, a study of Japanese national character writ-ten by the prominent anthropologist Ruth Benedict, was the most influential prod-uct of these wartime projects.[4] Its publication in 1946 came at a critical moment in the history of U.S.-Japan relations. Before the book came out, there existed books and articles written for an academic audience, but few works to which the general American reader could refer to learn about Japanese culture. The books on Japan-ese culture written at the turn of the century by male Japanologists such as Lafcadio Hearn, Ernest Fenollosa, Percival Lowell, and Edward Morse never became "pop-ular" among the general public. World War II heightened public awareness about the Japanese psyche—however biased the American interest—while Japan's defeat and subsequent occupation by the Allied forces called for a sound and comprehen-sive understanding of Japanese culture and society and created a receptive audi-ence for Benedict's work. With its accessible language and style, *The Chrysanthe-mum and the Sword* gave a clear and incisive picture of Japanese culture and social structure, which were foreign to most American readers. Benedict explained such things as the role of the Emperor in nationalist ideology and daily life, structures of interpersonal relations, moral codes and methods of social control, and childrear-ing practices. She also gave suggestions for the treatment of postwar Japan under Occupation.

In addition to providing information, *The Chrysanthemum and the Sword* was sig-nificant in its interventions in America's gendered discourse about Japan and its construction of Japanese national character based on the theoretical framework Benedict shared with her fellow anthropologists. The text reinforced the dominant Western notion of Japan as emasculated and feminized through a process much dif-ferent from earlier approaches to Japan, which focused on the feminine aspects of Japanese society. Benedict "feminized" Japanese culture, not by looking at Japanese women's lives, but by looking at the masculine. She constructed a normative model of Japanese character based on male figures and male renditions of social structure, and diagnosed it as deviant from Western norms of masculinity, thereby rendering Japanese society emasculated and feminized. Like her peers in the study of national character, Benedict used the contemporary anthropological paradigm of "culture" to explain Japanese gender relations and sexuality. Although Benedict's uses of the concepts of culture and gender differed from the ways in which some of the other American women examined in the previous chapters thought about the issues, her paradigm of culture and the place she assigned to gender within that paradigm vali-dated and naturalized the existing association between Japanese culture and particular notions of gender and sexuality. As a consequence, the anthropologists' replacement of racial determinism with a culture paradigm brought about the familiar result of gendering the Other.

The title of the book, *The Chrysanthemum and the Sword*, epitomizes what Benedict considered to be most symbolic representations of Japanese culture: the Japanese imperial family and the feudal system of *samurai*. They are also gendered metaphors. The chrysanthemum is associated with femininity, fragility, and delicacy, the sword with masculinity, strength, and aggressiveness. In many ways, the book proves that these are apt metaphors for understanding seemingly contradictory aspects of Japanese culture. However, when one pays closer attention to the way in which Benedict unfolds these metaphors and their function in the overall scheme of the book, it becomes clear that the gendered meanings inherent in the title—whether or not Benedict was conscious of all of the meanings—are more complex than a simple binary between femininity and masculinity.

The metaphors of the chrysanthemum and the sword are introduced only toward the end of the book, after Benedict has already explicated her model of Japanese culture that is based on the system of hierarchy and social order. The symbolic meaning of the chrysanthemum, closely intertwined with the rigidly charted structures of obligation in Japanese social life, is explored through her discussion of the autobiography of a Japanese woman. A daughter of a prestigious *samurai* family is sent to learn English at a mission school in Tokyo, where her teacher allows each girl to have a plot of wild ground and any seeds she asks for. The plant-as-you-please garden gives her a "wholly new feeling of personal right," and she decides to plant potatoes while all other girls plant flowers. She juxtaposes this "sense of reckless freedom which this absurd act gave [her]" with the carefully calculated and tamed aesthetic of the Japanese garden, in which the chrysanthemum is grown in pots with tiny wire racks inserted in the living flower.[5] In Benedict's account, the chrysanthemum, requiring wire racks and constant pruning, symbolizes the meticulous constraints and rules governing Japanese life and its lack of freedom and naturalness.[6] Like the delicate and fragile femininity associated with the Japanese woman, the flower represents the intensely rigid and drastic forms of discipline and social order which constitute the masculinist ideal in Japanese life. In its way, the chrysanthemum is also the ultimate masculinist symbol of Japan's "old" order, the imperial family. By seeing the emperor as the "father symbol" of the Japanese nation, Benedict and other scholars understood the chrysanthemum to stand for the man who represents and governs the nation. However, her prescription ultimately curtails Japan's aggressive masculinist symbol and recommends the maintenance of the emperor in postwar Japan under the tutelage of the U.S. administration. By using the symbol of the chrysanthemum to suggest that Japan's masculinist ideology of imperialism will be defeated by the American notion of freedom and democracy, Benedict not only feminizes Japan but also feminizes the *masculine* Japan.

The metaphor of the sword also carries complex gendered meanings. Benedict argues that the Japanese virtue of self-responsibility can help the Japanese to make the transition to a greater freedom.

> As the wearer of a sword is responsible for its shining brilliancy, so each man must accept responsibility for the outcome of his acts. He must acknowledge and accept all natural consequences of his weakness, his lack of persistence, his ineffectualness. Self-responsibility is far more drastically interpreted in Japan than in free America. In this Japanese sense the sword becomes, not a symbol of aggression, but a simile of ideal and self-responsible man. . . . Today the Japanese have proposed 'to lay aside the sword' in the Western sense. In their Japanese sense, they have an abiding strength in their concern with keeping an inner sword free from the rust which always threatens it. In their phraseology of virtue the sword is a symbol they can keep in a freer and more peaceful world.[7]

While Benedict validates Japan's masculinist ethos of self-responsibility, she also acknowledges that Japan's postwar decision (made by the Americans) "to lay aside the sword"—that is, to demilitarize—is taken as an act of emasculation. By allowing Japan to keep the masculinist symbol of the sword as "not a symbol of aggression but a simile of ideal and self-responsible man," she makes demilitarization less demeaning to the Japanese and redefines the masculinist symbol.

The study of Japanese character and the writing of *The Chrysanthemum and the Sword* came relatively late in Benedict's career, when she was already known as a prominent anthropologist specializing in Native American myths and folklore. Benedict was not an Asian specialist and did not have either fieldwork experience or language training in Asian countries.[8] A close disciple of Franz Boas, she was an anti-racist and cultural relativist and wrote numerous articles and pamphlets about the lack of scientific basis for many of the widely-held views about race and condemning racial prejudice and discrimination.[9]

Benedict's involvement in the study of Japanese character was part of her job at the Office of War Information (OWI) where she worked from 1943 to 1945. Established by Executive Order in June 1942, the OWI disseminated news about the war on the homefront, while using propaganda to help win the war overseas.[10] Benedict was recruited to be the Head Analyst in the Cultural Analysis and Research Division of the Bureau of Overseas Intelligence, and her job description read:[11]

1. Library study of national cultures   25%
2. Collecting material on these countries available at other Government agencies   7%
3. Interviewing nationals of these cultures   10%
4. Supervising collection of materials by consultants   5%
5. Reading current cables, and press news from these countries   8%
6. Preparing reports on these cultures   35%
7. Preparing suggestions for P.W. [psychological warfare] based on above studies   5%
8. Preparing operational summaries of these investigations   5%

The range of projects Benedict worked on at the OWI shows that she was hired not as a specialist in a particular nation or culture, but as a cultural analyst who could put together general reports on different cultures based on resources available in Washington. She conducted a cultural survey of Thailand to help design plans for psychological warfare that provided a broad historical and geographical overview, followed by a discussion of adult life and the formation of national character.[12] This method became a skeletal model for her later study on Japan. She also conducted similar studies on Burma and Rumania.[13] At the end of 1943, she collaborated with her colleague David Rodnick to study the culture and personality of Germany, which resulted in a report entitled, "German Defeatism at the Beginning of the Fifth Winter of War."[14] She also worked on short reports on Finland, Denmark, Norway, Holland, France, Poland, and Italy.

As the focus of the war shifted from Europe to the Pacific, it became imperative for the U.S. government to gain an understanding of the Japanese in order to counter their propaganda and their will to "fight until the very end." For this purpose, the Foreign Morale Analysis Division (FMAD) was established in the OWI in August 1944. Furthering the work done by Commander Alexander Leighton of U.S. Navy Medical Corps in gathering information on Japanese morale in the Poston Japanese Relocation Camp, the FMAD brought together about thirty staff members, including anthropologists, psychologists, psychiatrists, sociologists, political scientists, and Japan specialists.[15] Benedict was assigned to the FMAD to study Japan in September. With no previous background or training in Japanese studies, Benedict would have less than a year to research the Japanese before the final surrender.

Wartime circumstances severely restricted the sources and methods Benedict could use for her study, a factor that greatly shaped her analysis. She used three types of evidence in researching and understanding Japanese culture. First, she conducted interviews of so-called "native informants": Japanese who were currently in the United States, Japanese Americans, and non-Japanese people who had lived in Japan. Second, she studied several dozen films written and produced in Japan. Finally, she reviewed literature of and about Japan, written both by Japanese and Westerners. Each of these sources had its strengths and limitations as anthropological evidence, and Benedict was aware of some but not of others.

The most critical, although certainly not the most extensive, of Benedict's sources were the interviews she and her colleagues conducted with Japanese informants. She considered these a crucial aspect of her research, the scholarly validation of her anthropological work.

> As a cultural anthropologist . . . , I had confidence in certain techniques and postulates which could be used. At least I did not have to forego the anthropologist's great reliance upon face-to-face contact with the people he is studying. There were plenty of Japanese in this country who had been reared in Japan and I could ask them about the concrete facts of their own experiences, find out how they judged them, fill in from their descriptions many gaps in our knowledge which as an anthropologist I believed were essential in understanding any culture. Other social scientists who were studying Japan were using libraries, analyzing past events or statistics, following developments in the written or spoken word of Japanese propaganda. I had confidence that many of these answers they sought were embedded in the rules and values of Japanese culture and could be found more satisfactorily by exploring that culture with people who had really lived it.[16]

Although it is unclear from the documents how many of these interviews were conducted by Benedict herself and how much she relied on reports submitted by her colleagues, Benedict's handwritten notes suggest that she did conduct a number of interviews herself in 1944 and 1945, and the experience provided her with professional confidence and scholarly credibility.[17] While Benedict acknowledged the limited access she had to the object of her study, she did not spell out what exactly she meant by "people who had really lived [Japanese culture]." She showed no concern with the sampling of the interviewees, although her informants were varied in their positions and relationships to Japanese culture. Some were Japanese prisoners of war, some were Japanese or Japanese Americans who worked for the OWI, and some were Americans who had previously lived in Japan. She did not differentiate among these interviewees' social, political, and ideological positions or comment on their mental state at the time of the interviews. Furthermore, she did not theorize the relationship between the "concrete facts of their own experiences" and "how they judged them."

Another group of sources available to Benedict were films produced in Japan. Although one would expect that the visual images presented in the films would have given her a sense of Japanese life unavailable from literature and interviews, Benedict focused on the narratives and themes of the films and did not comment on any aspect of visuality. Describing how she discussed the films with Japanese friends who "saw the hero and the heroine and the villain as the Japanese see them, not as [she] saw them," Benedict says:

> When I was at sea, it was clear that they were not. The plots, the motivations were not as I saw them, but they made sense in terms of the way the movie was constructed. As with the novels, there was much more difference than met the eye between what they meant to me and what they meant to the Japanese-reared.[18]

During Benedict's research, the Office of Strategic Services surveyed twenty Japanese films, and Benedict studied the report of the survey. The researchers' concern with Japanese wartime mentality and the films' propaganda value shaped the ways in which the films were classified and described. The films' "basic themes" are categorized as the "dominant theme," which is "the spirit of sacrifice or the subjection of self to pattern"; "theme of filial piety," "theme of the faithful wife," "theme of patriotism," and "theme of Japan's role in Greater East Asia." The "psychological content" is divided into "attitude towards life," "attitude towards love," "attitude towards fatherland and Emperor," "attitude towards war," "attitude towards death," and "attitude towards religion."[19] In addition to such a politically charged approach to the films, Benedict's interest in "how one regulates one's life in Japan" also shaped her reading of the films in her own research.

The most extensive group of sources, which was unique to Benedict's study as an anthropological project, was the literature of and about Japan. Anthropology was still considered to be primarily a study of "primitive" cultures, many of which had no written language. Studying a culture like Japan—which had had a written tradition for more than a thousand years and whose history, literature, art, and politics had been written about by hundreds of Westerners—was a relatively new project not only for Benedict but also for anthropology as a discipline. Benedict states in *The Chrysanthemum and the Sword* that "[t]he vast literature on the Japanese and the great number of good Occidental observers who have lived in Japan gave me an advantage which no anthropologist has when he goes to the Amazon headwaters or the New Guinea highlands to study a non-literate tribe."[20] Benedict studied an amazingly wide range of literature, written mostly between the turn of the century and the 1940s, including travel narratives, histories of Japanese religion, novels, myths and folklore, sociological studies, military and strategic analyses, and psychological studies of sexual behavior.[21]

While the wide-ranging literature greatly informed Benedict, her use of written materials as a resource was limited by her inability to read Japanese. Her reading was therefore restricted to works written in English or to Japanese works that had been translated into English. These English-language sources included, but were not limited to, works by male "authorities" on Japan, such as William Griffis, Lafcadio Hearn, Percival Lowell, Ernest Fenollosa, Ezra Pound, and George Sansom; recent sociological, historical, or strategic studies of Japanese society had been written by scholars such as E. H. Norman, Hugh Borton, Miriam Farley, Sidney Gulick, Harley Farnsworth MacNair, and Lt. Col. Paul W. Thompson; and Japanese literature in translation, primarily works by canonical male writers and intellectuals, such as Natsume Soseki, Kikuchi Kan, Nitobe Inazo, Tanizaki Jun'ichiro, and Watsuji Tetsuro. Benedict's inability to reach beyond the existing English-language sources prevented her from breaking free of the dominant discourse about Japan.

These limitations on Benedict's sources and methods significantly affected her analysis of Japanese culture, causing later critics to undermine the validity and credibility of her accounts.[22] Practically every work that discusses *The Chrysanthemum and the Sword*, even the ones that give a more tempered and favorable view of Benedict's work, note that it was a "study of culture at a distance," and that Benedict lacked both the experience of doing fieldwork in Japan and Japanese language skills. Many critics have also been concerned with the question of "accuracy" and "authenticity." They argue that Benedict's representation of Japan is inaccurate, skewed, or dated, and thus lacks validity as an account of contemporary Japanese culture. Japanese scholars and intellectuals, who were invested in the "accurate" portrayal of Japan in the eyes of the foreigners—like the Chinese intellectuals who critiqued Buck's portrayals of China—raised most of these criticisms.[23]

However, these critiques miss the point. Benedict, as a prominent American anthropologist, had a specific "assignment" to fulfill, and for that goal she took the best advantage she could of the sources and tools to which she had access. Thus, rather than criticizing Benedict for not using the sources and methods she had no access to, a more useful task is to assess how the sources she used became available to her and the discourse in which such sources were embedded as well as to examine her treatment of the sources and her processes of theorization about Japanese culture.

In writing *The Chrysanthemum and the Sword*, Benedict constructed a gendered model of Japanese culture. What was unique about Benedict's study, however, was not so much that she produced a gendered narrative about Japan—which, as I have already shown, existed long before Benedict—but that she took a different path from the one taken by many other Orientalists to reach the same conclusion about the feminized Japan. Rather than feminizing Japan by focusing on women, gender relations, or the domestic sphere, Benedict feminized Japan by looking at the masculine. While many white women gained their position in Orientalist discourse by capitalizing on their access to the female sphere which male Orientalists could not reach, Benedict's profession as an anthropologist studying an enemy culture at a distance granted her a unique entry into, and authority on, Japan's male sphere. She thus constructed her model of normative Japanese character out of male figures and mapped her pattern of Japanese social order based on male, public spheres of life. She then characterized them as deviant from Western norms of masculinity, which are associated with individualism, democracy, and freedom. Benedict feminized Japan by diagnosing the Japanese male as lacking in proper forms of masculinity.

Benedict's construction of the normative Japanese character based on male figures largely resulted from the gendered nature of her evidence, which was most evident in the composition of her "native informants." Of the existing documents on these interviews, all but one (which is a report of an interview with a Japanese couple) record interviews with men. Of this informant pool, particularly important were the Japanese soldiers who either became prisoners of war or deserted their troops. Although Benedict by no means drew all of her arguments from these interviews, it would be safe to say that the gender composition and social position of her informant pool significantly affected Benedict's narrative about Japanese culture, particularly with regard to Japan's nationalist and imperialist ideology and the Japanese attitude toward the Emperor.

To supplement the limited number of interviews she conducted, Benedict also consulted the "community analyses" written by anthropologists working in Japanese internment camps.[24] Under the auspices of the War Relocation Authority, a group of anthropologists investigated social structures and behavior patterns of the Japanese in relocation camps on the West Coast. This Japanese Evacuation and Resettlement Study (JERS), under the directorship of sociologist Dorothy S. Thomas, produced several important works on Japanese culture, the most notable of which was Weston La Barre's "Some Observations on Character Structure in the Orient: The Japanese"[25] and a community analysis in Poston Japanese Relocation Center in the Colorado River Valley.[26] Leighton noted how gender might have affected the contours of his project, mentioning that while the anthropologists involved in the Poston project included women, the Japanese evacuee staff, trained to penetrate the community in a manner impossible for white project members, included only two women.[27] Although there is no record of Benedict visiting the Japanese internment camps and/or interviewing the internees herself, she did rely on the WRA's community analysis surveys as a substitute for fieldwork, and the gendered nature of these surveys certainly affected her analysis.

But the gendering of Japanese character in Benedict's model was also a result of the theoretical assumptions and analytical processes she shared with the contemporary scholars of national character. The most illustrative example of such assumptions and processes can be seen in Geoffrey Gorer's manuscript, "Japanese Character Structure," which was the single most influential analysis of Japanese national character presented before Benedict's study. Gorer's study was "a first attempt to give a systematic and dynamic description of the average Japanese character structure, with the aim of giving direction to future propaganda programmes by radio, insofar as these may be addressed to the Japanese."[28] Gorer's theoretical assumptions reveal the gendered way in which national character studies, including Benedict's work, constructed the "average," "normative" Japanese character. First of all, Gorer saw the "typical" Japanese as being male. In the beginning of the manuscript, Gorer outlines four boundaries of social dichotomy in Japan: (1) male vs. female, (2) common people (*heimin*) vs. the nobility on the one hand and the *eta* [outcasts] on the other; (3) moderate means vs. very poor and very rich; (4) urban vs. rural. Based on this categorization, Gorer states that the "typical Japanese" is taken in his study to be a "moderately well-off male of the common people living in a city." He justifies this by arguing that:

> Owing to the very considerable political and social subordination of women, men are the predominant formers of opinion and carriers of the culture. To a very large degree, Japan can be considered a "male culture." The contrast in typical character between men and women is very strong; it is above all the men's character which it is desirable to understand in the present situation.[29]

The "political and social subordination of women" and the social and cultural divisions according to gender were certainly a visible reality in Japan. However, differential social norms for men and women, gendered divisions of labor, and sexism in Japanese society do not in themselves validate Gorer's conclusion that the portrayal of the typical Japanese should be based on a male character. The premise that it was most important to study the characters of the male Japanese who shaped and embodied the ideologies of the public sphere was passed onto the next cohort of scholars of national character, including Benedict.

Gorer not only used a male figure as the normative Japanese individual, but also based his analysis of Japanese social order upon male social relations. Reflecting the Freudian psychoanalytic and child-development theories that dominated national character studies in this period, he described a culture in which Japanese boys were aware of their subordinate position, compliant with the patterns of the male universe, and heavily punished for deviance.[30] He portrayed the female world in Japan as the one that was controlled or dominated by male aggression, and at the same time is sentimentally loved, ill treated, and despised—so despised that no male wishes to identify himself with it.[31] Based upon this premise of sexual division of character and the assumption that social institutions and political organizations are explicable through the psychology of the individual, Gorer attributes the reasons for the Japanese aggression in war to "every Japanese man['s] urge to *control the environment.*"

In addition to constructing the normative model of Japanese national character out of the male figure and the male sphere of social order, Gorer used a highly gendered and sexualized perspective and language in his argumentation. Rather than ascribing gendered and sexualized meaning to Japanese culture, Gorer turned the model around and claimed that "to the contemporary Japanese other races and societies are viewed as either male or female; as groups to be followed and obeyed implicitly, or as groups to be forced to yield by aggression or threats of aggression."[32] Gorer's account of the Japanese "sexing" of races and nations obscured the fact that Americans and Europeans used the same gendered and sexualized frameworks and stereotypes in talking about Japan, and that Gorer himself was doing precisely that. Gorer called for the retrieval of Western masculinity—that is, U.S. military and political domination over Japan—in order to teach the Japanese that their "sexing" of the nation was incorrect: "it is essential that by every symbolic means possible we should attempt to reestablish ourselves in male roles. This means the complete abandonment of threats, cajolery and appeals to pity, which all indicate the female; and adopting instead the calm certainty of obedience, sanctioned by mockery, which indicated the male."[33] While he attributed the act of "sexing" of races and nations to the Japanese, Gorer himself assigned explicitly gendered and sexualized meanings to U.S.-Japan relations to reestablish the feminine—and thus subordinate—position of the Japanese.

Benedict's work came out of the political and academic discourse on Japan which relied on gendered and sexualized perspectives like Gorer's. In December 1944, the Institute of Pacific Relations, a major international organization founded in 1925 which brought together a large number of prominent scholars from nations of the Pacific Rim, held a conference specifically on Japanese character structure.[34] The conference exemplified the contemporary discourse, commonly called "Culture and Personality" studies, that brought together the methodologies of the applied behavioral and social sciences such as anthropology, sociology, psychology, and psychiatry, to systematically study and understand the character of other cultures. The participants consisted of government experts concerned with present and future plans in relation to Japan, those with experience in and knowledge of Japan, and anthropologists such as Benedict, who had no direct experience in Japanese culture but were accustomed to applying a systematic approach to the problems of personality and culture.[35] Using materials such as a diary of a Japanese prisoner of war and the Japanese films, the participants discussed issues such as the Japanese attitude toward death, conformism to patterns of group life, and sense of inadequacy, and decided that there is a distinct analogy between Japanese character structure and the American adolescent, particularly the gangster. The psychoanalytic and developmental approach used in the discussion rendered the male figure as the normative model of both individual development and national character.

The modeling of the Japanese character on a male figure took on a more conspicuous meaning when the conference moved to the discussion of propaganda strategies and postwar treatment of Japan, whose traces are clearly seen in *The Chrysanthemum and the Sword*. The participants spent a significant amount of time debating whether or not the "elder-brother, younger-brother relationship" of the Confucian family would be effective as American propaganda for the Japanese.[36] The discussion generally revolved around the question of whether Americans could or should appropriately assume the role of Japan's elder brother. Gorer commented that "[w]e can't expect the Japanese to think that we are elder brothers unless we think of them as younger brothers."[37] The boy-adolescent-brother model developed through these discussions manifested in various U.S. policies and attitudes during and after the postwar occupation of Japan.[38]

Although Benedict's relationship to the psychoanalytical and developmental approaches was somewhat ambivalent and her relative silence during the IPR conference shows her distance from the dominant method, Benedict worked within such discourses about Japan, in which gender and sexuality functioned not only as categories of analysis but also as the language and lens through which to critique Japan. Benedict used similarly gendered assumptions and argumentations in her account of Japanese culture, and constructed a model based on a male figure and male sphere of life. Furthermore, by stressing the undemocratic, anti-individualist aspects of Japanese male culture, Benedict implicitly suggested that Japanese masculinity deviated from Western notions of masculinity.

At the core of Benedict's "pattern" of Japanese culture was an intricate social hierarchy, in which individuals have their "proper place" and act according to their differential "obligations" to other members of the social matrix. Benedict saw this hierarchical social arrangement as the most Japanese element of Japanese culture, and interpreted all personal behaviors, cultural ethos, social structures, and historical development through this lens. Early in the book, Benedict states that:

> For a long, long time Japan will necessarily keep some of her inbred attitudes and one of the most important of these is her faith and confidence in hierarchy. It is alien to equality-loving Americans but it is nevertheless necessary for us to understand what Japan meant by hierarchy and what advantages she has learned to connect with it.[39]

With each example — ranging from bowing practices, patriarchal gender relations and marital arrangements, to filial piety, Emperor Worship and Japan's military aggression in Asia — Benedict constructed a Japanese "pattern" of hierarchy.

Benedict's interest in hierarchy, compounded by the book's purpose of studying wartime ideology and individual mentality, led her attention particularly to the most hierarchical and most masculinist sphere of Japanese life: men in military service and their attitudes toward the Emperor. In the chapter outlining Japanese behavior during the war, she describes how the Japanese prioritize spirit over material circumstances, providing a rather extreme example that "[i]n battle, spirit surmounted even the physical fact of death." She describes the tale of a hero-pilot: he had been fatally shot in his chest and had been dead for quite some time, yet his spirit drove him to report to the Commanding Officer at Headquarters, and he dropped to the ground cold as ice as soon as he made the report.[40] Much of the chapter is also devoted to the discussion of the Japanese attitude toward the Emperor. Using anecdotal examples of military and civilian men who willingly died in the name of the Emperor, Benedict depicts how the Emperor "was all things to all men," and that the Emperor was still "inseparable from Japan."[41] This unconditional and unrestricted loyalty to the Emperor, which seemed to Westerners to be conspicuously at odds with Japanese criticisms of all other persons and groups, epitomized her view of Japanese culture.

Benedict founded her model of normative Japanese character and mentality on a figure of the soldier ready to die for the Emperor or male civilians who were equally loyal to the Emperor and the nationalist and imperialist ideology. The archetype is most vividly manifested in the interview records of Suetsugu Shoji.[42] A 26-year-old single man from Hokkaido who had not graduated from upper grammar school and had been a welder, Suetsugu had been in service for four years in China, Malay, and Burma where he was captured in May 1944. Suetsugu's answers to the interrogations show what is to become Benedict's normative Japanese attitude toward the war. He regards the capture as "a discredit to the Emperor." "*And* he was also shamed," the reporter stressed, "because his captors were the inferior Chinese." He maintained his faith in victory, the purposes of the war, the reliability of news, and the production front. He said that he had never considered surrendering; he had never heard of a Japanese surrendering. He did not wish to return to live in Japan, fearing that he would be punished if he did, and intended to "live alone in mountains of Burma till the war is over and then start a new life in Asia."[43]

Benedict's emphasis on the stories told by soldiers notwithstanding, Japanese women were mobilized into wartime nationalist ideology. They embraced the imperial doctrines, assisted wartime economy, and supported the nationalist goals on the home front. Just as Western women were complicit in the masculinist project of Western imperialism and Orientalism, Japanese women were an integral part of Japanese imperialism. Still, men in uniform had a different relationship to the nationalist and imperialist ideology than women did. Men enacted Japan's imperialist ideology not just militarily but in the practice of conducting daily affairs within the rigid hierarchy of the military, governing surveillance, interactions with and violence against the natives, and sexual violence against native women. Furthermore, trained under the no-surrender policy, they were expected and willing to give their lives in the name of the Emperor. Their interviews informed and shaped Benedict's view on "official" wartime Japanese morale, including the soldiers' faith in the purpose of the war, attitude toward the Emperor, and attitude toward death.[44]

The fact that Benedict constructed—and naturalized—the model of Japanese character based on a male figure did not mean that she did not pay attention to Japanese women or that she did not deal with the issue of gender. She did not see women as exempt from the Japanese system of hierarchy or the "official" nationalist and imperialist ideology. Benedict knew that Japanese women's lives were also embedded within axes of hierarchical order, the most obvious one of which was patriarchy. She supplemented her own limited knowledge on Japanese women by reading cultural accounts and memoirs such as Alice Mabel Bacon's *Japanese Girls and Women* (1902), Sumie MISHIMA's *My Narrow Isle* (1941), and Etsu Inagaki SUGIMOTO's *A Daughter of the Samurai* (1926).[45]

What was unique about Benedict's approach to the issue of gender was that she used the paradigm of "culture" to explain gender. Instead of foregrounding gender as a category of analysis in explaining women's experiences, she placed gender under the larger cultural pattern of hierarchy and saw gender relations as a symptom or an effect of culture. Whereas Pearl Buck, for example, used "gender" to explain "culture," Benedict's anthropological discourse used "culture" to explain "gender." But while the two approaches to, and narrativizations of, gender were quite different from one another, they ultimately had the same effect of reinforcing the link between culture and gender and validating the association between Asia and particular types of gender and sexuality.

Benedict treats gender as a subcategory of the larger hierarchical patterns in Japanese life that promote the virtue of "taking one's proper station" in Japanese life.

> Whatever one's age, one's position in the hierarchy depends on whether one is male or female. The Japanese woman walks behind her husband and has a lower status. Even women who on occasions when they wear American clothes walk alongside and precede him through a door, again fall to the rear when they have donned their kimonos. The Japanese daughter of the family must get along as best she can while the presents, the attentions, and the money for education go to her brothers. Even when higher schools were established for young women the prescribed courses were heavily loaded with instruction in etiquette and bodily movement.[46]

While she thus calls attention to the strict gender inequality in Japanese society, Benedict also mentions that Japanese women still have greater freedom than women in most other Asian countries, since they are permitted to walk around the town, are responsible for the household finances, have a great say in their children's marriages, and run the household once they become mothers-in-law. But rather than using gender as a social category or an analytical category, Benedict treats gender inequality and patriarchal ideology as one manifestation of Japan's hierarchical cultural pattern and thus naturalizes it as being "Japanese."

Benedict also explains the Japanese family structure and domestic relations within the larger context of hierarchy rather than focusing on the specific issue of gender. She explains Japanese family structure by demonstrating how in respectable Japanese families the parents select their son's wife, and the good son's repayment of indebtedness to his parents does not allow him to question the parental decision; furthermore, if the mother-in-law finds fault with the wife, she may send the wife away and break up the marriage even when the husband is happy with his wife. She illustrates a case where a mother forces her pregnant young daughter-in-law to leave her grieving husband. When the child was born, the mother-in-law came accompanied by her silent and submissive son to claim the baby, and disposed of it immediately to a foster home. Rather than discussing the gender relations involved in this case, Benedict explains it in terms of filial piety and the payment of indebtedness: "In the United States all such stories are taken as instances of outside interference with an individual's right to happiness. Japan cannot consider this interference as 'outside' because of her postulate of indebtedness. Such stories in Japan . . . are tales of the truly virtuous, of persons who have earned their right to respect themselves, who have proved themselves strong enough to accept proper personal frustrations."[47] This account of filial piety and payment of indebtedness to parents is entirely based on the son's point of view and does not allow any discussion of the status of the bride.

Along with the issues of gender relations and patriarchy, sexuality is also embedded within Benedict's larger mapping of the Japanese social order. For example, in her discussion of the forms of payment for one's debt to others, Benedict cites a letter sent to the advice column of a journal of psychoanalysis. An elderly widowed man confesses that after his wife died he dallied with a young prostitute, bought her freedom and took her to his home, taught her etiquette and kept her as a maid. His children and children-in-law look down on him for this act and treat him as a stranger. The girl's parents, who initially wanted the girl to return home so she could get married, have consented that she may continue in the situation. Although the girl herself wants to remain by his side until his death, he sometimes considers sending her home, because the girl is his daughter's age. Afflicted with a chronic illness, he asks for advice on what course to take. The doctor makes a judgmental diagnosis on the man's character, stating that he should have told his children that he had to live with a woman rather than making them indebted to him for remaining unmarried for their sake. The doctor obfuscates the interrelated issues of obligations between parent and children, sexual desire, financial interests involved in the arrangement, and the man's aging. Benedict sees this case as "thoroughly Japanese." According to her, "the doctor regards this as a clear case of the old man's having put too heavy an *on* [indebtedness; obligation] upon his children."[48] By focusing on the issue of obligation and by characterizing the case as specifically "Japanese," she treats such issues as gender relations, sexuality, and patriarchy as part of larger cultural paradigm of Japanese national character.

When Benedict more explicitly and directly discusses the issue of sexuality, it is also within the context of "proper station." In the chapter on "The Circle of Human Feelings," she describes various physical pleasures in which the Japanese indulge and argues that

> The Japanese do not condemn self-gratification. They are not Puritans. They consider physical pleasures good and worthy of cultivation. They are sought and

valued. Nevertheless, they have to be kept in their place. They must not intrude upon the serious affairs of life.[49]

Benedict explains that the Japanese are not as moralistic as Americans are regarding erotic pleasure, since "Sex, like any other 'human feeling,' they regard as thoroughly good in its minor place in life."[50] She argues that whereas Americans consider love and marriage as one and the same thing, for the Japanese love and erotic pleasure are fenced off from one another as separate provinces, not by the division between the public and the surreptitious, but by the division between a man's major obligations and his minor relaxation. She accounts for the accepted practice of upper-class men keeping a mistress or a more general custom of men visiting geishas or prostitutes as activities falling within the latter domain. Pointing out the difference between such practices and "the whole Oriental arrangement of polygamy," Benedict states that "the Japanese keep family obligations and 'human feelings' even spatially apart."[51] She renders her explanation wholly through the male point of view, and apart from a cursory remark that a man's search for erotic pleasure outside of the home is openly acknowledged by his wife and that "[s]he may be unhappy about it but that is her own affair,"[52] she does not delve into the cultural meanings or social arrangements of sexuality for Japanese women. For Benedict, the question of sexuality was no more or less than one piece of evidence for her thesis that the Japanese kept everything in its proper place.

Benedict used the pattern of Japanese culture she mapped in order to explain gender relations, patriarchy, domestic life, and sexuality, subsuming them under the general rubric of the hierarchical order in Japanese life. While the relationship she depicted between "culture" and "gender" was different from the approaches taken by some of the other producers of American discourse about Asia—Pearl Buck, for example, used the category of gender and domesticity to describe and explain Chinese-ness—Benedict's analysis produced the same effect as the studies that preceded hers. The link drawn between culture and gender resulted in affirming the association between Asia and particular types of gender relations (patriarchy) and sexuality (licentious, extramarital).

Benedict's use of a cultural paradigm to discuss gender and sexuality was reflective of contemporary anthropological discourse and practice. Tied to wartime political conditions and needs and given extensive government support and funding, leading anthropologists—such as Benedict, Margaret Mead, Gregory Bateson, Edward Sapir, Clyde Kluckhohn, Alexander Leighton, and Geoffrey Gorer—engaged in so-called "applied anthropology." Although there was a significant debate within the discipline as to the uses of anthropology for wartime purposes, by 1943 it was estimated that over one-half of professional anthropologists were involved full-time in the war effort, believing that their work ultimately led to the creation of "scientific humanism" or "humanistic science."[53]

At the core of their intellectual and political pursuits was a commitment to revising the concept of "race" and to foregrounding "culture" as the determining factor in people's behaviors. As disciples of Franz Boas, who had been the extremely influential mentor of Benedict and Mead, this group of anthropologists renounced the theories of biological determinism, or scientific racism, which dominated nineteenth-century American racial thinking. Many of the scholars who came to be associated with Culture and Personality studies repudiated theories of biologically engendered superiority or inferiority in intellect or character. Race, they argued, was not a determining factor in behavior. Rather, integrated cultural patterns, the unconscious logic of sentiments and assumptions, and the processes of enculturation were the keys to understanding people's behaviors. Culture was inherited from the past, but had to be learned by each generation, and was capable of being altered. In many ways, the scholars of Culture and Personality studies replaced "race" with "culture" as a paradigm for understanding human behavior.[54]

As a pioneer in this approach, she explicated the theory and demonstrated the methods of the "culture" paradigm in her earlier work, most notably *Patterns of Culture*. Based on the assumption that individual behaviors, beliefs, and customs are always interconnected and constitute a piece of a holistic culture, Benedict maintained that individual behaviors are always defined and constrained by culture. *The Chrysanthemum and the Sword* applied this general approach, as the book's subtitle, *Patterns of Japanese Culture*, suggests. According to Benedict, the book "examines Japanese assumptions about the conduct of life," and "describes these assumptions as they have manifested themselves whatever the activity in hand. It is about what makes Japan a nation of Japanese."[55]

The anthropologists' foregrounding of "culture" over "race" had a highly significant impact on the discourse about race and racism in the United States and contributed much to repudiating biological determinism. However, the anthropologists' replacement of "race" with "culture" brought about the same consequences as many of the preceding approaches and discourses about the racial Other in terms of gendering. By making gender a symptom or an effect of culture, Benedict's culture paradigm naturalized certain forms of gender relations as constitutive elements of Japanese culture and society. As a result, it not only reinforced the link between gender and culture but also "scientifically" validated the association between particular types of gender relations and sexuality and Japan. Ironically enough, Benedict's work in scientific anti-racism and the use of the culture paradigm resulted in re-gendering Japan as the feminized racial Other.

The Chrysanthemum and the Sword had a tremendous impact politically, intellectually, and culturally. It was read enthusiastically in Washington, particularly because Benedict praised the work of the U.S. occupation of Japan, "administered with skill" by General MacArthur.[56] The American administration's decision to keep the Emperor and the Japanese government intact and to promote labor organization in Japan was in line with Benedict's analysis of the sentiments and needs of the Japanese people. She recommended Japanese disarmament as the best future course in order to reconstruct the Japanese economy, a course which was ultimately followed by the occupation policymakers. The Chief of the Advisory Study Group, Plans and Operation Division, War Department General Staff, wrote to Benedict that his group had studied *The Chrysanthemum and the Sword* with interest and gained "insight into pertinent problems now facing the U.S."[57] But beyond the praise for her recommendations for the American administration in Japan, Benedict's book was popular in Washington because, according to Margaret Mead, "It was the kind of book that colonels could mention to generals and captains to admirals without fear of producing an explosion against 'jargon,'" and was also "safe to put in the hands of congressmen alert to resist the 'schemes of long-haired intellectuals.'"[58]

On the intellectual level, Benedict's study had a strong influence on the subsequent development of "culture and personality studies" and "national character studies." As one of the first attempts to apply anthropological methods to a modern, industrialized culture, and also to "study culture at a distance" interdisciplinarily without recourse to fieldwork, *The Chrysanthemum and the Sword* soon became a classic in the field of anthropology, pointing to new methodological and thematic directions. The book also had a tremendous impact on American understanding of the hierarchical nature of Japanese social structure and the pressure for conformity, which became a long-standing theme in many areas of Japanese Studies.

The publication of *The Chrysanthemum and the Sword* was greeted with much enthusiasm in Japan as well and was given a canonical status in the literatures about Japanese culture. Japanese scholars and public intellectuals have treated the book with serious attention and have repeatedly held debates about its value.[59] Benedict's argument about the hierarchy of Japanese society had an important influence on scholars of so-called *nihonjin-ron* (studies of Japanese-ness) that burgeoned in postwar Japan, particularly prominent anthropologists and sociologists such as Watsuji Tetsuro, Nagai Michio, and Nakane Chie. The book continues to be widely read in Japan, and while shifts in the field of anthropology have led most American scholars to give the book little attention today beyond that of a classic, Japanese scholars and public intellectuals have demonstrated a sustained interest in and engagement with the text, producing a number of new studies on the book.[60]

The book also exerted a significant cultural influence on American public opinion about Japan. During the 1930s and 1940s, existing Orientalist discourse about Japan and the wartime fear of the aggressive enemy had generated blatantly racist and prejudiced views of the Japanese in the American mind.[61] Benedict herself claimed that "The Japanese were the most alien enemy the United States ever fought in all-out struggle. In no other war with a major foe had it been necessary to take into account such exceedingly different habits of acting and thinking."[62] In such a climate, Benedict explained Japan's cultural and social foundations so that Americans could see the Japanese as "human," rather than incomprehensibly barbarous and cruel. On the other hand, as many later critics have pointed out, the observations and analyses Benedict made in *The Chrysanthemum and the Sword* did not depart fundamentally from the existing dominant view of Japan as being undemocratic and unindividualistic. As historian John Dower argues,

> [Although the series of national character studies produced in this period] may have helped make the Japanese a more complex people in Western eyes, they also gave a patina of scholarly credibility to the impression that the Japanese were unique in unattractive ways, almost totally lacking in diversity or individuality. . . culturally and socially primitive, infantile or childish as individuals and as a group, collectively abnormal in the psychological and psychiatric sense, and tormented at every level by an overwhelming inferiority complex. . . . They remained odd and alien—and, in rather precise ways, stunted.[63]

Benedict's book fit into this larger framework, and by appealing to a wide general audience as well as to academic readers, it reinforced the dominant stereotypes about Japan. Influencing those in intellectual and high policy circles as well as a mass audience, Benedict's work bridged the gap between the populist approach taken by Pearl Buck with regard to China and the intellectual orientation of the Japanologists who preceded her.

*T*he story of *Madame Butterfly* has had tremendous cultural power far beyond the period covered in this book. Innumerable Euro-American cultural texts—ranging from literature, art, theater, opera, and film, to political documents, journalism, and scholarly research— have drawn upon *Madame Butterfly* to construct and reconstruct a gendered and sexualized vision of East-West relations. *Madame Butterfly* quickly became not just a powerful fictional icon but also a trope used to refer to real events and relationships. Only a few years after the publication of Long's original story, *The World* reported on the story of "A 'Madame Butterfly' of the Philippines: The Romantic Problem that Confronts Uncle Sam in His Far Eastern Islands." Lieutenant Sydney Barbank of the United States Infantry left a sweetheart behind in his Kansas hometown when he was sent to the Philippines; when he came back to the U.S., he left another in the "far eastern islands," a "Filipino girl." Unlike Madame Butterfly who patiently waited for Pinkerton's return, the "girl" traveled to San Francisco in search of the Lieutenant. Although her search ended in vain, the case resulted in a complicated legal case involving the War Department in Washington and the Judge Advocate-General.[1]

In the century to follow, *Madame Butterfly* served as a popular American icon used in diverse ways to construct the meanings and fantasies of Western relationship with Asia. In the film *Sayonara*, a 1957 adaptation of James Michener's novel, the interracial romance between an American officer and a Japanese actress in an all-female theater troupe played out the complex racial, gender, sexual, and class politics under the U.S. Occupation of Japan after World War II. In his *M. Butterfly*,

Asian American playwright David Henry Hwang used the real story of a French diplomat's 20-year affair with a beautiful Chinese diva—who turned out to be not only a spy but also a man—to expose and challenge the sexualized Orientalist fantasies long held by Western men. The melodrama of interracial romance was again put on stage in the Broadway musical *Miss Saigon*, set during and after U.S. involvement in the Vietnam War.

These gendered and sexualized tropes and rhetoric reflected and shaped domestic racial and gender ideology in the West on the one hand and the unequal power relations between the Western powers and their colonized subjects on the other. The circulation of such symbolism functioned to justify and endorse Western power, while constituting a unique mix of exoticism and fear, desire and contempt, admiration and domination for the East as the racial Other. A gendered and sexualized vision of the East was particularly apt for negotiating and fulfilling these mixed interests, as it was a medium of both affect and power.

The issue of gender and sexuality in U.S.-Asian relations, however, is not simply a trope used in fictional narratives and discursive constructions. The "real" gender and sexual politics in U.S.-Asian relations have taken place within the context of power dynamics between the two regions. In fact, gender and sexuality are major arenas in which power relations between races and nations have been enacted in both explicit and subtle ways. Even in the time of *Madame Butterfly* when racist sentiments and antimiscegenation laws were solidly operative, marriage or extramarital relationships between American men and Asian women were not unusual. In addition to amorous servicemen such as the fictional Pinkerton or real Lieutenant Barbank, some of the "classic" American officials and Asia specialists, such as the first U.S. consul Townsend Harris and the acclaimed Japanologist Lafcadio Hearn, had Japanese wives or mistresses; many American male travelers to Asia boasted of their visits to brothels and their sexual adventures with native women.[2] The series of war in the Pacific in the twentieth century produced many war brides, "Miss Saigons," and fatherless Amerasian children. The sex industry catering specifically to foreign customers has proliferated around ports and military bases as well as in urban centers of underdeveloped Asian countries during and after the Cold War.[3] While these different manifestations of gender and sexuality in U.S.-Asian relations are shaped by their specific historical, political, and economic contexts, they all point to the close connections between sexual politics and international relations.

While it is easy to denounce the cross-Pacific patriarchy that fosters and maintains these structures, paying attention to the roles of white women in these relations presents a more complex and disturbing picture. A number of scholars in the last two decades have looked at white women's roles in Euroamerican empire-building. While Edward Said rightly demonstrated that Orientalism was a white, upper-class, masculinist discourse, these scholars have complicated and revised

Said's formulation by demonstrating that the discourse and practice of empire has been created, challenged, and/or reinforced by women as well as men, and that white women benefited from their complicity and participation in the culture of empire.[4] White women—both European and American—explored areas of the world foreign to them as missionaries, teachers, administrators, artists, anthropologists, wives of colonial officers, and tourists. The mobility of Western women across national boundaries was the product of specific historical, socioeconomic, and geopolitical circumstances, as well as of various intersecting ideologies about race, class, and gender.[5] As feminist political scientist Cynthia Enloe argues:

> To describe colonization as a process that has been carried on solely by men overlooks the ways in which male colonizers' success depended on some women's complicity. Without the willingness of 'respectable' women to see that colonization offered them an opportunity for adventure, or a new chance of financial security or moral commitment, colonization would have been even more problematic.[6]

These women held complex positions in relation to both the dominant ideology of the West and the racial and cultural Other. On the one hand, Orientalism as a masculinist Western discourse marginalized white women in its public sphere and simultaneously used the status of white women and Western gender relations as a symbol of the superiority of the Western civilization over the rest of the world. Many marginalized women saw themselves in alliance with the racially oppressed, geopolitically dominated, socioeconomically exploited peoples of the colonies, and voiced their anti-imperialist positions. On the other hand, Western overseas expansion and imperial enterprise offered many white, middle-class women the opportunity to gain social and economic autonomy, independence, and status, and to exercise an agency and power denied them in the conventions of Western society. As imperial subjects, white women were situated in a position of superiority vis-à-vis the "natives." As such, many women actively contributed to the imperial enterprise and the culture of Orientalism through their various works in relation to the peoples their nations dominated.[7]

White women's relationship to Orientalism was manifested not only in the "Orient" itself. The ideology, discourse, and culture of Orientalism were ubiquitous within Western societies.[8] The images and ideas about the "Orient" circulated widely within Western societies in the form of "official" documents, media, education, art, literature, popular and consumer culture. White women who stayed "at home" were thus drawn into and became part of the culture of Orientalism.[9] Middle-class women of the late nineteenth century embraced Orientalism through various social and cultural activities, the most widespread of which was the purchase and consumption of commodities. The New Woman of the early twentieth century actively sought contact with foreign cultures and peoples through her profession, social work, cultural endeavors, and leisure.[10] Some New Women devoted their careers to studying foreign cultures, some dedicated themselves to the betterment of the lives of poor immigrants, some produced arts and literatures with foreign settings or motifs, and some tried on those "exotic" styles in their own ways of dressing, housing, or eating.

While scholars have examined such relationships between white women and Orientalism, most of these studies have focused on European women, and the location of American women in the U.S. empire-building, especially vis-à-vis Asia, has rarely been theorized in the same context.[11] This is partly due to the ambivalent relationship U.S. history and historiography have had with "imperialism," as cultural critic Amy Kaplan has discussed, and consequently the questions about the applicability of the term "Orientalism" to U.S.-Asian relations.[12] It is also partly due to the fact that, until recently, the study of race relations in the United States, and particularly the theorizations of the relationship between gender and racial constructions, tended to focus on white-black relations, and the presence of Asians in this matrix has been largely neglected. In this context, the study of white women and American Orientalism allows us to look at the history of white American women in a new light.

Through their engagement with Orientalism, white American women made several gains. First, white women working with "Asian" objects, ideas, themes, and methods found new media of expression. Using foreign settings, figures, and/or styles, women could explore new ways of representing—and thus understanding—the world. While the degree to which such attempts "truly" captured Asian culture varied widely, these engagements certainly contributed to the creative power of American culture. Orientalism has been a highly productive engagement and exploration in the West, and white women played an important role in these productions.

Second, white women in Orientalist discourse gained authority and power that they would otherwise not have had. Orientalism—and the structures that supported it—allowed white women to earn and exercise their power in multiple ways. In relation to their own American society, women often gained access to, and recognition in, the male-dominated world of arts and letters or institutions of scholarly and professional knowledge. Vis-à-vis Asian women, white women possessed material power sustained by racial and class differences and exercised discursive power by performing the roles of, or representing, Asian women. White women also often used Asian men as "native informants" to assert their own cultural authority. Having power over Asian men elevated white women's material and discursive status and bestowed them with masculinist power.

Finally, by going to Asia—either physically or vicariously—white women gained freedom from the conventions of Western gender and sexual relations. For some, the performance of "Asian" gender roles and sexuality was a temporary play that enhanced their own identities as modern American women. For others, it was a way to envision alternatives to gender oppression at home. Differences in motivations and modes of these performances notwithstanding, the crossing of racial and cultural lines allowed white women to explore different forms of womanhood.

In short, by embracing the East white women found new ways of being women. In this sense, Orientalism offered liberation and empowerment for white women. Yet their class, educational, and cultural backgrounds, as well as their individual characters, attitudes, and intellectual and/or political orientations, differently shaped each woman's relationship to Asia. In the preceding chapters, I have illustrated the diversity of those subject positions, discursive strategies, and social and cultural conditions which shaped women's relationship to Asia. I hope to have also portrayed the individual agency and power these women exercised with regard to their own life and work as well as their position in the dominant Orientalist discourse.

In order to fully appreciate what Orientalism offered to women's sense of identity and to American culture as well as understand how such gains were achieved, we need a method that balances the humanist and the materialist perspectives. To understand both the larger ideological context and specific interventions by individual women in that context, we need concrete narratives of cultural history and discourse analyses based on close textual reading. To analyze how the encounter with the foreign is often articulated through a gendered vocabulary and framework, we must integrate the history of foreign relations with the history of gender. To realize the range and diversity of the ways in which a discourse such as Orientalism is expressed, we have to look at different sites of cultural production and understand how each material or genre is governed by its own internal logic while engaging in a dialogue with a larger culture. Toward these goals, I have attempted to use an interdisciplinary approach that bridges these concerns.

It is easy to interpret white women's "contribution" to—or "complicity" in— American Orientalism as their racism and to dismiss or to make a totalizing critique of their work by seeing their interest in, treatment of, and commitment to Asia as uniquely a negative, perhaps hypocritical, preoccupation. It is also tempting to try to rescue these women from such unflattering charges and to insist on the "genuine" interest, "profound" love, and "serious" commitment the women held toward Asian cultures and peoples. In order to turn such inclinations to analytically useful questions, it is important to place these women's positions in their historical and ideological context.

The women who appeared in this book were incredibly serious about their pursuit. It was not a casual or whimsical pastime for a woman to build or renovate her house in Oriental style, pluck her eyebrows and dress in kimonos to learn the manners of Japanese women, or study Chinese and Japanese poetry and compose her own *haikus*. Nor was it common for a woman to move to China and spend years with the Chinese Communists on their Long March, or read hundreds of books on Japan and write an anthropological study of the country. What I sought to interrogate in this book is why these women were so interested in countries that were so geographically and culturally distant from their American homes. Why were they so committed to the causes of men and women so far away, when they saw and experienced severe social problems at home? What drove them to immerse themselves so deeply in Asian arts and letters when Asia was, to say the least, on the wild frontiers of American intellectual life? I have tried to tackle these questions by analyzing the nature of white women's interest in Asia. Serious engagements with Asia were not simply idiosyncratic occurrences of women who "happened" to be interested in Asian affairs; rather, their interest and commitment emerged out of specific historical and ideological circumstances.

Furthermore, none of the women I have discussed were blatant racists who consciously portrayed Asians in a negative light or used their involvement in Asian cultures for selfish personal gain. These women had genuine, "well-intentioned" motives to promote cross-cultural understanding and took great pains to achieve that goal, and my critique is not meant to trivialize their efforts. However, we must make an analytical distinction between intentionality and strategic positioning. We are always situated in an ideological and material context that defines dominant interests, even when we are not conscious of it or when our own beliefs and interests are in conflict with the dominant ones. Through an analysis of different subject positions and discursive devices the women used, we can unfold the web of ideologies that informed and shaped these women as well as the ways in which the women strategically responded to those ideologies.

Finally, these women's endeavors did not necessarily have a negative effect on the actual lives of Asians or on U.S.-East Asian relations. In fact, many of the women's pursuits had a very positive impact in that they not only spread knowledge about Asia to a wide American audience but often created a favorable—often more personal than existing ones—image of Asia in the American mind. Some of the women's works brought tangible social or cultural benefits to Asia and, as in the cases of Agnes Smedley and Ruth Benedict, many have been and continue to be much appreciated by Asians themselves. Thus, the effects of women's activities and pursuits were diverse in quality as well as in quantitative impact. However, the varying effects of their pursuits do not undermine the importance of ideological and discursive forces that underlay individual endeavors. What I attempted to do in this book is not to assess the effects of women's activities but to analyze their roles in shaping American Orientalism as an ideology and discourse.

My project is not to chastise or champion any of the women I have discussed, but rather to critically analyze a set of ideologies that defined the discourse and the agency of individual women in redefining it. American Orientalism is a discourse that both shapes and is shaped by the material reality of U.S.-Asian relations, and one that is constantly revised by those that are not necessarily central to the making of America's "official" narratives about Asia. By locating white women's place in the discourse, I aimed to map out the racial and gendered contours of American Orientalism and to interrogate the power and appeal—as well as the problems and limitations—of cross-cultural encounters in women's explorations of their identities.

Introduction

1. John Luther Long, *Madame Butterfly*, Japanese ed. (New York: Century Co., 1903).

2. Ibid., 142.

3. Ibid., 145.

4. Matthew Frye Jacobson, *Whiteness of a Different Color: European Immigrants and the Alchemy of Race* (Cambridge: Harvard University Press, 1998).

5. Jane Hunter, *The Gospel of Gentility: American Women Missionaries in Turn-of-the-Century China* (New Haven: Yale University Press, 1984); Kohiyama Rui, *Amerika Fujin Senkyoshi: Rainichi no Haikei to Sono Eikyo [American Women Missionaries: The Background and Influence of Their Coming to Japan]* (Tokyo: University of Tokyo Press, 1992).

6. John Kuo Wei Tchen, *New York before Chinatown: Orientalism and the Shaping of American Culture, 1776–1882* (Baltimore and London: Johns Hopkins University Press, 1999).

7. James C. Thomson, Jr., et al., *Sentimental Imperialists: The American Experience in East Asia* (New York: Harper & Row, 1981), 7.

8. Jonathan Goldstein, "Cantonese Artifacts, Chinoiserie, and Early American Idealization of China," in *America Views China: American Images of China Then and Now*, eds. Jonathan Goldstein, et al. (Bethlehem: Lehigh University Press, 1991), 43–55; Ellen Paul Denker, *After the Chinese Taste: China's Influence in America, 1730–1930* (Salem, MA: Peabody Museum of Salem, 1985); Hugh Honour, *Chinoiserie: The Vision of Cathay* (London: John Murray, 1961); Oliver Impey, *Chinoiserie: The Impact of Oriental Styles on Western Art and Decoration* (Oxford: Oxford University Press, 1977).

9. Thomson, Jr., et al., *Sentimental Imperialists*, 44–60, 93–133; Hunter, *Gospel of Gentility*.

10. Beongcheon Yu, *The Great Circle: American Writers and the Orient* (Detroit: Wayne State University Press, 1983), 77–91; T. J. Jackson Lears, *No Place of Grace: Antimodernism*

and the Transformation of American Culture, 1880–1920 (Chicago: University of Chicago Press, 1981), 218–260.

11. Tchen, *New York before Chinatown*.

12. Carol C. Clark, *American Japonism: Contacts between America and Japan, 1854–1910* (Cleveland: Cleveland Museum of Art, 1975); William Hosley, *The Japan Idea: Art and Life in Victorian America* (Hartford, CT: Wadsworth Atheneum, 1990); Clay Lancaster, *The Japanese Influence in America* (New York: Walton H. Rawls, 1963); Julia Meech and Gabriel Weisberg, *Japonisme Comes to America: The Japanese Impact on the Graphic Arts, 1876–1925* (New York: Harry N. Abrams, 1990); Sally Mills, *Japanese Influences in American Art* (Williamstown, MA: Sterling and Francine Clark Art Institute, 1981); *"A Pleasing Novelty": Bunkio Matsuki and the Japan Craze in Victorian Salem* (Salem, MA: Peabody & Essex Museum, 1993); Jane Converse Brown, "The 'Japanese Taste': Its Role in the Mission of the American Home and in the Family's Presentation of Itself to the Public as Expressed in Published Sources, 1876–1916," (Ph.D. Diss., University of Wisconsin, 1987).

Chapter One

1. Louisa May Alcott, *Eight Cousins; or, The Aunt-Hill.* [1875] (New York: Books, Inc., 1946).

2. "Introduction," in Louisa May Alcott, *Alternative Alcott*, ed. Elaine Showalter (New Brunswick and London: Rutgers University Press, 1988), xxiii.

3. Alcott, *Eight Cousins*, 1.

4. Ibid., 62.

5. Ibid., 67–68.

6. Ibid., 69–70.

7. Ibid., 82.

8. John Kuo Wei Tchen, *New York before Chinatown: Orientalism and the Shaping of American Culture, 1776–1882* (Baltimore and London: Johns Hopkins University Press, 1999), esp. 63–163.

9. A number of cultural historians have investigated the world's fairs from such a perspective. Among the best accounts are Robert Rydell, *All the World's a Fair: Visions of Empire at American International Expositions, 1876–1916* (Chicago and London: University of Chicago Press, 1984); Paul Greenhalgh, *Ephemeral Vistas: The Exposition Universelles, Great Exhibitions and World's Fairs, 1851–1939* (Manchester: Manchester University Press, 1988); Yoshimi Shunya, *Hakurankai no Seiji-gaku: Manazashi no Kindai [The Politics of World's Fairs: Modernity of the Gaze]* (Tokyo: Chuo-koron-sha, 1992).

10. Rydell, *All the World's a Fair*, 38–71; John F. Kasson, *Amusing the Million: Coney Island at the Turn of the Century* (New York: Hill and Wang, 1978); Alan Trachtenberg, *Incorporation of America: Culture and Society in the Gilded Age* (New York: Hill and Wang, 1982), 230–232; Curtis M. Hinsley, "The World as Marketplace: Commodification of the Exotic at the World's Columbian Exposition, Chicago, 1893," in *Exhibiting Cultures: The Poetics and Politics of Museum Display*, eds. Ivan Karp and Steven D. Lavine (Washington: Smithsonian Institution Press, 1991), 351–363; Gail Bederman, *Manlines and Civilization: A Cultural History of Gender and Race in the United States, 1880–1917* (Chicago: University of Chicago Press, 1995), Chap. 1.

11. Rydell, *All the World's a Fair*, 49–50; *Official Guide to the Midway Plaisance*, (Chicago: The Columbian Guide Co., 1893), 27–28.

12. On Japanese exhibits at the fair, see Notoji Masako, "Ferisu Kanransha to Ho-ö-den: 1893-nen Shikago Hakurankai ni Miru Nichibei no Nashonarizumu," [Ferris Wheel and Ho-ö-den: U.S. and Japanese Nationalisms in 1893 Chicago World's Fair] in *Gendai Amerika-zo no Saikochiku: Seiji to Bunka no Gendai-shi [Reconstructing the Image of Contemporary America: Contemporary History of Politics and Culture]*, eds. Homma Nagayo, et al. (Tokyo: Tokyo Daigaku Shuppan Kai, 1990), 123–139; Neil Harris, "All the World a Melting Pot? Japan at American Fairs, 1876–1904," in *Mutual Images: Essays in American-Japanese Relations*, ed. Akira IRIYE (Cambridge: Harvard University Press, 1975), 37–46; Clay Lancaster, *The Japanese Influence in America* (New York: Walton H. Rawls, 1963), 76–83.

13. Lancaster, *The Japanese Influence*, 77–83; Harris, "All the World a Melting Pot?" 39–40; Notoji, "Ferisu Kanransha," 132–135. Okakura Kakuzo [sic], who directed the design and decoration of the building, provided a detailed description of the structure in Okakura Kakudzo [sic], *The Hö-ö-den (Pheonix Hall): An Illustrated Description of the Buildings Erected by the Japanese Government at the World's Columbian Exposition, Jackson Park, Chicago* (Tokyo: K. Ogawa, 1893).

14. Lancaster, *The Japanese Influence*, 83.

15. Quoted in Harris, "All the World a Melting Pot?" 39–40.

16. Quoted in Rydell, *All the World's a Fair*, 50.

17. On Asian art collections in American museums, see Warren I. Cohen, *East Asian Art and American Culture: A Study in International Relations* (New York: Columbia University Press, 1992), esp. Chap. 2. On the politics of museum exhibits in general, see Karp and Lavine, eds., *Exhibiting Cultures*; Barbara Kirshenblatt-Gimblett, *Destination Culture: Tourism, Museums, and Heritage* (Berkeley: University of California Press, 1998).

18. Quoted in Morris Carter, *Isabella Stewart Gardner and Fenway Court*, 2nd ed. (Boston and New York: Houghton Mifflin, 1925), 62.

19. Quoted in Louise Hall Tharp, *Mrs. Jack: A Biography of Isabella Stewart Gardner* (Boston: Little, Brown, & Co., 1965), 254.

20. *Books in the Library of Nelson W. Aldrich, Warwick, Rhode Island*, 2 vols. (Boston: The Merrymount Press, 1914).

21. Carol S. Cook, *Travel and Exploration: A Catalogue of the Providence Athenaeum Collection* (Providence: Providence Athenaeum, 1988).

22. Susan Anderson Hay, "Providence, Paris, Kyoto, Peking: Lucy Truman Aldrich and Her Collections," in *Patterns and Poetry: No Robes from the Lucy Truman Alcrich Collection at the Museum of Art, Rhode Island School of Design*, ed. Susan Anderson Hay (Providence: Museum or Art, Rhode Island School of Design, 1992), 12–14.

23. Lucy Truman Aldrich to Abby Aldrich Rockefeller, May 12, 1919. Rockefeller Foundation Archives, RG3. 2AA. Box 7. Letter C.

24. Ibid.

25. Lucy Truman Aldrich to Abby Aldrich Rockefeller, April 15, 1923. Rockefeller Foundation Archives, RG3. 2AA. Box 7. No. 41.

26. Hay, "Providence," 19–20. When Aldrich sailed to Shanghai and took the train to Beijing, bandits took over the Shanghai-to-Beijing express. Although she and other passengers were safely rescued after threats of force by the Western powers, Aldrich lost some of

her jewelry and two pieces of antique Chinese brocade purchased in Shanghai. One story holds that when the Chinese government paid reparations, she spent the money on her collection of Chinese textiles, indicating her persistent passion for her textile collection. Ibid., 11.

27. Ibid., 19.

28. Sadamura Tadashi, "Rokkuferah Korekushon no Oitachi [The life of the Rockefeller Collection]," in *Yomigaeru Bi—Hana to Tori to: Rokkuferah Ukiyoe Korekushon Ten* (Tokyo: Bun-yu-sha, 1990), 143–145.

29. Ian Quimby, "Oriental Influence on American Decorative Arts," *Journal of the Society of Architectural Historians* 35 (1976): 300–308; William Hosley, *The Japan Idea: Art and Life in Victorian America* (Hartford, CT: Wadsworth Atheneum, 1990), 117–153.

30. Mary Blanchard, *Oscar Wilde's America: Counterculture in the Gilded Age* (New Haven and London: Yale University Press, 1998), xiii.

31. Kristin Hoganson, "Cosmopolitan Domesticity: Importing the American Dream, 1965–1920," *American Historical Review* 107 (2002): 55–83.

32. Roger B. Stein, "Artifact as Ideology: The Aesthetic Movement in Its American Cultural Context," in *In Pursuit of Beauty: Americans and the Aesthetic Movement* (New York: Metropolitan Museum of Art, 1986), 27.

33. Blanchard, *Oscar Wilde's America*, 88.

34. T. J. Jackson Lears, *No Place of Grace: Antimodernism and the Transformation of American Culture, 1880–1920* (Chicago: University of Chicago Press, 1981), 218–241.

35. Karen Halttunen, *Confidence Men and Painted Women: A Study of Middle-Class Culture in America, 1830–1870* (New Haven and London: Yale University Press, 1982).

36. Jane Converse Brown, "The 'Japanese Taste': Its Role in the Mission of the American Home and in the Family's Presentation of Itself to the Public as Expressed in Published Sources, 1876–1916," (Ph.D. Diss., University of Wisconsin-Madison, 1987).

37. Charles H. Carpenter, Jr., *Gorham Silver, 1831–1981* (New York: Dodd, Mead, & Co., 1982).

38. Gorham Manufacturing Company, *Photographs of Silver Ware, Manufactured by the Gorham Manufacturing Company* (Providence: Gorham Mfg. Co., 1875). Gorham Collection, John Hay Library, Brown University [hereafter GC].

39. Gorham Mfg. Co., *Photo Book—Silver Hallow Ware* (Providence: Gorham Mfg. Co., [1879]). GC.

40. Gorham Mfg. Co., *Photo Book—Silver Halloware Catalog* (Providence: Gorham Mfg. Co., [1883]); Gorham Mfg. Co., *Photo Book—Silver Holloware, 1880–1884* (Providence: Gorham Mfg. Co., [1884]). GC.

41. Lancaster, *The Japanese Influence*, 37–50.

42. [Gorham Mfg. Co.,] *American Sterling Silver Ware: A Sketch of the Gorham Manufacturing Company, of Providence & New York, U. S. A.* (n.p.: Gorham Mfg. Co., [1876]), 10–11. GC.

43. Charles L. Venable, *Silver in America, 1840–1940: A Century of Splendor* (Dallas: Dallas Museum of Art, 1994), 151.

44. [Gorham Mfg. Co..] *Women's Work at the Gorham Manufacturing Company, Silversmiths, Providence and New York* (n.p.: Gorham Mfg. Co., n.d.). GC.

45. On the production and consumption of goods in the gendered market, see Regina Lee Blaszczyk, "Cinderella Stories: The Glass of Fashion and the Gendered Marketplace,"

in *His and Hers: Gender, Consumption, and Technology*, eds. Roger Horowitz and Arwen Mohun (Charlottesville: University Press of Virginia, 1998), 139–164.

46. Advertisements for "Jap Rose Soap," *Ladies' Home Journal* 20 no. 6 (May 1903), 48; 20 no. 7 (June 1903), 38; 20 no. 8 (July 1903), 35; 20 no. 10 (September 1903), 40; 20 no. 11 (October 1903), 44; 20 no. 12 (November 1903), 59; 21 no. 2 (January 1904), 38; 21 no. 3 (February 1904), 46; 21 no. 4 (March 1904), 51; 21 no. 5 (April 1904), 52.

47. Glidden Varnish Co., *Jap-a-lac* (Cleveland: Glidden Varnish Co., [c.1910]). Winterthur Library.

48. Ibid., 11.

49. Ibid., 3.

50. *"A Pleasing Novelty": Bunkio Matsuki and the Japan Craze in Victorian Salem* (Salem, MA: Peabody & Essex Museum, 1993); Cynthia A. Brandimarte, "Japanese Novelty Stores," *Winterthur Portfolio* 26 (1991): 1–25.

51. William Leach, *Land of Desire: Merchants, Power, and the Rise of a New American Culture* (New York: Vintage, 1993), esp. 104–111.

52. Inderpal Grewal has demonstrated this in terms of British women's relationship to imperialism in *Home and Harem: Nation, Gender, Empire, and the Cultures of Travel* (Durham and London: Duke University Press, 1996), 127.

53. Obituary, Ashley A. Vantine, *New York Times* (January 26, 1890), 3.

54. A. A. Vantine, *Illustrated Catalogue of A. A. Vantine & Co., Importers from the Empires of Japan, China, India, Turkey, Persia, and the East* (New York: A. A. Vantine & Co., n.d. [189-]). Winterthur Library.

55. Ibid., 3.

56. A. A. Vantine & Co., *The Wonder Book* (New York: A. A. Vantine's, n. d.). Winterthur Library.

57. Ibid., n.p.

58. A. A. Vantine, *Entrance to Vantine's: The House of the Orient* (New York: A. A. Vantine's, n.d.). Winterthur Library.

59. *New York Times* (March 20, 1895), 8.

60. *New York Times* (May 18, 1898), 5.

61. *Illustrated Catalogue of A. A. Vantine & Co.*, 4.

62. *Entrance to Vantine's*, n. p.

63. *New York Times* (February 4, 1894), 9.

64. *New York Times* (October 21, 1894), 17.

65. *New York Times* (October 18, 1896), 13.

66. Yamanaka & Co., Ko Yamanaka Sadajiro O Den Hensan Kai [The Editorial Committee for the Biography of Late Yamanaka Sadajiro], ed., *Yamanaka Sadajiro O Den [The Biography of Late Sadajiro Yamanaka]* (Osaka: Yamanaka & Co., 1939), 91–104.

67. Yamanaka & Co., *Catalogue of Room Decorations and Artistic Furniture* (Osaka, Japan: Yamanaka & Co., 1905). Winterthur Library.

68. An exemplary study from such a perspective is Timothy Mitchell, *Colonising Egypt* (Cambridge: Cambridge University Press, 1988).

69. *Yamanaka Sadajiro O Den*, 280–281. [My translation]

70. See, for example, Yamanaka & Co., *Catalogue of Room Decorations and Artistic Furniture* (Osaka, Japan: Yamanaka & Co., 1905), n. p.; Yamanaka & Co., *Illustrated Catalogue of a Remarkable Collection of Early Chinese Pottery, Porcelains, and Bronzes of the*

Han, T'ang, Sung, Yuan, and Ming Dynasties, including Many Mortuary Objects which Rank in Archaeological Importance with the Specimens Found in Egyptian Tombs, and Other Rare Objects which Are of Uncommon Interest to Connoisseurs, Amateurs, and Art Institutions (New York: Yamanaka & Co., 1912). Winterthur Library.

71. *New York Times* (April 17, 1927), 5; *New York Times* (Dec. 7, 1929), 13; *New York Times* (Dec. 8, 1929), 24.

72. *New York Times* (May 13, 1934), Sec. IX, 7.

73. *New York Times* (Sept. 9, 1934), Sec. IX, 6.

74. *New York Times* (Jan. 12, 1936), Sec., IX, 10.

75. Frederic A. Sharf, "Bunkio Matsuki: Salem's Most Prominent Japanese Citizen," in *"A Pleasing Novelty": Bunkio Matsuki and the Japan Craze in Victorian Salem* (Salem, MA: Peabody & Essex Museum, 1993), 7–33.

76. Hina HIRAYAMA, "Curious Merchandise: Bunkio Matsuki's Japanese Department," in *"A Pleasing Novelty,"* 97.

77. Ibid., 103.

78. Bunkio MATSUKI, *Catalogue of Japanese Artists' Materials* (Boston: Bunkio Matsuki, 1904); Bunkio Matsuki, *Supplement to Catalogue of Japanese Artists' Materials* (Boston: Bunkio Matsuki, 1904); Bunkio Matsuki, *Catalogue of Japanese Artists' Materials* (Boston: Bunkio Matsuki, 1908). Winterthur Library.

79. *Lotus* 1 (December 1903): n. p. Winterthur Library.

80. Hosley, *The Japan Idea*, 43–44; Kenneth Trapp, "Rookwood and the Japanese Mania in Cincinnati," *Cincinnati Historical Society Bulletin* 39 (1987): 51–75; Brandimarte, "Japanese Novelty Stores."

81. Brown, "The 'Japanese Taste,'" xi.

82. "Fashion Novelties in New York Shops," *Godey's Lady's Book* 130 no. 775 (January 1895), 224.

83. "Much in Little Space," *The House Beautiful* (1878), 108.

84. V. G. Reinhardt, "Illuminating," *Harper's New Monthly Magazine* 73 (1886), 935.

85. "A Japanese Room," *Ladies' Home Journal* 12 (1895), 13.

86. "Screens for the Clever Woman to Make," *Ladies' Home Journal* 25 (1908), 51.

87. Quoted in Martha Crabill McClaugherty, "Household Art: Creating the Artistic Home, 1868–1893," *Winterthur Portfolio* 18 (1983): 8.

88. Hosley, *The Japan Idea*, 137.

89. *In Pursuit of Beauty: Americans and the Aesthetic Movement* (New York: Metropolitan Museum of Art, 1986), 39, 120–127.

90. *Good Furniture* 7 (September 1916): 129.

Chapter Two

1. Jean-Christophe Agnew, "A House of Fiction: Domestic Interiors and the Commodity Aesthetic," in *Consuming Visions: Accumulation and Display in America, 1880–1920*, ed. Simon J. Bronner (New York: W.W. Norton & Co., 1989), 144.

2. Eunyoung Cho, "The Selling of Japan: Race, Gender, and Cultural Politics in the American Art World, 1876–1915," (Ph.D. Diss., University of Delaware, 1998), esp. Chap. 5.

3. Linda Nochlin, *Representing Women* (New York: Thames and Hudson, 1999), 185–186.

4. Griselda Pollock, *Mary Cassatt: Painter of Modern Women* (London: Thames and Hudson, 1998), 16.

5. Nochlin, *Representing Women*, 194.

6. Nancy Mowll Mathews, "The Color Prints in the Context of Mary Cassatt's Art," in *Mary Cassatt: The Color Prints*, eds. Nancy Mowll Mathews and Barbara Stern Shapiro (New York: Harry N. Abrams, 1989), 36; Pollock, *Mary Cassatt*, 166–167.

7. Tadashi KOBAYASHI, *Ukiyo-e: An Introduction to Japanese Woodblock Prints*, trans. Mark A. Harbison (Tokyo: Kondansha International, 1982).

8. Mathews, "The Color Prints," 38–39.

9. Barbara Stern Shapiro, "Mary Cassatt's Color Prints and Contemporary French Printmaking," in *Mary Cassatt: The Color Prints*, eds. Mathews and Shapiro, 64.

10. Anne Higonnet, *Berthe Morisot's Images of Women* (Cambridge: Harvard University Press, 1992), 188–191.

11. Ibid., 186–187; Pollock, *Mary Cassatt*, 176–177.

12. Kathleen McCarthy, *Women's Culture: American Philanthropy and Art, 1830–1930* (Chicago: University of Chicago Press, 1991), 52. Also see Kirsten Swinth, *Painting Professionals: Women Artists and the Development of Modern American Art, 1870–1930* (Chapel Hill: University of North Carolina Press, 2001).

13. Mary Warner Blanchard, *Oscar Wilde's America: Counterculture in the Gilded Age* (New Haven and London: Yale University Press, 1998), xiii, 46.

14. Reina Lewis, *Gendering Orientalism: Race, Femininity, and Representation* (London and New York: Routledge, 1996).

15. Mary Evans O'Keefe Gravalos and Carol Pulin, *Bertha Lum* (Washington: Smithsonian Institution Press, 1990), 7–32.

16. Meike Bal and Norman Bryson, "Semiotics and Art History," *Art Bulletin* 73 (1991): 199.

17. Linda Nochlin, *The Politics of Vision: Essays in Nineteenth-Century Art and Society* (New York: Harper & Row, 1989), 35–36.

18. Gravalos and Pulin, *Bertha Lum*, 16.

19. Bertha Lum, *Gangplanks to the East* (New York: The Henkle-Yewdale House, Inc., 1936), 79–80.

20. Peter Lum, *My Own Pair of Wings* (San Francisco: Chinese Materials Center, Inc., 1981), 150–151.

21. Arnold Genthe, *Pictures of Old Chinatown*, with text by Will Irwin (New York: Moffat, Yard, & Co., 1908), 4, 30–31.

22. For an insightful reading of Genthe's photographs of Chinatown, see James S. Moy, *Marginal Sights: Staging the Chinese in America* (Iowa City: University of Iowa Press, 1993), Chap. 6.

23. Bertha E. Jaques, *Helen Hyde and Her Work: An Appreciation* (Chicago: The Libby Company, 1922), 7.

24. Ibid., 10.

25. Mabel Hyde, *Jingles from Japan: As Set Forth by the Chinks*, illustrated by Helen Hyde (San Francisco: A. M. Robertson, 1901).

26. On the ideological and cultural work of the notion of "the coolie" in nineteenth-century America, see Robert G. Lee, *Orientals: Asian Americans in Popular Culture* (Philadelphia: Temple University Press, 1999), Chap. 2.

27. Jaques, *Helen Hyde and Her Work*, 18.

28. Ibid., 21.

29. William Hosley, *The Japan Idea: Art and Life in Victorian America* (Hartford, CT: Wadsworth Atheneum, 1990), 164.

30. Nancy Elizabeth Owen, *Rookwood and the Industry of Art: Women, Culture, and Commerce, 1880–1913* (Athens: Ohio University Press, 2001); *In Pursuit of Beauty: America and the Aesthetic Movement* (New York: The Metropolitan Museum of Art, 1986), 31–32; On examples of women artists working with Asian art in media such as china painting and textiles, see Cynthia Brandimarte, "Somebody's Aunt and Nobody's Mother: The American China Painter and Her Work, 1870–1920," *Winterthur Portfolio* 23 (1988): 203–224; Kenneth Trapp, "Rookwood and the Japanese Mania in Cincinnati," *Cincinnati Historical Society Bulletin* 39 (1987): 51–75; Marcene Jean Edmiston, "Candace Wheeler and the Associated Artists: American Aesthetic Interiors and Their Textiles" (M.A. Thesis, George Washington University, 1990).

Chapter Three

1. James S. Moy, *Marginal Sights: Staging the Chinese in America* (Iowa City: University of Iowa Press, 1993), Chap. 7.

2. Angela C. Pao, *The Orient of the Boulevards: Exoticism, Empire, and Nineteenth-Century French Theater* (Philadelphia: University of Pennsylvania Press, 1998)

3. On studies of racial-crossing in black-white context, see Eric Lott, *Love and Theft: Blackface Minstrelsy and the American Working-Class* (New York and Oxford: Oxford University Press, 1993); Michael Rogin, *Blackface, White Noise: Jewish Immigrants in the Hollywood Melting Pot* (Berkeley: University of California Press, 1996); Susan Gubar, *Racechanges: White Skin, Black Face in American Culture* (New York and Oxford: Oxford University Press, 1997); Gayle Wald, *Crossing the Line: Racial Passing in Twentieth-Century U.S. Literature and Culture* (Durham and London: Duke University Press, 2000). The racial lines crossed through performance were not limited to the black-white binary. See, for example, Philip J. Deloria, *Playing Indian* (New Haven: Yale University Press, 1998).

4. Montrose J. Moses, introduction to *Madame Butterfly*, in David Belasco, *Six Plays: Madame Butterfly, Du Barry, The Darling of the Gods, Adrea, the Girl of the Golden West, The Return of Peter Grimm* (Boston: Little, Brown, and Company, 1928), 6.

5. David Belasco, "Star Making: A Confession of the Theater," *Liberty* (July 25, 1925), 22. David Belasco Papers, New York Public Library for the Performing Arts, [hereafter DBP], Box 1, Folder 57.

6. Gayle Wald discusses the question of "race" knowledge and the agency of vision in cinematic representation of racial passing in her *Crossing the Line*, 93–94.

7. *Telegraph* [New York] (March 6, 1900?); *Evening World* [New York] (n.d.?) DBP, Microfilm Reel 16.

8. "This 'Butterfly' a Winged Jewel: Belasco's Little Play Earns Distinct Success—Blanche Bates, Relieved from Farce, Shows Once More Her Remarkable Capabilities," *The New York Press* (March 6, 1900), n.p. DBP, Microfilm Reel 16.

9. "Morris Gest Now Enters the Motion Picture Field," *Review* (April 24, 1926). DBP, Microfilm Reel 16.

10. Belasco, "The Darling of the Gods," in *Six Plays*, 177.

11. Ibid., 221.

12. n.t., *Mobile Register* (October 4, 1903?), n.p. DBP, Microfilm Reel 16.

13. "Fond of the Jap Traits — Blanche Bates Acquainted with Race Early in Life — Has Many Moments to Remind Her of Flowery Kingdom — Not Possible to Act as a Real Mongolian Woman — 'Darling of the Gods' Is Equipped with Beautiful Scenery," *Chicago Chronicle* (February 16, 1904), n.p. DBP, Microfilm Reel 16.

14. On Asian immigrants' labor as domestic workers, see Evelyn Nakano Glenn, *Issei, Nisei, War Bride: Three Generations of Japanese American Women in Domestic Service* (Philadelphia: Temple University Press, 1986); Evelyn Nakano Glenn, "From Servitude to Service Work: Historical Continuities in the Racial Division of Paid Reproductive Labor," *Signs* 18 (1992): 1–43; Yen Le Espiritu, *Asian American Women and Men* (Thousand Oaks: Sage, 1997), Chap. 2; Mitziko Sawada, *Tokyo Life, New York Dreams: Urban Japanese Visions of America, 1890–1924* (Berkeley: University of California Press, 1996).

15. Wendell Phillips Dodge, "A Chat with Blanche Bates," *Theatre Magazine* 18 (July/Dec 1913): 24.

16. [n.t., n.d.]; "Blanche Bates to Nurse Japs," [*InterOcean*, Feb. 11, 1904]; "Blanche Bates to Aid the Japanese," [*Philadelphia Item*, Feb. 11, 1904]. DBP, Microfilm Reel 7.

17. "How a Yankee Girl Becomes a Japanese Maiden," *Boston Sunday Journal* (November 29, 1903), n.p. DBP, Reel 16.

18. n.t., *Boston Transcript* (November 25, 1903), n.p. DBP, Microfilm Reel 16.

19. "Old Japan in Modern Boston: 'The Darling of the Gods' Is Doing All Kinds of 'Stunts' with Our Talk," *Boston Evening News* (November 25, 1903), n.p. DBP, Microfilm Reel 16.

20. "How a Yankee Girl Becomes a Japanese Maiden," *Boston Sunday Journal* (November 29, 1903), n.p. DBP, Microfilm Reel 16.

21. "Fond of the Jap Traits — Blanche Bates Acquainted with Race Early in Life — Has Many Moments to Remind Her of Flowery Kingdom — Not Possible to Act as a Real Mongolian Woman — 'Darling of the Gods' Is Equipped with Beautiful Scenery," *Chicago Chronicle* (February 16, 1904), n.p. DBP, Microfilm Reel 16.

22. Blanche Bates, "The Role and the Soul," n.t. n.d. DBP, Microfilm Reel 16.

23. "If the Japanese Portrayed Us," *St. Louis Globe Democrat* (December 4, 1904), n.p. DBP, Microfilm Reel 16.

24. On the racialized and gendered nature of the discourse of "civilization," see Gail Bederman, *Manliness and Civilization: A Cultural History of Gender and Race in the United States, 1880–1917* (Chicago: University of Chicago Press, 1995).

25. Albert Auster, *Actresses and Suffragists: Women in the American Theater, 1890–1920* (New York: Praeger, 1984), 6. Some exemplary scholarship on the New Woman includes: Nancy Cott, *The Grounding of Modern Feminism* (New Haven: Yale University Press, 1987); Kathy Peiss, *Cheap Amusements: Working Women and Leisure at the Turn-of-the-Century New York* (Philadelphia: Temple University Press, 1986); Christina Simmons, "Modern Sexuality and the Myth of Victorian Repression," in *Gender and American History since 1890*, ed. Barbara Melosh (New York: Routledge, 1992), 17–42; Ellen Wiley Todd, "Art, the 'New Woman,' and Consumer Culture," in ibid., 127–154; Christine Stansell, *American Moderns: Bohemian New York and the Creation of a New Century* (New York: Henry Holt & Co., 2000).

26. The Japanese name for Madame Butterfly is spelled "Cho-Cho-San" in Long's and Belasco's texts, "Cio-Cio-San" in Illica and Giacosa's libretto for the opera.

27. "Puccini and 'Madama Butterfly,'" *Metropolitan Opera House, Grand Opera Season 1914–1915* [published by the Theatre Magazine Co., New York], 26. Geraldine Farrar Collection [hereafter GFC], Library of Congress, Box 16.

28. Contract between the Metropolitan Opera Company and Geraldine Farrar, June 1908, Clause V. GFC, Box 12. "When Stars of the Opera Sings at Concerts: Their Earnings from Important Items in Incomes Reaching the $100,000 Mark," n.t., n.d., Scrapbook 1908–1909, 47. GFC, Box 22; "Opera Singers' Salaries: Estimates of What Some Leading Metropolitan Artists Make in Season," [*Musical America.*, n.d.] Scrapbook 1910, 47, GFC, Box 24.

29. "Miss Farrar's Art Aids Puccini Opera: Success of Madame Butterfly Due Largely to Popularity of Singer," [n.t., n.d.], Scrapbook 1909–1910, 90, GFC, Box 23. Also see "Geraldine Farrar's 'Butterfly,'" [n.t., n.d.], Scrapbook 1909–1910, p. 91. GFC, Box 23.

30. Victor Talking Machine Company, Statement of Royalty Due on Selections by Geraldine Farrar, February 1, 1924. GFC, Box 12. Other popular recordings included "Habanera" from *Carmen*, which sold 2,104 copies in the same year, and *"Vissi d'arte e d'amor"* from *Tosca*, which sold 1,743 copies.

31. For cultural studies approaches to musicology that analyze opera's ability to construct various, often competing, meanings at once through musical as well as narrative, visual, and histrionic means, see Catherine Clément, *Opera, or the Undoing of Women* Trans. Betsy Wing (Minneapolis: University of Minnesota Press, 1988 [1979]); Susan McClary, *Feminine Endings: Music, Gender, and Sexuality* (Minneapolis: University of Minnesota Press, 1991); Edward Said, *Musical Elaborations* (New York: Columbia University Press, 1991); Jonathan Bellman, *The Exotic in Western Music* (Boston: Northeastern University Press, 1998).

32. Elizabeth Nash, *Always First Class: The Career of Geraldine Farrar* (Washington, DC: University Press of America, 1981), 1.

33. Ibid., 238.

34. Ibid., 67.

35. Contract between the Metropolitan Opera Company and Geraldine Farrar, June 1908, Clause XI. GFC, Box 12. Since the nineteenth century, it was common practice for performers to provide their own costumes. See Auster, *Actresses and Suffragists*, 54.

36. Nash, *Always First Class*, 67; Geraldine Farrar, *Such Sweet Compulsion: The Autobiography of Geraldine Farrar* (New York: The Greystone Press, 1938), 102–103; Geraldine Farrar, *Geraldine Farrar: The Story of an American Singer, by Herself* (Boston: Houghton Mifflin, 1915), 92–94.

37. Geraldine Farrar, "Farrar's Real Opinion of Puccini's Butterfly: 'Difficult but Pleasing' Is Judgment of American Prima Donna on Role of Cio-Cio-San," n.t., n.d., Scrapbook 1907–1908, n.p., GFC, Box 21.

38. Dennis Hendricks [The Greystone Press] to Geraldine Farrar, August 26, 1938; Dennis Hendricks to Geraldine Farrar, September 1, 1938. GFC, Box 9.

39. "Farrar in 'Mme. Butterfly,'" n.t., [April 16, 1909], Scrapbook 1909–1910, 12. GFC, Box 23.

40. n.t. n.d., Scrapbook 1908–1909, 30. GFC, Box 22.

41. "Farrar and Martinelli in 'Butterfly,'" [*Musical America*, November 29, 1913], n.p. Scrapbook 1910–, No. 3, n.p. GFC, Box 25.

42. n.t., [*Musical America*, April 4, 1914], n.p. Scrapbook 1910–, No.3, n.p. GFC, Box 25.

43. n.t., [*Musical America*, May 9, 1914], n.p. Scrapbook 1910–, No.3, n.p. GFC, Box 25.

44. Clara S. Boyden, n.t., [*Musical America*, May 2, 1914], n.p. Scrapbook 1910-, No.3, n.p. GFC, Box 25.

45. n.t., [*Musical America*, April 18, 1914], n.p. Scrapbook 1910–, No.3, n.p. GFC, Box 25.

46. Miller Uler, "Miss Geraldine Farrar's Chicago: American Woman Outshines Rivals in 'Butterfly,'" [n.t., n.d.], Scrapbook 1907–1908, n.p. GFC, Box 21.

47. "Madama Butterfly," [n.t., n.d.], Scrapbook, 1908–1909, 16. GFC, Box 22.

48. "Bohemian Singer Wants Star Role: Prima Donna Angry because American Was Preferred for 'Madame Butterfly,'" [n.t., n.d.], Scrapbook 1908–1909, 23. GFC, Box 22; n.t., n.d. [1909], Scrapbook, n.p. GFC, Box 24.

49. Miller Uler, "Miss Geraldine Farrar's Chicago: American Woman Outshines Rivals in 'Butterfly,'" [n.t., n.d.], Scrapbook 1907–1908, n.p. GFC, Box 21.

50. n.t., n.d., Scrapbook 1909–1910, 11. GFC, Box 23.

51. Farrar, *Geraldine Farrar*, 94.

52. Terry Castle, "In Praise of Brigitte Fassbaender: Reflections on Diva-Worship," in *En Travesti: Women, Gender Subversion, Opera* eds. Corinne E. Blackmer and Patricia Juliana Smith (New York: Columbia University Press, 1995), 22, 24–25; Nash, *Always First Class*, 200. Joseph Horowitz also points out that the cult of Wagner in America between the late nineteenth century and WWI powerfully infiltrated the women's movement and activated emerging New Women. See Joseph Horowitz, *Wagner Nights: An American History* (Berkeley: University of California Press, 1994).

53. *The Radcliffe Magazine* 3 (1900): 69–77; *The Orientals: An Operetta in Two Acts* Music and Lyrics, Josephine Sherwood, Libretto, Katharine Berry ([Cambridge, MA]: n.p., 1898); Josephine Hull, diary, 1898, Josephine Hull Papers, Box 1, Vol. 10, Schlesinger Library, Radcliffe College.

54. *Japanese-American Commercial Weekly* 9 no. 389 (December 26, 1908), 7; Ibid. 10 no. 390 (January 2, 1909), 4.

55. Amy Kaplan's *The Social Construction of American Realism* (Chicago: University of Chicago Press, 1988), 94–96, provides an insightful analysis of tableaux vivants as used in Edith Wharton's *The House of Mirth*.

56. Margaret Hayden Rector, *Alva, That Vanderbilt-Belmont Woman* (Wickford, RI: The Dutch Island Press, 1992). On Belmont's involvement in the suffrage movement, see Cott, *The Grounding of Modern Feminism*, 55–56.

57. Antoinette F. Downing, *The Chinese Teahouse at Marble House* (Newport, RI: The Preservation Society of Newport County, 1982).

58. *Town Topics* [New York] 72 no. 2 (July 9, 1914), 1.

59. *Town Topics* 72 no. 4 (July 23, 1914), 5.

60. *The New York Times* (July 25, 1914), 7.

61. Inderpal Grewal, *Home and Harem: Nation, Gender, Empire, and the Cultures of Travel* (Durham and London: Duke University Press, 1996), Chap. 2.

Chapter Four

1. Michael North, *The Dialect of Modernism: Race, Language, and Twentieth-Century Literature* (New York: Oxford University Press, 1994).

2. Cynthia Stamy, *Marianne Moore and China: Orientalism and a Writing of America* (Oxford: Oxford University Press, 1999), 24.

3. Ezra Pound, "The Renaissance," in *Literary Essays*, ed. T. S. Eliot (London: Farber and Farber, 1968), 215.

4. S. Foster Damon, *Amy Lowell: A Chronicle, with Extracts from Her Correspondence* (Boston and New York: Houghton Mifflin, 1935), 587.

5. On Pound, see Zhaoming Qian, *Orientalism and Modernism: The Legacy of China in Pound and Williams, 1913–1923* (Durham: Duke University Press, 1995); Beongcheon Yu, *The Great Circle: American Writers and the Orient* (Detroit: Wayne State University Press, 1983), Chap. 10; Earl Miner, *The Japanese Tradition in British and American Literature* (Princeton: Princeton University Press, 1966), 108–112.

6. On the life of Amy Lowell, see Damon, *Amy Lowell*; Richard Benvenuto, *Amy Lowell* (Boston: Twayne Publishers, 1985), Chap. 1; Glenn Richard Ruihley, *The Thorn of a Rose: Amy Lowell Reconsidered* (Hamden, CT: Archon Books, 1975); Horace Gregory, *Amy Lowell: Portrait of the Poet in Her Time* (New York: Thomas Nelson & Sons, 1958); Jean Gould, *Amy: The World of Amy Lowell and the Imagist Movement* (New York: Dodd, Mead, & Co., 1975).

7. Damon, *Amy Lowell*, 196.

8. Quoted in Benvenuto, *Amy Lowell*, 13.

9. David Strauss, *Percival Lowell: The Culture and Science of a Boston Brahmin* (Cambridge: Harvard University Press, 2001).

10. Florence Ayscough and Amy Lowell, *Fir-Flower Tablets* (Boston and New York: Houghton Mifflin, 1921). On the process through which Ayscough and Lowell collaborated on the translation, see Harley Farnsworth MacNair, ed., *Florence Ayscough and Amy Lowell: Correspondence of a Friendship* (Chicago: University of Chicago Press, 1945); also see Lowell's preface to *Fir-Flower Tablets*.

11. Steven Bradbury, "Through the Open Door: American Translations of Chinese Poetry and the Translations of Empire," (Ph.D. Diss., University of Hawai'i, 1997), 129.

12. MacNair, ed., *Florence Ayscough and Amy Lowell*, 104.

13. Ibid., 175.

14. Ayscough and Lowell, *Fir-Flower Tablets*,10.

15. Ibid., 180.

16. Ibid., 28.

17. Ezra Pound, *Personae. Collected Shorter Poems of Ezra Pound* (New York: New Directions, 1971), 130.

18. Ayscough and Lowell, *Fir-Flower Tablets*, 190.

19. Pound, *Personae*, 130.

20. Ayscough and Lowell, *Fir-Flower Tablets*, 29.

21. Ibid., 190.

22. Amy Lowell, *Pictures of the Floating World* (New York: Macmillan, 1919), vii–viii. Other references to the book are made parenthetically in the text.

23. Amy Lowell, *Can Grande's Castle* (New York: Macmillan, 1918), x–xi. On a critical analysis of Lowell's idea of polyphonic prose and her uses of it in *Can Grande's Castle*, see Conrad Aiken, "The Technique of Polyphonic Prose: Amy Lowell," in *Scepticisms: Notes on Contemporary Poetry* [1919] (Freeport, NY: Essay Index Reprint Series, 1967), 115–125.

24. Amy Lowell, "Guns as Keys: and the Great Gate Swings," in *Can Grande's Castle*, 51–52. Subsequent references to the poem are made parenthetically in the text.

25. Benvenuto, *Amy Lowell*, 105.

26. Frederic Jameson, "Modernism and Imperialism," in *Nationalism, Colonialism, and Literature*, Terry Eagleton et al. (Minneapolis: University of Minnesota Press, 1990), 48.

27. Amy Lowell to Linda Hawley Brigham, November 4, 1919. Quoted in Damon, *Amy Lowell*, 475; also see Benvenuto, *Amy Lowell*, 106.

28. Preface to *Can Grande's Castle*, xvi.

Chapter Five

1. Agnes Smedley, *Daughter of Earth* ([1929] New York: The Feminist Press, 1987).

2. Ibid., 287–288.

3. Marge Piercy, "Agnes Smedley: Dirt Poor Daughter of Earth," *The New Republic* (December 14, 1974), 20.

4. Smedley, *Daughter of Earth*, 377–378.

5. Janice R. MacKinnon and Stephen R. MacKinnon, *Agnes Smedley: The Life and Times of an American Radical* (Berkeley: University of California Press, 1988), 177.

6. On the discourse of race, gender, and civilization, see Gail Bederman, *Manliness and Civilization: A Cultural History of Gender and Race in the United States, 1880–1917* (Chicago: University of Chicago Press, 1995); Louise Michele Newman, *White Women's Rights: The Racial Origins of Feminism in the United States* (New York: Oxford University Press, 1999).

7. Agnes Smedley, *China Fights Back: An American Woman with the Eighth Route Army* (New York: The Vanguard Press, 1938), 197.

8. Agnes Smedley to Margaret Sanger, Oct. 12, 1929; Nov. 21, 1929. Margaret Sanger Papers. Microfilm edition. Widener Library, Harvard University.

9. Smedley, *China Fights Back*, 232.

10. Smedley to Margaret Sanger, June 13, 1929. Margaret Sanger Papers.

11. Smedley to Karin Michaelis, April 2, 1930, quoted in MacKinnon and MacKinnon, *Agnes Smedley*, 145.

12. Smedley to Karin Michaelis, June 23, 1930, quoted in MacKinnon and MacKinnon, *Agnes Smedley*, 145–146.

13. Agnes Smedley, *Battle Hymn of China* (New York: Knopf, 1943), 52.

14. MacKinnon and MacKinnon, *Agnes Smedley*, 143, 254.

15. On her relationship with Hu Shih, she wrote to Margaret Sanger: "Between just you and me, I'm capable of trying to break up his home—which wouldn't mean much because it's unhappy." Smedley to Margaret Sanger, Aug. 10, 1929 and Oct. 12, 1929. Margaret Sanger Papers.

16. Agnes Smedley, *China Fights Back*, 22–23.

17. Ibid., 248.

18. MacKinnon and MacKinnon, *Agnes Smedley*, 187.

19. Ibid., 190.

20. Ibid., 192.

21. On the gender ideology of evangelist missions in China, see Jane Hunter, *The Gospel of Gentility: American Women Missionaries in Turn-of-the-Century China* (New Haven: Yale University Press, 1984).

22. Smedley, *China Fights Back*, 112.

23. Ibid., 250–251.

24. Freda Utley, *Odessey of a Liberal* (Washington: Washington National Press, 1970), 206–207.

25. Smedley, *Battle Hymn of China*, 473–444.

26. Ibid., 474.

27. Ibid., 475.

28. Smedley, *China Fights Back*, 506.

29. Smedley, *Chinese Destinies*, 68–69.

30. Ibid., 76.

31. Ibid., 88–89.

32. Smedley, *China's Red Army Marches* (Westport, CT: Hyperion Press, 1977), 173–184.

33. Ibid., 173, emphasis added.

34. Marge Piercy, "Agnes Smedley"; Carolyn Nizzi Warmbold, "Women of the Mosquito Press: Louise Bryant, Agnes Smedley, and Margaret Randall as Narrative Guerrillas," (Ph.D. Diss., University of Texas at Austin, 1990), 202.

35. Ibid., 203.

36. "Hsu Mei-ling," in Agnes Smedley, *Chinese Destinies: Sketches of Present-Day China* ([1933]; Westport, CT: Hyperion Press, 1977), 9. First published in the *New Republic*.

37. Ibid., 11.

38. Ibid., 13.

39. Ibid., 13.

40. Ibid., 253.

41. Ibid., 35.

42. Ibid., 42.

43. Smedley, *Battle Hymn of China*, 32–33.

Chapter Six

1. Janice R. MacKinnon and Stephen R. MacKinnon, *Agnes Smedley: The Life and Times of an American Radical* (Berkeley and Los Angeles: University of California Press, 1988), 254.

2. Peter Conn, *Pearl S. Buck: A Cultural Biography* (Cambridge and New York: Cambridge University Press, 1996).

3. Harold Isaacs, *Scratches on Our Minds: American Images of China and India* (New York: The John Day Co., 1958), 162.

4. Michael H. Hunt, "Pearl Buck—Popular Expert on China, 1931–1949," *Modern China* 3 (1977): 33–64.

5. Isaacs, *Scratches on Our Minds*, 155.

6. Ibid., 97–140; Robert McClellan, *The Heathen Chinee: A Study of American Attitudes toward China, 1890–1905* (Columbus, OH: Ohio State University Press, 1971); Stuart

Creighton Miller, *The Unwelcome Immigrant: The American Image of the Chinese, 1785–1882* (Berkeley: University of California Press, 1969).

7. James C. Thomson, Jr., "Pearl S. Buck and the American Quest for China," in *The Several Worlds of Pearl S. Buck: Essays Presented at a Centennial Symposium, Randolph-Macon Woman's College, March 26–28, 1992*, eds. Elizabeth J. Lipscomb et al. (Westport, CT: Greenwood Press, 1994), 13.

8. Carl Van Doren, *The American Novel 1789–1939* rev. ed. (New York: Macmillan, 1940), 353.

9. J. Donald Adams, *The Shape of Books to Come* (New York: Viking, 1944), 125.

10. Kiang Kang-hu, review of *The Good Earth, The New York Times Book Review* (Jan. 15, 1933) 2, 6.

11. Sophia Chen Zen, review of *The Good Earth, Pacific Affairs* 4 (1931): 915.

12. Dominika Ferens provides an insightful analysis of similar functions of ethnographic discourse in the writings of Edith Eaton (Sui Sin Far) and Winnifred Eaton (Onoto Watanna) in her *Edith & Winnifred Eaton: Chinatown Missions and Japanese Romances* (Urbana and Chicago: University of Illinois Press, 2002).

13. Pearl Buck, *The Good Earth* (New York: John Day, 1931), 3–4. Other references to the novel are made parenthetically in the text.

14. Paul Atkinson, *The Ethnographic Imagination: Textual Constructions of Reality* (London: Routledge, 1990), 46; Mary Louise Pratt, "Fieldwork in Common Places," in *Writing Culture: The Poetics and Politics of Ethnography*, eds. James Clifford and George E. Marcus (Berkeley: University of California Press, 1986), 32.

15. James Clifford, "On Ethnographic Allegory," in *Writing Culture: The Poetics and Politics of Ethnography*, eds. James Clifford and George E. Marcus (Berkeley: University of California Press, 1986), 98–121.

16. Cao-Ly Doàn, "The Images of the Chinese Family in Pearl Buck's Novels," (Ph.D. Diss., St. John's University, 1964), 78; Phyllis Bentley, "The Art of Pearl S. Buck," *English Journal* 24 (December 1935): 794.

17. Pearl S. Buck, Response to Kiang Kang-Hu's review of *The Good Earth, The New York Times Book Review* (January 15, 1933), 2.

18. Ibid., 2.

19. Such a debate over accuracy is one of the pitfalls of the discussions of Orientalism. See James Clifford, *Predicament of Culture: Twentieth-Century Ethnography, Literature, and Art* (Cambridge: Harvard University Press, 1988), 260.

20. On the prehistory and early development of modern anthropology, see George W. Stocking, Jr., *The Ethnographer's Magic and Other Essays in the History of Anthropology* (Madison: University of Wisconsin Press, 1992).

21. See Henry Yu, *Thinking Orientals: Migration, Contact, and Exoticism in Modern America* (New York: Oxford University Press, 2001), 19–30.

22. Conn, *Pearl S. Buck*, 1–44.

23. Jane Hunter, *The Gospel of Gentility: American Women Missionaries in Turn-of-the-Century China* (New Haven: Yale University Press, 1984).

24. On women in anthropology, see Peggy Golde, ed., *Women in the Field: Anthropological Experiences*, 2nd ed. (Berkeley: University of California Press, 1986); Micaela di Leonardo, *Exotics at Home: Anthropologies, Others, American Modernity* (Chicago: University of Chicago Press, 1998). Also see Rosalind Rosenberg, *Beyond Separate*

Spheres: Intellectual Roots of Modern Feminism (New Haven: Yale University Press, 1982).

25. Pearl S. Buck, *Sons* (New York: John Day, 1932).

26. Pearl S. Buck, *A House Divided* (New York: John Day, 1935). Other references to the novel are made parenthetically in the text.

27. Malcom Cowley, "Wang Lung's Children," *New Republic* (May 10, 1939), 24.

28. Paul A. Doyle, *Pearl S. Buck*, rev. ed. (Boston: Twayne Publishers, 1980), 55–56.

29. John Sedges [Pearl S. Buck], *The Townsman* (New York: John Day, 1945); *The Angry Wife* (New York: John Day, 1947); *The Long Love* (New York: John Day, 1949); *Bright Procession* (New York: John Day, 1952); *Voices in the House* (New York: John Day, 1953).

30. For details on Buck's career, see Conn, *Pearl S. Buck*.

31. Pearl S. Buck, unpublished memorandum on the East and West Association (n.d.), Pearl S. Buck Family Trust Archives. Quoted in Conn, *Pearl S. Buck*, 245.

32. Pearl S. Buck to Edward Carter, February 3, 1942, Institute of Pacific Relations Papers, Butler Library, Columbia University.

Chapter Seven

1. Harold Isaacs, *Scratches on Our Minds: American Images of China and India* (New York: J. Day Co., 1958), 164–176.

2. "How to Tell Your Friends from the Japs," *Time* (Dec. 22, 1941), 33; "How to Tell the Japs from the Chinese," *Life* (Dec. 22, 1941), 7.

3. John W. Dower, *War without Mercy: Race and Power in the Pacific War* (New York: Pantheon Books, 1986), 119.

4. Ruth Benedict, *The Chrysanthemum and the Sword: Patterns of Japanese Culture* ([1946]; Boston: Houghton Mifflin, 1989)

5. Etsu Inagaki SUGIMOTO, *A Daughter of the Samurai* (New York: Doubleday, 1926), 136; quoted in Benedict, *The Chrysanthemum and the Sword*, 294. Karen Kelsky traces the genealogy of Japanese women's "internationalist" narrative exemplified by Sugimoto's text in her *Women on the Verge: Japanese Women, Western Dreams* (Durham: Duke University Press, 2001), chap. 1.

6. Benedict, *Chrysanthemum*, 296.

7. Ibid., 296.

8. Ruth Benedict, *Patterns of Culture* (Boston and New York: Houghton Mifflin Co., 1934)

9. Ruth Benedict, *Race: Science and Politics* (New York: Modern Age Books, 1940); Ruth Benedict and Gene Weltfish, *In Henry's Backyard: The Races of Mankind* (New York: H. Schuman, 1947).

10. Allan M. Winkler, *The Politics of Propaganda: The Office of War Information, 1942–1945* (New Haven: Yale University Press, 1978).

11. Ruth Benedict Position Description, Ruth Benedict Papers [hereafter RBP], Vassar College Library.

12. Ruth Benedict, *Thai Culture and Behavior* Data Paper No. 4 [1943] (Ithaca: Southeast Asia Program, Cornell University, 1952). RBP.

13. Ruth Benedict, "Background for a Basic Plan for Burma," (September 13, 1943); "Rumanian Culture and Behavior" (Reproduced and distributed by Institute for Intercultural Studies, Inc., 1943), RBP.

14. "German Defeatism at the Beginning of the Fifth Winter of War," Office of War Information, Bureau of Overseas Intelligence, December 15, 1943, RBP.

15. Dr. Katherine Spencer, "The Development of the Research Methods of the Foreign Morale Analysis Division [OWI]," Interim International Information Service, Report No. 29 (November 30, 1945), 223–225; Alexander L. Leighton, *Human Relations in a Changing World: Observations on the Use of the Social Sciences* (New York: E. P. Dutton and Co., 1949), Appendix D.

16. Benedict, *Chrysanthemum*, 6.

17. Miscellaneous records of interviews with Robert Hashima (OWI staff); record of interview with Mr. and Mrs. Shirahata (conducted by H. C. Hu, March 1945); record of interview with Mr. Okami (OWI, New York); record of interview with Mr. Bergher (OWI, New York, July 6, 1945), RBP.

18. Benedict, *Chrysanthemum*, 8.

19. Office of Strategic Services, Research and Analysis Branch, Report No. 1307 "Japanese Films: A Phase of Psychological Warfare, An analysis of the themes, psychological content, technical quality, and propaganda value of twenty recent Japanese films." (March 1944), RBP.

20. Benedict, *Chrysanthemum*, 6.

21. Pauline Kent has compiled an extensive bibliography of sources used by Benedict. See "Ruth Benedict and Her Wartime Studies: Primary Materials and References," 1995-nendo Monbusho Kagaku Kenkyu-hi Hojokin Shourei Kenkyu (A) Kenkyu Seika Houkokusho, 07710166 ([Tokyo]: Monbusho, 1996), 235–242.

22. For example, see Alfred R. Lindsmith and Anselm L. Strauss, "A Critique of Culture-Personality Writings," *American Sociological Review* 15 (1950): 587–600; John Bennet and Michio NAGAI, "The Japanese Critique of the Methodology of Benedict's *Chrysanthemum and the Sword*," *American Anthropologist* 55 (1953): 404–411; Richard H. Minear, "Cross-Cultural Perception and WWII: American Japanists of the 1940s and Their Images of Japan," *International Studies Quarterly* 24 (1980): 555–580; Richard Minear, "The Wartime Studies of Japanese National Character," *Japan Interpreter* (Summer 1980): 36–59; Peter T. Suzuki, "Anthropologists in the Wartime Camps for Japanese Americans: A Documentary Study," *Dialectical Anthropology* 6 (1981): 23–60; Peter T. Suzuki, "A Retrospective Analysis of a Wartime 'National Character' Study," *Dialectical Anthropology* 5 (1980): 33–46. See also John W. Dower, *War without Mercy*, Chaps. 5, 6.

23. The most extreme example of such critique is by Watsuji Tetsuro, an eminent Japanese ethnologist. "Kagaku-teki Kachi ni taisuru Gimon [Questions as to the Scientific Value]," *Minzokugaku Kenkyu* 14 (1950): 23–27.

24. On the implications of these community analyses in the postwar theories of Japanese culture, see Caroline Chung Simpson, *An Absent Presence: Japanese Americans in Postwar American Culture, 1945–1960* (Durham: Duke University Press, 2001), Chap. 2.

25. Weston La Barre, "Some Observations on Character Structure in the Orient: The Japanese," *Psychiatry: Journal of Biology and the Pathology of Interpersonal Relations* 8 (1945): 319–342.

26. Alexander H. Leighton, *The Governing of Men: General Principles and Recommendations Based on Experience at a Japanese Relocation Camp* (Princeton: Princeton University Press, 1945); Dorothy S. Thomas, *The Salvage* (Berkeley: University of California Press, 1952); Dorothy S. Thomas and Richard S. Nishimoto, *The Spoilage* (Berkeley: Uni-

versity of California Press, 1946); U.S. Department of Interior, War Relocation Authority, *Impounded People: Japanese Americans in the Relocation Centers* (Washington: Government Printing Office, 1946). For the details of these studies in the internment camps, see Yuji Ichioka, ed., *Views from Within: The Japanese American Evacuation and Resettlement Study* (Los Angeles: UCLA Asian American Studies Center, 1989).

27. Leighton, *The Governing of Men*, 376.

28. Geoffrey Gorer, *Japanese Character Structure*, 2nd ed. (New York: Distributed by the Institute for Intercultural Studies, 1942), 1.

29. Ibid., 4.

30. Ibid., 17.

31. Ibid., 18.

32. Ibid., 18.

33. Ibid., 19.

34. John N. Thomas, *The Institute of Pacific Relations: Asian Scholars and American Politics* (Seattle: University of Washington Press, 1974); Paul F. Hooper, ed., *Rediscovering the IPR: Proceedings of the First International Research Conference on the Institute of Pacific Relations, University of Hawaii, August 9–10, 1993* (Honolulu: Center for Arts and Humanities, University of Hawaii at Manoa, Department of American Studies, 1994).

35. Margaret Mead, "Provisional Analytical Summary of Institute of Pacific Relations Conference on Japanese Character Structure, December 16–17, 1944," IPR Papers, Butler Library, Columbia University.

36. Ibid., 15–18.

37. Significantly, some participants made sound comments, such as the one by Ernst Kris that "[i]f American propaganda is going to assume the elder-brother role, it isn't feasible to continue the sub-human image of the Japanese in our home-front propaganda. Japanese are becoming more sub-human in American public opinion and this makes the pattern of superior but friendly relationship very difficult."

38. See Yukiko Koshiro, *Trans-Pacific Racisms and the U.S. Occupation of Japan* (New York: Columbia University Press, 1999); John W. Dower, *Embracing Defeat: Japan in the Wake of World War II* (New York: The New Press, 1999); Naoko Shibusawa, *America's Geisha Ally: Gender, Race, and Maturity in Reimagining the Japanese* (Harvard University Press, forthcoming).

39. Benedict, *Chrysanthemum*, 22.

40. Ibid., 25.

41. Ibid., 31–32.

42. OWI interview records. "Suetsugu Shoji." RBP.

43. For a similar story, also see OWI interview notes on "POW Masuda," June 30, 1944. RBP.

44. The FMAD's "Morale Handbook," which outlines the questions to be asked during the interviews and how to record the answers, shows that in addition to factual information about the interviewee's background, military affiliation, and circumstances of capture, the interviewers were instructed to assess the informants' attitude toward capture (divided into seventeen categories, such as "indifference," "disgrace," "fear of future punishment in Japan," "antagonistic," "requests or desired to be executed or killed," "glad to be prisoner and out of war," etc.), and to quote answers on the questions including:

U. Faith in Purpose:

1. War

2. Victory

4. [*sic*] Japanese nation or race.

5. Japan as savior of Asia, or liberator; includes "Asian for Asiatics" philosophy.

x. Others

V. Faith in Leaders:

1. Emperor

2. Political leaders (Tojo Incl.)

3. Higher command.

4. Immediate superiors

5. Reliability of news (Leaders, or govt.)

x. Others.

W. Faith in each other:

1. Platoon or immediate associates or larger unit or division.

3. [*sic*] Armed forces. Army or Navy, Air force-Navy or rest of armed forces.

6. [*sic*] People at home

7. Germans

8. Koreans

9. Formosans

10. Natives (inhabitants of invaded area; write specific group on back)

x. Others.

[FMAD], "Morale Handbook," (n.d.) RBP.

45. Alice Mabel Bacon, *Japanese Girls and Women* (Boston: Houghton Mifflin, 1902); Sumie Seo MISHIMA, *My Narrow Isle: The Story of a Modern Woman in Japan* (New York: John Day, 1941); Sugimoto, *A Daughter of the Samurai*. Benedict also consulted a manuscript put together by Baroness Ishimoto on biographical sketches of diverse Japanese women including ancient mythological figures, writers, educators, social workers, and political activists.

46. Benedict, *Chrysanthemum*, 53–54.

47. Ibid., 121–122.

48. Ibid., 109–110.

49. Ibid., 177.

50. Ibid., 183.

51. Ibid., 185.

52. Ibid., 186.

53. George W. Stocking, Jr., *The Ethnographer's Magic and Other Essays in the History of Anthropology* (Madison: University of Wisconsin Press, 1992), 165–168; John Embree, "Applied Anthropology and Its Relation to Anthropology," *American Anthropologist* 47 (1945): 516–539; Laura Thompson, "Some Perspectives on Applied Anthropology," *Applied Anthropology* 3 (1944): 12.

54. For a critique of "culture" paradigm in anthropology, see Christopher Shannon, "A World Made Safe for Differences: Ruth Benedict's *The Chrysanthemum and the Sword*," *American Quarterly* 47 (1995): 659–680.

55. Benedict, *Chrysanthemum*, 13.

56. Ibid., 297.

57. Quoted in Margaret M. Caffrey, *Ruth Benedict: Strangers in This Land* (Austin: University of Texas Press, 1989), 325.

58. Margaret Mead, ed., *An Anthropologist at Work: Writings of Ruth Benedict* ([1959]; New York: Avon Books, 1973), 428.

59. The Japanese translation of *The Chrysanthemum and the Sword* is still in print in paperback today. *Kiku to Katana [The Chrysanthemum and the Sword]* (Tokyo: Shakai Shisosha, 1967). See *Minzokugaku Kenkyu* [Studies in Ethnology], the leading Japanese journal of ethnology, published a special issue on *The Chrysanthemum and the Sword* in 1949. *Minzokugaku Kenkyu* 14 (1949): 1–35.

60. For example, see Soeda Yoshiya, *Nihon Bunka Shiron: Benedict "Kiku to Katana" wo Yomu* ([Tokyo]: Shinyosha, 1993); Fukui Nanako, "'Kiku to Katana' to 'Botchan,'" *This Is Yomiuri* (March 1996), 230–235, Nanako FUKUI and Ueda Y., "From 'Japanese Behavior Patterns' to 'The Chrysanthemum and the Sword,'" in *Collection of Papers from the Faculty of Letters, Kansai University: Commemorating the 70th Anniversary of the Establishment of the Faculty* 44 (1995): 555–580.

61. Dower, *War without Mercy*.

62. Benedict, *Chrysanthemum*, 1.

63. Dower, *War without Mercy*, 122.

Conclusion

1. "A 'Madame Butterfly' of the Philippines: The Romantic Problem that Confronts Uncle Sam in His Far Eastern Islands," *The World* [New York] (June 7, 1903), 1.

2. Carl Dawson, *Lafcadio Hearn and the Vision of Japan* (Baltimore: Johns Hopkins University Press, 1992); Yoji Hasegawa, *Lafcadio Hearn's Japanese Wife: Her Memoirs and Her Early Life* (Tokyo: Micro Printing Co., 1988); Robert Rosenstone, *Mirror in the Shrine: American Encounters with Meiji Japan* (Cambridge: Harvard University Press, 1988); Beongcheon Yu, *An Ape of Gods: The Art and Thought of Lafcadio Hearn* (Detroit: Wayne State University Press, 1964).

3. An excellent pioneering study of gender dimension in international relations is Cynthia Enloe, *Bananas, Beaches, and Bases: Making Feminist Sense of International Politics* (Berkeley: University of California Press, 1990). For examples of studies of international relations in Asia-Pacific that use gender and sexuality as a central category of analysis, see Kristin L. Hoganson, *Fighting for American Manhood: How Gender Politics Provoked the Spanish-American and Philippine-American Wars* (New Haven: Yale University Press, 1998); Katharine H. S. Moon, *Sex among Allies: Military Prostitution in U.S.-Korea Relations* (New York: Columbia University Press, 1997); Lenore Manderson and Margaret Jolly, eds., *Sites of Desire, Economies of Pleasure: Sexualities in Asia and the Pacific* (Chicago: University of Chicago Press, 1997); Saundra Pollock Sturdevant and Brenda Stoltzfus, *Let the Good Times Roll: Prostitution and the U.S. Military in Asia* (New York: The New Press, 1992). See also Rosemary Foot, "Where Are the Women? The Gender Dimension in the Study of International Relations," *Diplomatic History* 14 (1990): 615–622; Andrew J. Rotter, "Gender Relations, Foreign Relations: The United States and South Asia, 1947–1964," *Journal of American History* 81 (1994): 518–542.

4. Reina Lewis, *Gendering Orientalism: Race, Femininity and Representation* (London: Routledge, 1996); Billie Melman, *Women's Orients: English Women and the Middle East, 1718–1918* (Ann Arbor: University of Michigan Press, 1992); Mary Louise Pratt, *Imperial Eyes: Travel Writing and Transculturation* (London: Routledge, 1992); Sara Mills, *Discourses of Difference: An Analysis of Women's Travel Writing and Colonialism* (London: Routledge, 1991); Lisa Lowe, *Critical Terrains: French and British Orientalisms* (Ithaca: Cornell University Press, 1991).

5. For theoretical discussions of western women's travel, see Caren Kaplan, *Questions of Travel: Postmodern Discourses of Displacement* (Durham: Duke University Press, 1996); Inderpal Grewal and Caren Kaplan, eds., *Scattered Hegemonies: Postmodernity and Transnational Feminist Practices* (Minneapolis: University of Minnesota Press, 1994); Inderpal Grewal, *Home and Harem: Nation, Gender, Empire, and the Cultures of Travel* (Durham and London: Duke University Press, 1996); Nupur Chaudhuri and Margaret Strobel, eds., *Western Women and Imperialism: Complicity and Resistance* (Bloomington and Indianapolis: Indiana University Press, 1992).

6. Enloe, *Bananas, Beaches, and Bases*, 16.

7. Some of the recent scholarship on Western women and imperialism include Laura Wexler, *Tender Violence: Domestic Visions in an Age of U.S. Imperialism* (Chapel Hill: University of North Carolina Press, 2000); Rosemary Marangoly George, *The Politics of Home: Postcolonial Relocations and Twentieth-Century Fiction* (Berkeley: University of California Press, 1999); Anne McClintock, *Imperial Leather: Race, Gender, and Sexuality in the Colonial Contest* (New York: Routledge, 1995); Kumari Jayawardena, *The White Woman's Other Burden: Western Women and South Asia during British Colonial Rule* (New York: Routledge, 1995); Gail Bederman, *Manliness and Civilization: A Cultural History of Gender and Race in the United States, 1880–1917* (Chicago: University of Chicago Press, 1995); Jenny Sharpe, *Allegories of Empire: The Figure of Woman in the Colonial Text* (Minneapolis: University of Minnesota Press, 1993); Ann Laura Stoler, "Carnal Knowledge and Imperial Power: Gender, Race, and Morality in Colonial Asia," in *Gender at the Crossroads of Knowledge: Feminist Anthropology in the Postmodern Era*, ed. Micaela di Leonardo (Berkeley: University of California Press, 1991), 51–101; Ann Laura Stoler, "Rethinking Colonial Categories: European Communities and the Boundaries of Rule," *Comparative Studies in Society and History* 31 (1989): 134–161; Laura Donaldson, *Decolonizing Feminism: Race, Gender, and Empire-Building* (Chapel Hill: University of North Carolina Press, 1992); Vron Ware, *Beyond the Pale: White Women, Racism, and History* (New York: Verso, 1992); Enloe, *Bananas, Beaches, and Bases*; Chaudhuri and Strobel, eds., *Western Women and Imperialism*; Margaret Strobel, *European Women and the Second British Empire* (Bloomington: Indiana University Press, 1991); Helen Callaway, *Gender, Culture, and Empire: European Women in Colonial Nigeria* (Urbana and Chicago: University of Illinois Press, 1987).

8. On the relationship between women and imperialism within the western metropole, see McClintock, *Imperial Leather*; also see Grewal, *Home and Harem*, 4.

9. Although it does not deal specifically with Orientalism, for a sophisticated analysis of imperialism and domesticity, see Amy Kaplan, "Manifest Domesticity," *American Literature* 70 (1998): 581–606.

10. On the "New Woman," see Nancy Cott, *The Grounding of Modern Feminism* (New Haven: Yale University Press, 1987); Kathy Peiss, *Cheap Amusements: Working Women and*

Leisure in Turn-of-the-Century New York (Philadelphia: Temple University Press, 1986); Kathryn Kish Sklar, "Hull House in the 1890s: A Community of Women Reformers," in *Women and Power in American History*, Vol. II, eds. Kathryn Kish Sklar and Thomas Dublin (Englewood Cliffs, NJ: Prentice-Hall, 1991), 54–68; Estelle Freedman, "Separatism as Strategy: Female Institution Building as American Feminism, 1870–1930," in ibid., 10–24; Christina Simmons, "Companionate Marriage and the Lesbian Threat," in ibid., 183–194.

11. For example, Nupur Chaudhuri and Margaret Strobel., eds., *Western Women and Imperialism*, includes only one article that pertains to American women. A rare study of white women's role in American colonialism vis-à-vis Asia is Vicente L. Rafael, "Colonial Domesticity: White Women and United States Rule in the Philippines," *American Literature* 67 (1995): 639–666.

12. Amy Kaplan, "'Left Alone with America': The Absence of Empire in the Study of American Culture," in *Cultures of United States Imperialism*, eds. Amy Kaplan and Donald E. Pease (Durham: Duke University Press, 1993), 3–21.

BIBLIOGRAPHY ·

Archives Consulted

Brown University. John Hay Library. Gorham Manufacturing Company Papers. [GC]
Harvard University. Widener Library. Margaret Sanger Papers, Microfilm edition.
——. Theater Collection.
Library of Congress. Music Division. Geraldine Farrar Collections. [GFC]
New York Public Library for the Performing Arts. Theater Collection. David Belasco Papers. [DBP]
Rhode Island Historical Society.
Radcliffe College. Arthur and Elizabeth Schlesinger Library.
Vassar College Library. Ruth Benedict Papers. [RBP]
Winterthur Library.

Primary and Secondary Sources
(Archival sources are cited in the notes.)

"A 'Madame Butterfly' of the Philippines: The Romantic Problem that Confronts Uncle Sam in His Far Eastern Islands." *The World* [New York] 7 June 1903: 1.
"A Pleasing Novelty": Bunkio Matsuki and the Japan Craze in Victorian Salem. Salem, MA: Peabody & Essex Museum, 1993.
Adams, J. Donald. *The Shape of Books to Come*. New York: Viking, 1944.
Agnew, Jean-Christophe. "A House of Fiction: Domestic Interiors and the Commodity Aesthetic." In *Consuming Visions: Accumulation and Display in America, 1880–1920*. Ed. Simon J. Bronner. New York: W.W. Norton & Co., 1989. 133–155.
Ahmad, Aijaz. *In Theory: Classes, Nations, Literatures*. London: Verso, 1992.
Aiken, Conrad. "The Technique of Polyphonic Prose: Amy Lowell." In *Scepticisms: Notes on Contemporary Poetry*. Freeport, NY: Essay Index Reprint Series, [1919] 1967. 115–125.

Alcott, Louisa May. *Eight Cousins; or, The Aunt-Hill.* [1875] New York: Books, Inc., 1946.

Appadurai, Arjun, ed. *The Social Life of Things: Commodities in Cultural Perspective.* Cambridge: Cambridge University Press, 1986.

Arac, Jonathan and Harriet Ritvo, eds. *Macropolitics of Nineteenth-Century Literature: Nationalism, Exoticism, Imperialism.* Philadelphia: University of Pennsylvania Press, 1991.

Armstrong, Nancy. *Desire and Domestic Fiction: A Political History of the Novel.* New York: Oxford University Press, 1987.

Atkinson, Paul. *The Ethnographic Imagination: Textual Constructions of Reality.* London: Routledge, 1990.

Auster, Albert. *Actresses and Suffragists: Women in the American Theater, 1890–1920.* New York: Praeger, 1984.

Ayscough, Florence and Amy Lowell. *Fir-Flower Tablets.* Boston and New York: Houghton Mifflin, 1921.

Bacon, Alice Mabel. *Japanese Girls and Women.* Boston: Houghton Mifflin, 1902.

Bal, Meike and Norman Bryson. "Semiotics and Art History." *Art Bulletin* 73 (1991): 174–208.

Bederman, Gail. *Manlines and Civilization: A Cultural History of Gender and Race in the United States, 1880–1917.* Chicago: University of Chicago Press, 1995.

Belasco, David. *Six Plays: Madame Butterfly, Du Barry, The Darling of the Gods, Adrea, The Girl of the Golden West, The Return of Peter Grimm.* Boston: Little, Brown, and Company, 1928.

Bellman, Jonathan. *The Exotic in Western Music.* Boston: Northeastern University Press, 1998.

Benedict, Ruth. *The Chrysanthemum and the Sword: Patterns of Japanese Culture* Boston: Houghton Mifflin, [1946] 1989.

——. *Race: Science and Politics.* New York: Modern Age Books, 1940.

——. *Patterns of Culture.* Boston and New York: Houghton Mifflin Co., 1934.

Benedict, Ruth and Gene Weltfish. *In Henry's Backyard: The Races of Mankind.* New York: H. Schuman, 1947.

Bennet, John and Michio NAGAI. "The Japanese Critique of the Methodology of Benedict's *Chrysanthemum and the Sword.*" *American Anthropologist* 55 (1953): 404–411.

Bentley, Phyllis. "The Art of Pearl S. Buck." *English Journal* 24 (1935): 794.

Benvenuto, Richard. *Amy Lowell.* Boston: Twayne Publishers, 1985.

Bernstein, Matthew and Gaylyn Studlar, eds. *Visions of the East: Orientalism in Film.* New Brunswick, NJ: Rutgers University Press, 1997.

Blanchard, Mary. *Oscar Wilde's America: Counterculture in the Gilded Age.* New Haven and London: Yale University Press, 1998.

Blaszczyk, Regina Lee. "Cinderella Stories: The Glass of Fashion and the Gendered Marketplace." In *His and Hers: Gender, Consumption, and Technology.* Eds. Roger Horowitz and Arwen Mohun. Charlottesville: University Press of Virginia, 1998. 139–164.

Books in the Library of Nelson W. Aldrich, Warwick, Rhode Island. 2 vols. Boston: The Merrymount Press, 1914.

Bradbury, Steven. "Through the Open Door: American Translations of Chinese Poetry and the Translations of Empire." PhD. Diss. University of Hawai'i, 1997.

Brandimarte, Cynthia A. "Japanese Novelty Stores." *Winterthur Portfolio* 26 (1991): 1–25.

——. "Somebody's Aunt and Nobody's Mother: The American China Painter and Her Work, 1870–1920." *Winterthur Portfolio* 23 (1988): 203–224.

Bronner, Simon J., ed. *Consuming Visions: Accumulation and Display of Goods in America, 1880–1920*. New York: Norton, 1989.

Brown, Gillian. *Domestic Individualism: Imagining Self in Nineteenth-Century America*. Berkeley: University of California Press, 1990.

Brown, Jane Converse. "The 'Japanese Taste': Its Role in the Mission of the American Home and in the Family's Presentation of Itself to the Public as Expressed in Published Sources, 1876–1916." PhD. Diss. University of Wisconsin, 1987.

Buck, Pearl S. *A House Divided*. New York: John Day, 1935.

——. *Sons*. New York: John Day, 1932.

——. *The Good Earth*. New York: John Day, 1931.

Butler, Judith. *Gender Trouble: Feminism and the Subversion of Identity*. New York: Routledge, 1990.

Caffrey, Margaret M. *Ruth Benedict: Strangers in This Land*. Austin: University of Texas Press, 1989.

Callaway, Helen. *Gender, Culture, and Empire: European Women in Colonial Nigeria*. Urbana and Chicago: University of Illinois Press, 1987.

Carpenter, Charles H. Jr. *Gorham Silver, 1831–1981*. New York: Dodd, Mead, & Co., 1982.

——. "Tiffany Silver in the Japanese Style." *The Connoisseur*. 200 (1979): 42–47.

Carter, Morris. *Isabella Stewart Gardner and Fenway Court*. 2nd ed. Boston and New York: Houghton Mifflin, 1925.

Castle, Terry. "In Praise of Brigitte Fassbaender: Reflections on Diva-Worship." In *En Travesti: Women, Gender Subversion, Opera*. Eds. Corinne E. Blackmer and Patricia Juliana Smith. New York: Columbia University Press, 1995. 20–58.

Chaudhuri, Nupur and Margaret Strobel, eds. *Western Women and Imperialism: Complicity and Resistance*. Bloomington and Indianapolis: Indiana University Press, 1992.

Chisolm, Lawrence W. *Fenollosa: The Far East and American Culture*. New Haven: Yale University Press, 1963.

Cho, Eunyoung. "The Selling of Japan: Race, Gender, and Cultural Politics in the American Art World, 1876–1915." PhD. Diss. University of Delaware, 1998.

Clark, Carol C. *American Japonism: Contacts between America and Japan, 1854–1910*. Cleveland: Cleveland Museum of Art, 1975.

Clément, Catherine. *Opera, or the Undoing of Women*. Trans. Betsy Wing. Minneapolis: University of Minnesota Press, 1988 [1979].

Clifford, James. *Predicament of Culture: Twentieth-Century Ethnography, Literature, and Art*. Cambridge: Harvard University Press, 1988.

——. "On Ethnographic Allegory." In *Writing Culture: The Poetics and Politics of Ethnography*. Eds. James Clifford and George E. Marcus. Berkeley: University of California Press, 1986. 98–121.

Clifford, James and George E. Marcus, eds. *Writing Culture: The Poetics and Politics of Ethnography*. Berkeley: University of California Press, 1986.

Cohen, Paul. *Discovering History in China: American Historical Writing on the Recent Chinese Past*. New York: Columbia University Press, 1984.

Cohen, Warren I. *East Asian Art and American Culture: A Study in International Relations*. New York: Columbia University Press, 1992.

Conn, Peter. *Pearl S. Buck: A Cultural Biography*. Cambridge and New York: Cambridge University Press, 1996.

Cook, Carol S. *Travel and Exploration: A Catalogue of the Providence Athenaeum Collection*. Providence: Providence Athenaeum, 1988.

Cott, Nancy. *The Grounding of Modern Feminism*. New Haven: Yale University Press, 1987.

Cowley, Malcolm. "Wang Lung's Children." *New Republic* 10 May 1939: 24.

Damon, S. Foster. *Amy Lowell: A Chronicle, with Extracts from Her Correspondence*. Boston and New York: Houghton Mifflin, 1935.

Dawson, Carl. *Lafcadio Hearn and the Vision of Japan*. Baltimore: Johns Hopkins University Press, 1992.

Deloria, Philip J. *Playing Indian*. New Haven: Yale University Press, 1998.

Denker, Ellen Paul. *After the Chinese Taste: China's Influence in America, 1730–1930*. Salem, MA: Peabody Museum of Salem, 1985.

Di Leonardo, Micaela. *Exotics at Home: Anthropologies, Others, American Modernity*. Chicago: University of Chicago Press, 1998.

Doàn, Cao-Ly. "The Images of the Chinese Family in Pearl Buck's Novels." PhD. Diss. St. John's University, 1964.

Donaldson, Laura. *Decolonizing Feminism: Race, Gender, and Empire-Building*. Chapel Hill: University of North Carolina Press, 1992.

Dower, John W. *Embracing Defeat: Japan in the Wake of World War II*. New York: The New Press, 1999.

——. *War without Mercy: Race and Power in the Pacific War*. New York: Pantheon Books, 1986.

Downing, Antoinette F. *The Chinese Teahouse at Marble House*. Newport, RI: The Preservation Society of Newport County, 1982.

Downs, Jacques M. "The Commercial Origins of American Attitudes toward China, 1784–1844." In *America Views China: American Images of China Then and Now*. Eds. Jonathan Goldstein, et al. Bethlehem: Lehigh University Press, 1991. 56–66.

Doyle, Paul A. *Pearl S. Buck*. Rev. ed. Boston: Twayne Publishers, 1980.

Edmiston, Marcene Jean. "Candace Wheeler and the Associated Artists: American Aesthetic Interiors and Their Textiles." M.A. Thesis. George Washington University, 1990.

Embree, John. "Applied Anthropology and Its Relation to Anthropology." *American Anthropologist* 47 (1945): 516–539.

Enloe, Cynthia. *Bananas, Beaches, and Bases: Making Feminist Sense of International Politics*. Berkeley: University of California Press, 1990.

Espiritu, Yen Le. *Asian American Women and Men*. Thousand Oaks: Sage, 1997.

Fabian, Johannes. *Time and the Other: How Anthropology Makes Its Object*. New York: Columbia University Press, 1983.

Farrar, Geraldine. *Such Sweet Compulsion: The Autobiography of Geraldine Farrar*. New York: The Greystone Press, 1938.

——. *Geraldine Farrar: The Story of an American Singer, by Herself*. Boston: Houghton Mifflin, 1915.

Ferens, Dominika. *Edith & Winnifred Eaton: Chinatown Missions and Japanese Romances*. Urbana and Chicago: University of Illinois Press, 2002.

Foley, Barbara. "Women and the Left in the 1930s." *American Literary History* 2 (1990): 150–169.

Foot, Rosemary. "Where Are the Women? The Gender Dimension in the Study of International Relations." *Diplomatic History* 14 (1990): 615–622.

Freedman, Estelle. "Separatism as Strategy: Female Institution Building as American Feminism, 1870–1930." In *Women and Power in American History*. Vol. II Eds. Kathryn Kish Sklar and Thomas Dublin. Englewood Cliffs, NJ: Prentice Hall, 1991. 10–24.

Fukui, Nanako. "'Kiku to Katana' to 'Botchan.'" *This Is Yomiuri* March 1996: 230–235.

Fukui, Nanako and Ueda Y. "From 'Japanese Behavior Patterns' to 'The Chrysanthemum and the Sword.'" In *Collection of Papers from the Faculty of Letters, Kansai University: Commemorating the 70th Anniversary of the Establishment of the Faculty* 44 (1995): 555–580.

Garber, Marjorie. *Vested Interests: Cross-Dressing and Cultural Anxiety*. New York: Routledge, 1992.

Genthe, Arnold. *Pictures of Old Chinatown*. With text by Will Irwin. New York: Moffat, Yard, & Co., 1908.

George, Rosemary Marangoly. *The Politics of Home: Postcolonial Relocations and Twentieth-Century Fiction*. Berkeley: University of California Press, 1999.

Glenn, Evelyn Nakano. "From Servitude to Service Work: Historical Continuities in the Racial Division of Paid Reproductive Labor." *Signs* 18 (1992): 1–43.

——. *Issei, Nisei, War Bride: Three Generations of Japanese American Women in Domestic Service*. Philadelphia: Temple University Press, 1986.

Golde, Peggy, ed. *Women in the Field: Anthropological Experiences*. 2nd ed. Berkeley: University of California Press, 1986.

Goldstein, Jonathan. "Cantonese Artifacts, Chinoiserie, and Early American Idealization of China. " In *America Views China: American Images of China Then and Now*. Eds. Jonathan Goldstein, et al. Bethlehem: Lehigh University Press, 1991. 43–55.

Gorer, Geoffrey. *Japanese Character Structure*. 2nd ed. New York: Distributed by the Institute for Intercultural Studies, 1942.

Gould, Jean. *Amy: The World of Amy Lowell and the Imagist Movement*. New York: Dodd, Mead, & Co., 1975.

Gravalos, Mary Evans O'Keefe and Carol Pulin. *Bertha Lum*. Washington: Smithsonian Institution Press, 1990.

Greenhalgh, Paul. *Ephemeral Vistas: The Exposition Universelles, Great Exhibitions and World's Fairs, 1851–1939*. Manchester: Manchester University Press, 1988.

Gregory, Horace. *Amy Lowell: Portrait of the Poet in Her Time*. New York: Thomas Nelson & Sons, 1958.

Grewal, Inderpal. *Home and Harem: Nation, Gender, Empire, and the Cultures of Travel*. Durham and London: Duke University Press, 1996.

Grewal, Inderpal and Caren Kaplan, eds. *Scattered Hegemonies: Postmodernity and Transnational Feminist Practices*. Minneapolis: University of Minnesota Press, 1994.

Gubar, Susan. *Racechanges: White Skin, Black Face in American Culture*. New York and Oxford: Oxford University Press, 1997.

Halttunen, Karen. *Confidence Men and Painted Women: A Study of Middle-Class Culture in America, 1830–1870*. New Haven and London: Yale University Press, 1982.

Harris, Neil. "All the World a Melting Pot? Japan at American Fairs, 1876–1904." In *Mutual Images: Essays in American-Japanese Relations*. Ed. Akira IRIYE. Cambridge: Harvard University Press, 1975. 37–46.

Harris, Theodore. *Pearl S. Buck: A Biography*. New York: John Day, 1969–1971.

Hasegawa, Yoji. *Lafcadio Hearn's Japanese Wife: Her Memoirs and Her Early Life*. Tokyo: Micro Printing Co., 1988.

Hay, Susan Anderson. "Providence, Paris, Kyoto, Peking: Lucy Truman Aldrich and Her Collections." In *Patterns and Poetry: No Robes from the Lucy Truman Alcrich Collection at the Museum of Art, Rhode Island School of Design*. Ed. Susan Anderson Hay. Providence: Museum or Art, Rhode Island School of Design, 1992. 10–27.

Henning, Joseph M. *Outposts of Civilization: Race, Religion, and the Formative Years of American-Japanese Relations*. New York: New York University Press, 2000.

Higonnet, Anne. *Berthe Morisot's Images of Women*. Cambridge: Harvard University Press, 1992.

Hinsley, Curtis M. "The World as Marketplace: Commodification of the Exotic at the World's Columbian Exposition, Chicago, 1893." In *Exhibiting Cultures: The Poetics and Politics of Museum Display*. Eds. Ivan Karp and Steven D. Lavine. Washington: Smithsonian Institution Press, 1991. 351–363.

Hirayama, Hina. "Curious Merchandise: Bunkio Matsuki's Japanese Department." In *"A Pleasing Novelty": Bunkio Matsuki and the Japan Craze in Victorian Salem*. Salem, MA: Peabody & Essex Museum, 1993. 88–103.

Hobsbawm, Eric. *The Age of Empire, 1875–1914*. New York: Random House, 1987.

Hoffman, Nancy. "A Journey into Knowing: Agnes Smedley's *Daughter of Earth*." *Tradition and the Talents of Women*. Ed. Florence Howe. Urbana and Chicago: University of Illinois Press, 1991. 171–182.

Hoganson, Kristin L. "Cosmopolitan Domesticity: Importing the American Dream, 1865–1920." *American Historical Review* 107 (2002): 55–83.

———. *Fighting for American Manhood: How Gender Politics Provoked the Spanish-American and Philippine-American Wars*. New Haven: Yale University Press, 1998.

Honour, Hugh. *Chinoiserie: The Vision of Cathay*. London: John Murray, 1961.

Hooper, Paul F. ed. *Rediscovering the IPR: Proceedings of the First International Research Conference on the Institute of Pacific Relations, University of Hawaii, August 9–10, 1993*. Honolulu: Center for Arts and Humanities, University of Hawaii at Manoa, Department of American Studies, 1994.

Horowitz, Joseph. *Wagner Nights: An American History*. Berkeley: University of California Press, 1994.

Hosley, William. *The Japan Idea: Art and Life in Victorian America*. Hartford, CT: Wadsworth Atheneum, 1990.

"How to Tell the Japs from the Chinese." *Life* 22 December 1941: 7.

"How to Tell Your Friends from the Japs." *Time* 22 December 1941: 33.

Hunt, Michael H. "Pearl Buck—Popular Expert on China, 1931–1949." *Modern China* 3 (1977): 33–64.

Hunter, Jane. *The Gospel of Gentility: American Women Missionaries in Turn-of-the-Century China*. New Haven: Yale University Press, 1984.

Hyde, Mabel. *Jingles from Japan: As Set Forth by the Chinks*. Illustrated by Helen Hyde. San Francisco: A. M. Robertson, 1901.

Ichioka, Yuji, ed. *Views from Within: The Japanese American Evacuation and Resettlement Study*. Los Angeles: UCLA Asian American Studies Center, 1989.

Impey, Oliver. *Chinoiserie: The Impact of Oriental Styles on Western Art and Decoration*. Oxford: Oxford University Press, 1977.

In Pursuit of Beauty: Americans and the Aesthetic Movement. New York: Metropolitan Museum of Art, 1986.

Iriye, Akira. *Pacific Estrangement: Japanese and American Expansion, 1897–1911*. Cambridge: Harvard University Press, 1972.

——. *Across the Pacific: An Inner History of American-East Asian Relations*. Cambridge: Harvard University Press, 1967.

Iriye, Akira, ed. *Mutual Images: Essays in American-Japanese Relations*. Cambridge: Harvard University Press, 1975.

Isaacs, Harold. *Scratches on Our Minds: American Images of China and India*. New York: The John Day Co., 1958.

Jacobson, Matthew Frye. *Barbarian Virtues: The United States Encounters Foreign Peoples at Home and Abroad, 1876–1917*. New York: Hill and Wang, 2000.

——. *Whiteness of a Different Color: European Immigrants and the Alchemy of Race*. Cambridge: Harvard University Press, 1998.

Jameson, Frederic. "Modernism and Imperialism." In *Nationalism, Colonialism, and Literature* Terry Eagleton, et al. Minneapolis: University of Minnesota Press, 1990. 43–66.

Jaques, Bertha E. *Helen Hyde and Her Work: An Appreciation*. Chicago: The Libby Company, 1922.

Jayawardena, Kumari. *The White Woman's Other Burden: Western Women and South Asia during British Colonial Rule*. New York: Routledge, 1995.

Kaplan, Amy. "Manifest Domesticity." *American Literature* 70 (1998): 581–606.

——. "'Left Alone with America': The Absence of Empire in the Study of American Culture." In *Cultures of United States Imperialism*. Eds. Amy Kaplan and Donald E. Pease. Durham: Duke University Press, 1993. 3–21.

——. "Romancing the Empire: The Embodiment of American Masculinity in the Popular Historical Novel of the 1890s." *American Literary History* 3 (1990): 659–690.

——. *The Social Construction of American Realism*. Chicago: University of Chicago Press, 1988.

Kaplan, Caren. *Questions of Travel: Postmodern Discourses of Displacement*. Durham: Duke University Press, 1996.

Karp, Ivan and Steven D. Lavine, eds. *Exhibiting Cultures: The Poetics and Politics of Museum Display*. Washington: Smithsonian Institution Press, 1991.

Kasson, John F. *Amusing the Million: Coney Island at the Turn of the Century*. New York: Hill and Wang, 1978.

Kelsky, Karen. *Women on the Verge: Japanese Women, Western Dreams*. Durham: Duke University Press, 2001.

Kent, Pauline. "Ruth Benedict and Her Wartime Studies: Primary Materials and References." 1995-nendo Monbusho Kagaku Kenkyu-hi Hojokin Shourei Kenkyu (A) Kenkyu Seika Houkokusho, 07710166 [Tokyo]: Monbusho, 1996.

Kert, Bernice. *Abby Aldrich Rockefeller: The Woman in the Family*. New York: Random House, 1993.

Kiang, Kang-hu. Review of *The Good Earth* by Pearl S. Buck. *The New York Times Book Review* 15 January 1933: 2, 6.

Kirshenblatt-Gimblett, Barbara. *Destination Culture: Tourism, Museums, and Heritage*. Berkeley: University of California Press, 1998.

Kobayashi, Tadashi. *Ukiyo-e: An Introduction to Japanese Woodblock Prints*. Trans. Mark A. Harbison. Tokyo: Kondansha International, 1982.

Kohiyama, Rui. *Amerika Fujin Senkyoshi: Rainichi no Haikei to Sono Eikyo*. [*American Women Missionaries: The Background and Influence of Their Coming to Japan*] Tokyo: University of Tokyo Press, 1992.

Koshiro, Yukiko. *Trans-Pacific Racisms and the U.S. Occupation of Japan*. New York: Columbia University Press, 1999.

La Barre, Weston. "Some Observations on Character Structure in the Orient: The Japanese." *Psychiatry: Journal of Biology and the Pathology of Interpersonal Relations* 8 (1945): 319–342.

La Feber, Walter. *The New Empire: An Interpretation of American Expansion, 1860–1898*. Ithaca: Cornell University Press, 1963.

Lancaster, Clay. *The Japanese Influence in America*. New York: Walton H. Rawls, 1963.

Leach, William. *Land of Desire: Merchants, Power, and the Rise of a New American Culture*. New York: Vintage, 1993.

Lears, T. J. Jackson. *No Place of Grace: Antimodernism and the Transformation of American Culture, 1880–1920*. Chicago: University of Chicago Press, 1981.

Lee, Robert G. *Orientals: Asian Americans in Popular Culture*. Philadelphia: Temple University Press, 1999.

Leighton, Alexander L. *Human Relations in a Changing World: Observations on the Use of the Social Sciences*. New York: E. P. Dutton and Co., 1949.

——. *The Governing of Men: General Principles and Recommendations Based on Experience at a Japanese Relocation Camp*. Princeton: Princeton University Press, 1945.

Lewis, Reina. *Gendering Orientalism: Race, Femininity, and Representation*. London and New York: Routledge, 1996.

Lindsmith, Alfred R. and Anselm L. Strauss. "A Critique of Culture-Personality Writings." *American Sociological Review* 15 (1950): 587–600.

Lipscomb, Elizabeth J., et al., eds. *The Several Worlds of Pearl S. Buck: Essays Presented at a Centennial Symposium, Randolph-Macon Woman's College, March 26–28, 1992*. Westport, CT: Greenwood Press, 1994.

Long, John Luther. *Madame Butterfly*. Japanese ed. New York: Century Co., 1903.

Lott, Eric. *Love and Theft: Blackface Minstrelsy and the American Working-Class*. New York and Oxford: Oxford University Press, 1993.

Lowe, Lisa. *Critical Terrains: French and British Orientalisms*. Ithaca: Cornell University Press, 1991.

Lowell, Amy. *Pictures of the Floating World*. New York: Macmillan, 1919.

——. *Can Grande's Castle*. New York: Macmillan, 1918.

Lum, Bertha. *Gangplanks to the East*. New York: The Henkle-Yewdale House, Inc., 1936.

Lum, Peter. *My Own Pair of Wings*. San Francisco: Chinese Materials Center, Inc., 1981.

Lutz, Catherine A. and Jane L. Collins. *Reading National Geographic*. Chicago: University of Chicago Press, 1993.

MacKinnon, Janice R. and Stephen R. MacKinnon. *Agnes Smedley: The Life and Times of an American Radical*. Berkeley: University of California Press, 1988.

MacKinnon, Stephen R. and Oris Friesen. *China Reporting: An Oral History of American Journalism in the 1930s and 1940s*. Berkeley: University of California Press, 1987.

MacNair, Harley Farnsworth, ed. *Florence Ayscough and Amy Lowell: Correspondence of a Friendship*. Chicago: University of Chicago Press, 1945.

McCarthy, Kathleen. *Women's Culture: American Philanthropy and Art, 1830–1930*. Chicago: University of Chicago Press, 1991.

McClary, Susan. *Feminine Endings: Music, Gender, and Sexuality*. Minneapolis: University of Minnesota Press, 1991.

McClaugherty, Martha Crabill. "Household Art: Creating the Artistic Home, 1868–1893." *Winterthur Portfolio* 18 (1983): 1–26.

McClellan, Robert. *The Heathen Chinee: A Study of American Attitudes toward China, 1890–1905*. Columbus, OH: Ohio State University Press, 1971.

McClintock, Anne. *Imperial Leather: Race, Gender, and Sexuality in the Colonial Contest*. New York: Routledge, 1995.

McCormick, Thomas. *The China Market: America's Quest for an Informal Empire*. Chicago: University of Chicago Press, 1967.

Manderson, Lenore and Margaret Jolly, eds. *Sites of Desire, Economies of Pleasure: Sexualities in Asia and the Pacific*. Chicago: University of Chicago Press, 1997.

March, Benjamin. *China and Japan in Our Museums*. Chicago: University of Chicago Press, 1929.

Mathews, Nancy Mowll. "The Color Prints in the Context of Mary Cassatt's Art." In *Mary Cassatt: The Color Prints*. Eds. Nancy Mowll Mathews and Barbara Stern Shapiro. New York: Harry N. Abrams, 1989. 19–55.

Mead, Margaret, ed. *An Anthropologist at Work: Writings of Ruth Benedict* New York: Avon Books, [1959] 1973.

Mead, Margaret and Rhoda Metraux, eds. *The Study of Culture at a Distance*. Chicago: University of Chicago Press, 1953.

Meech, Julia and Gabriel Weisberg. *Japonisme Comes to America: The Japanese Impact on the Graphic Arts, 1876–1925*. New York: Harry N. Abrams, 1990.

Meech-Pekarik, Julia. "Early Collectors of Japanese Prints and the Metropolitan Museum of Art." *The Metropolitan Museum Journal* 17 (1984): 93–118.

Melman, Billie. *Women's Orients: English Women and the Middle East, 1718–1918*. Ann Arbor: University of Michigan Press, 1992.

Miller, Stuart Creighton. *The Unwelcome Immigrant: The American Image of the Chinese, 1785–1882*. Berkeley: University of California Press, 1969.

Mills, Sally. *Japanese Influences in American Art*. Williamstown, MA: Sterling and Francine Clark Art Institute, 1981.

Mills, Sara. *Discourses of Difference: An Analysis of Women's Travel Writing and Colonialism*. London: Routledge, 1991.

Minear, Richard H. "Cross-Cultural Perception and WWII: American Japanists of the 1940s and Their Images of Japan." *International Studies Quarterly* 24 (1980): 555–580.

Minear, Richard H. "The Wartime Studies of Japanese National Character." *Japan Interpreter* (Summer 1980): 36–59

Miner, Earl. *The Japanese Tradition in British and American Literature*. Princeton: Princeton University Press, 1966.

Mishima, Sumie Seo. *My Narrow Isle: The Story of a Modern Woman in Japan*. New York: John Day, 1941.

Mitchell, Timothy. *Colonising Egypt*. Cambridge: Cambridge University Press, 1988.

Miyoshi, Masao. *Off Center: Power and Culture Relations between Japan and the United States*. Cambridge: Harvard University Press, 1991.

Modell, Judith Schachter. *Ruth Benedict: Patterns of a Life*. Philadelphia: University of Pennsylvania Press, 1983.

Moon, Katharine H.S. *Sex among Allies: Military Prostitution in U.S.-Korea Relations*. New York: Columbia University Press, 1997.

Morgan, Susan. *Place Matters: Gendered Geography in Victorian Women's Travel Books about Southeast Asia*. New Brunswick, NJ: Rutgers University Press, 1996.

Motz, Marilyn Ferris and Pat Browne, eds. *Making the American Home: Middle-Class Women and the Domestic Material Culture, 1840–1940*. Bowling Green, OH: Bowling Green State University Popular Press, 1988.

Moy, James S. *Marginal Sights: Staging the Chinese in America*. Iowa City: University of Iowa Press, 1993.

Nash, Elizabeth. *Always First Class: The Career of Geraldine Farrar*. Washington, DC: University Press of America, 1981.

Nelson, Christina. *Directly from China: Export Goods for the American Market, 1784–1930*. Salem, MA: Peabody Museum of Salem, 1984.

Newman, Louise Michele. *White Women's Rights: The Racial Origins of Feminism in the United States*. New York: Oxford University Press, 1999.

Nichols, Kathleen L. "The Western Roots of Feminism in Agnes Smedley's *Daughter of Earth*." In *Women and Western American Literature*. Eds. Helen Winter Stauffer and Susan J. Rosowski. Troy, NY: The Whiston Publishing Co., 1982. 114–123.

Nochlin, Linda. *Representing Women*. New York: Thames and Hudson, 1999.

———. *The Politics of Vision: Essays in Nineteenth-Century Art and Society*. New York: Harper & Row, 1989.

North, Michael. *The Dialect of Modernism: Race, Language, and Twentieth-Century Literature*. New York: Oxford University Press, 1994.

Notoji, Masako. "Ferisu Kanransha to Ho-ö-den: 1893-nen Shikago Hakurankai ni Miru Nichibei no Nashonarizumu." [Ferris Wheel and Ho-ö-den: U.S. and Japanese Nationalisms in 1893 Chicago World's Fair]. In *Gendai Amerika-zo no Saikochiku: Seiji to Bunka no Gendai-shi* [Reconstructing the Image of Contemporary America: Contemporary History of Politics and Culture]. Eds. Homma Nagayo, et al. Tokyo: Tokyo Daigaku Shuppan Kai, 1990. 123–139.

Official Guide to the Midway Plaisance. Chicago: The Columbian Guide Co., 1893.

Okakura, Kakudzo. *The Hö-ö-den (Pheonix Hall): An Illustrated Description of the Buildings Erected by the Japanese Government at the World's Columbian Exposition, Jackson Park, Chicago*. Tokyo: K. Ogawa, 1893.

Owen, Nancy Elizabeth. *Rookwood and the Industry of Art: Women, Culture, and Commerce, 1880–1913*. Athens: Ohio University Press, 2001.

Pao, Angela C. *The Orient of the Boulevards: Exoticism, Empire, and Nineteenth-Century French Theater*. Philadelphia: University of Pennsylvania Press, 1998.

Pascoe, Peggy. *Relations of Rescue: The Search for Female Moral Authority in the American West, 1874–1939*. New York: Oxford University Press, 1990.

Peiss, Kathy. *Cheap Amusements: Working Women and Leisure at the Turn-of-the-Century New York*. Philadelphia: Temple University Press, 1986.

Piercy, Marge. "Agnes Smedley: Dirt Poor Daughter of Earth." *The New Republic* 14 December 1974: 20.

Pollock, Griselda. *Mary Cassatt: Painter of Modern Women*. London: Thames and Hudson, 1998.

Porter, Dennis. "*Orientalism* and Its Problems." In *The Politics of Theory*. Eds. Francis Barker et al. Essex: Colchester, 1983. 179–193.

Pound, Ezra. *Personae. Collected Shorter Poems of Ezra Pound*. New York: New Directions, 1971.

——. "The Renaissance." In *Literary Essays*. Ed. T. S. Eliot. London: Farber and Farber, 1968. 214–226.

Powell, John W. "The Best and the Brightest—Western Reporting from Asia." *Bulletin of Concerned Asian Scholars* 22 (1990): 55–63.

Pratt, Mary Louise. *Imperial Eyes: Travel Writing and Transculturation* (London: Routledge, 1992.

——. "Fieldwork in Common Places." In *Writing Culture: The Poetics and Politics of Ethnography*. Eds. James Clifford and George E. Marcus. Berkeley: University of California Press, 1986. 27–50.

Price, Sally. *Primitive Art in Civilized Places*. Chicago: University of Chicago Press, 1989.

Qian, Zhaoming. *Orientalism and Modernism: The Legacy of China in Pound and Williams, 1913–1923*. Durham: Duke University Press, 1995.

Quimby, Ian. "Oriental Influence on American Decorative Arts." *Journal of the Society of Architectural Historians* 35 (1976): 300–308.

Rabinowitz, Paula. *Labor and Desire: Women's Revolutionary Fiction in Depression America*. Chapel Hill: University of North Carolina Press, 1991.

Rafael, Vicente L. "Colonial Domesticity: White Women and United States Rule in the Philippines." *American Literature* 67 (1995): 639–666.

Rand, Peter. *China Hands: The Adventures and Ordeals of the American Journalists Who Joined Forces with the Great Chinese Revolution*. New York: Simon & Schuster, 1995.

Rector, Margaret Hayden. *Alva, That Vanderbilt-Belmont Woman*. Wickford, RI: The Dutch Island Press, 1992.

Rogin, Michael. *Blackface, White Noise: Jewish Immigrants in the Hollywood Melting Pot*. Berkeley: University of California Press, 1996.

Rosenberg, Emily. *Spreading the American Dream: American Economic and Cultural Expansion, 1890–1945*. New York: Hill & Wang, 1982.

Rosenberg, Rosalind. *Beyond Separate Spheres: Intellectual Roots of Modern Feminism*. New Haven: Yale University Press, 1982.

Rosenstone, Robert. *Mirror in the Shrine: American Encounters with Meiji Japan*. Cambridge: Harvard University Press, 1988.

Rotter, Andrew J. "Gender Relations, Foreign Relations: The United States and South Asia, 1947–1964." *Journal of American History* 81 (1994): 518–542.

Ruihley, Glenn Richard. *The Thorn of a Rose: Amy Lowell Reconsidered*. Hamden, CT: Archon Books, 1975.

Rydell, Robert. *All the World's a Fair: Visions of Empire at American International Expositions, 1876–1916*. Chicago and London: University of Chicago Press, 1984.

Sadamura, Tadashi. "Rokkuferah Korekushon no Oitachi [The life of the Rockefeller Collection]." In *Yomigaeru Bi—Hana to Tori to: Rokkuferah Ukiyoe Korekushon Ten*. Tokyo: Bun-yu-sha, 1990.

Said, Edward. *Culture and Imperialism*. New York: Knopf, 1993.

——. *Musical Elaborations*. New York: Columbia University Press, 1991.

——. *Orientalism*. New York: Random House, 1978.

Sawada, Mitziko. *Tokyo Life, New York Dreams: Urban Japanese Visions of America, 1890–1924*. Berkeley: University of California Press, 1996.

Sedges, John. [Pearl S. Buck] *Voices in the House*. New York: John Day, 1953.

——. *Bright Procession*. New York: John Day, 1952.

——. *The Long Love*. New York: John Day, 1949.

——. *The Angry Wife*. New York: John Day, 1947.

——. *The Townsman*. New York: John Day, 1945.

Shannon, Christopher. "A World Made Safe for Differences: Ruth Benedict's *The Chrysanthemum and the Sword*." *American Quarterly* 47 (1995): 659–680.

Shapiro, Barbara Stern. "Mary Cassatt's Color Prints and Contemporary French Printmaking." In *Mary Cassatt: The Color Prints*. Eds. Nancy Mowll Mathews and Barbara Stern Shapiro. New York: Harry N. Abrams, 1989. 57–87.

Sharf, Frederic A. "Bunkio Matsuki: Salem's Most Prominent Japanese Citizen." In *"A Pleasing Novelty": Bunkio Matsuki and the Japan Craze in Victorian Salem*. Salem, MA: Peabody & Essex Museum, 1993. 7–33.

Sharpe, Jenny. *Allegories of Empire: The Figure of Woman in the Colonial Text*. Minneapolis: University of Minnesota Press, 1993.

Shewmaker, Kenneth. *Americans and Chinese Communists, 1927–1945: A Persuading Encounter*. Ithaca: Cornell University Press, 1971.

Shibusawa, Naoko. *America's Geisha Ally: Gender, Race, and Maturity in Reimagining the Japanese*. Cambridge: Harvard University Press, forthcoming.

Showalter, Elaine. "Introduction." In Louisa May Alcott, *Alternative Alcott*. Ed. Elaine Showalter. New Brunswick and London: Rutgers University Press, 1988.

Simmons, Christina. "Modern Sexuality and the Myth of Victorian Repression." In *Gender and American History since 1890*. Ed. Barbara Melosh. New York: Routledge, 1992. 17–42.

——. "Companionate Marriage and the Lesbian Threat." In *Women and Power in American History*. Vol. II. Eds. Kathryn Kish Sklar and Thomas Dublin. Englewood Cliffs, NJ: Prentice Hall, 1991. 183–194.

Simpson, Caroline Chung. *An Absent Presence: Japanese Americans in Postwar American Culture, 1945–1960*. Durham: Duke University Press, 2002.

Sklar, Kathryn Kish. "Hull House in the 1890s: A Community of Women Reformers." In *Women and Power in American History*. Vol. II. Eds. Kathryn Kish Sklar and Thomas Dublin. Englewood Cliffs, NJ: Prentice Hall, 1991. 54–68.

Smedley, Agnes. *China's Red Army Marches*. Westport, CT: Hyperion Press, 1977.

——. *Battle Hymn of China*. New York: Knopf, 1943.

——. *China Fights Back: An American Woman with the Eighth Route Army*. New York: The Vanguard Press, 1938.

——. *Chinese Destinies: Sketches of Present-Day China*. Westport, CT: Hyperion Press, [1933] 1977.

——. *Daughter of Earth*. New York: The Feminist Press, [1929] 1987.

Smith-Rosenberg, Carol. *Disorderly Conduct: Visions of Gender in Victorian America*. New York: Knopf, 1985.

Soeda, Yoshiya. *Nihon Bunka Shiron: Benedict "Kiku to Katana" wo Yomu*. [Tokyo]: Shinyosha, 1993.

Spurr, David. *The Rhetoric of Empire: Colonial Discourse in Journalism, Travel Writing, and Imperial Administration*. Durham: Duke University Press, 1993.

Stamy, Cynthia. *Marianne Moore and China: Orientalism and a Writing of America*. Oxford: Oxford University Press, 1999.

Stansell, Christine. *American Moderns: Bohemian New York and the Creation of a New Century*. New York: Henry Holt & Co., 2000.

Stein, Roger B. "Artifact as Ideology: The Aesthetic Movement in Its American Cultural Context." In *In Pursuit of Beauty: Americans and the Aesthetic Movement*. New York: Metropolitan Museum of Art, 1986.

Stocking, George W., Jr. *The Ethnographer's Magic and Other Essays in the History of Anthropology*. Madison: University of Wisconsin Press, 1992.

Stoler, Ann Laura. *Race and the Education of Desire: Foucault's History of Sexuality and the Colonial Order of Things*. Durham and London: Duke University Press, 1995.

——. "Carnal Knowledge and Imperial Power: Gender, Race, and Morality in Colonial Asia." In *Gender at the Crossroads of Knowledge: Feminist Anthropology in the Postmodern Era*. Ed. Micaela di Leonardo. Berkeley: University of California Press, 1991. 51–101.

——. "Rethinking Colonial Categories: European Communities and the Boundaries of Rule.' *Comparative Studies in Society and History* 31 (1989): 134–161.

Strauss, David. *Percival Lowell: The Culture and Science of a Boston Brahmin*. Cambridge: Harvard University Press, 2001.

——. "The 'Far East' in the American Mind, 1883–1894: Percival Lowell's Decisive Impact." *The Journal of American-East Asian Relations* 2 (1993): 217–241.

Strobel, Margaret. *European Women and the Second British Empire*. Bloomington: Indiana University Press, 1991.

Sturdevant, Saundera Pollock and Brenda Stoltzfus. *Let the Good Times Roll: Prostitution and the U.S. Military in Asia*. New York: The New Press, 1992.

Sugimoto, Etsu Inagaki. *A Daughter of the Samurai*. New York: Doubleday, 1926.

Suleri, Sara. *The Rhetoric of English India*. Chicago: University of Chicago Press, 1992.

Suzuki, Peter T. "Anthropologists in the Wartime Camps for Japanese Americans: A Documentary Study." *Dialectical Anthropology* 6 (1981): 23–60.

——. "A Retrospective Analysis of a Wartime 'National Character' Study." *Dialectical Anthropology* 5 (1980): 33–46.

Swinth, Kirsten. *Painting Professionals: Women Artists and the Development of Modern American Art, 1870–1930*. Chapel Hill: University of North Carolina Press, 2001.

Tchen, John Kuo Wei. *New York before Chinatown: Orientalism and the Shaping of American Culture, 1776–1882*. Baltimore and London: Johns Hopkins University Press, 1999.

Tharp, Louise Hall. *Mrs. Jack: A Biography of Isabella Stewart Gardner*. Boston: Little, Brown, & Co., 1965.

Thomas, Dorothy S. *The Salvage*. Berkeley: University of California Press, 1952.

Thomas, Dorothy S. and Richard S. Nishimoto. *The Spoilage*. Berkeley: University of California Press, 1946.

Thomas, John N. *The Institute of Pacific Relations: Asian Scholars and American Politics*. Seattle: University of Washington Press, 1974.

Thompson, Laura. "Some Perspectives on Applied Anthropology." *Applied Anthropology* 3 (1944): 12.

Thomson, James C., Jr. "Pearl S. Buck and the American Quest for China." In *The Several Worlds of Pearl S. Buck: Essays Presented at a Centennial Symposium, Randolph-Macon Woman's College, March 26–28, 1992*. Eds. Elizabeth J. Lipscomb, et al. Westport, CT: Greenwood Press, 1994. 7–15.

Thomson, James C., Jr., et al. *Sentimental Imperialists: The American Experience in East Asia*. New York: Harper & Row, 1981.

Todd, Ellen Wiley. "Art, the 'New Woman,' and Consumer Culture," In *Gender and American History since 1890*. Ed. Barbara Melosh. New York: Routledge, 1992. 127–154.

Tompkins, Jane. *Sensational Designs: The Cultural Work of American Fiction, 1790–1860*. New York: Oxford University Press, 1985.

Torgovnick, Marianna. *Gone Primitive: Savage Intellectuals, Modern Lives*. Chicago: University of Chicago Press, 1990.

Trachtenberg, Alan. *Incorporation of America: Culture and Society in the Gilded Age*. New York: Hill and Wang, 1982.

Trapp, Kenneth. "Rookwood and the Japanese Mania in Cincinnati." *Cincinnati Historical Society Bulletin* 39 (1987): 51–75.

U.S. Department of Interior, War Relocation Authority. *Impounded People: Japanese Americans in the Relocation Centers*. Washington: Government Printing Office, 1946.

Utley, Freda. *Odessey of a Liberal*. Washington: Washington National Press, 1970.

Van Doren, Carl. *The American Novel 1789–1939*. Rev. ed. New York: Macmillan, 1940.

Venable, Charles L. *Silver in America, 1840–1940: A Century of Splendor*. Dallas: Dallas Museum of Art, 1994.

Wald, Alan M. *Writing from the Left: New Essays on Radical Culture and Politics*. London: Verso, 1994.

Wald, Gayle. *Crossing the Line: Racial Passing in Twentieth-Century U.S. Literature and Culture*. Durham and London: Duke University Press, 2000.

Ware, Vron. *Beyond the Pale: White Women, Racism, and History*. New York: Verso, 1992.

Warmbold, Carolyn Nizzi. "Women of the Mosquito Press: Louise Bryant, Agnes Smedley, and Margaret Randall as Narrative Guerrillas." PhD Diss. University of Texas at Austin, 1990.

Watsuji, Tetsuro. "Kagaku-teki Kachi ni taisuru Gimon [Questions as to the Scientific Value]." *Minzokugaku Kenkyu* 14 (1950): 23–27.

Wexler, Laura. *Tender Violence: Domestic Visions in an Age of U.S. Imperialism*. Chapel Hill and London: University of North Carolina Press, 2000.

Wheeler, Candace. *Yesterdays in a Busy Life*. New York: Harper & Bros., 1918.

Winkler, Allan M. *The Politics of Propaganda: The Office of War Information, 1942–1945*. New Haven: Yale University Press, 1978.

Yamanaka & Co., Ko Yamanaka Sadajiro O Den Hensan Kai [The Editorial Committee for the Biography of Late Yamanaka Sadajiro], ed. *Yamanaka Sadajiro O Den [The Biography of Late Sadajiro Yamanaka]*. Osaka: Yamanaka & Co., 1939.

Yoshimi, Shunya. *Hakurankai no Seiji-gaku: Manazashi no Kindai [The Politics of World's Fairs: Modernity of the Gaze]*. Tokyo: Chuo-koron-sha, 1992.

Yu, Beongcheon. *The Great Circle: American Writers and the Orient*. Detroit: Wayne State University Press, 1983.

———. *An Ape of Gods: The Art and Thought of Lafcadio Hearn*. Detroit: Wayne State University Press, 1964.

Yu, Henry. *Thinking Orientals: Migration, Contact, and Exoticism in Modern America*. New York: Oxford University Press, 2001.

Zen, Sophia Chen. Review of *The Good Earth* by Pearl S. Buck. *Pacific Affairs* 4 (1931): 915.

INDEX

Tiffany & Co., 26, 28
translations, 102, 105–9
"Two Views of Japan" (poem), 32

ukiyo-e prints, 24, 50–52, 54–57, 61, 63, 71, 110
Utley, Freda, 137

Vanderbilt, William, 42
Van Doren, Carl, 151
Vantine's, A. A. (store), 31–36, 37, 38, 39, 41
"Vicarious" (poem), 113–14
Victorian era, 7, 25, 26, 47
Vorce, A. D. & Co., 40
vorticism, 104

Walsh, Richard, 152
Washington, George, 8
Watsuji Tetsuro, 188
Weston, Anna, 57
Wharton, Edith, 45
Wheeler, Candace, 72
Whistler, James Abbott McNeill, 18, 40
Wilde, Oscar, 114
Williams, William Carlos, 102
Winter (Lum), 60
Woman Adjusting Her Hair (Katsushika), 56

Woman Bathing (Cassatt), 54, 55
women
  Aesthetic Movement, 25, 56
  artists' "Asian" prints, 49–73
  Chinese, 141–43
  consumption of Asian objects, 15–43
  Japanese, 4–5, 92–93, 114, 183–84
  New Women, 78, 87, 95, 98, 100, 193–94
  performances of Asian heroines, 77–100
  relation to Orientalism, 7–8, 193–95
  role in American Orientalism, 6
  role in Euroamerican empire-building, 192–93
  role of white in American society, 7
woodcuts, 57, 58, 63
World's Columbian Exposition. *See* Columbian Exposition
world's fairs, 18–20
World War II, 171, 174–75
"Would You Like to Be a Coolie?" (poem), 66, 68

Xian Incident, 131
Xu Zhimo, 133, 150

Yamanaka & Co., 23, 24, 37–38, 39
Yamanaka Sadajiro, 24, 37